CW01499410

JFK ASSASSINATION AFTERMATH

JFK ASSASSINATION AFTERMATH

What Happened to Key Figures 1963-2024?

Dr. Diane Holloway Cheney

Tampa, Florida

The content associated with this book is the sole work and responsibility of the author. Gatekeeper Press had no involvement in the generation of this content.

JFK Assassination Aftermath:
What Happened to Key Figures 1963-2024?

Published by Gatekeeper Press
7853 Gunn Hwy., Suite 209
Tampa, FL 33626
www.GatekeeperPress.com

Copyright © 2024 by Dr. Diane Holloway Cheney
All rights reserved. Neither this book, nor any parts within it may be sold or reproduced in any form or by any electronic or mechanical means, including information storage and retrieval systems, without permission in writing from the author. The only exception is by a reviewer, who may quote short excerpts in a review.

Editorial work for this book is entirely the product of the author. Gatekeeper Press did not participate in and is not responsible for any aspect of these elements.

ISBN (paperback): 9781662952524
eISBN: 9781662952531

ALSO BY DR. DIANE HOLLOWAY CHENEY

The Mind of Oswald

Dallas and the Jack Ruby Trial

I Was a VIP on 11/22/63

Donald Trump, Robert Mueller, Christopher Steele: Mogul, Enforcer, Spy

American Police Dilemma: Protectors or Enforcers?

Analyzing Leaders, Presidents, and Terrorists

Famous Doctors and Famous Patients: Lives in Jeopardy?

Who Killed New Orleans?

Jacuzzi: A Father's Invention to Ease a Son's Pain

Sleep Problems: Food Solutions

American History in Song

Academy Award Winning Movies 1928-2020

I Did Not Burn the Church Down, I Only Started the Fire

Jesus, His Brother, and Paul

Arizona's Historic and Unique Hotels

Before You Say 'I Quit'

Oldest Restaurants in the USA and Europe

Interrupted Lives: Hood's Texas Brigade

This book is dedicated to Clint Hill who was the Secret Service agent who jumped on the limousine and covered the President after he was shot. Clint also protected Mrs. Kennedy and has written about that. Mr. Hill is appalled at the controversies and conspiracy theories that have distorted the truth. He wants people to know that Lee Oswald killed the President with no other aid, a truth which I also believe, and I support him in that wish. Thank you so very much for your work, Mr. Hill.

I also wish to thank Edgar Van Cott who was a rocket scientist for Raytheon but has been an able researcher helping me to explore ideas in my books. He is so patient and encouraging that I can never express enough thanks.

Table of Contents

Introduction

"The moving finger writes, and having writ,
Moves on: nor all thy piety nor wit
Shall lure it back to cancel half a Line,
Nor all thy tears wash out a word of it."
Omar Khayyam

The finality of the assassination of President John F. Kennedy gripped us all. I was inspired to write this book by Clint Hill of the Secret Service. As shots were fired on 11/22/63, he ran to the presidential limousine and threw his body over the President and Mrs. Kennedy just as she was trying to crawl out of the line of fire. He has just released a special version of his book *Five Days in November* with some important words:

> Right now, there are very few people left who were present that day and we'll all be gone soon and there will be no one left to tell the facts… It is my duty to bear witness, because by now, I have become the only person who knows or cares.

He has steadfastly believed that what happened on November 22nd, 1963, was "One man, one gun, three shots."

I believe that, too. I was involved with the psychological evaluation of the first victim Oswald tried to kill—Major General Edwin Walker, whom Oswald shot at on April 10th, 1963. That will be discussed later.

I also believe Oswald did it alone because I read all of Oswald's words in documents most people have never seen. When I was selected to serve as the Drug Czar of Dallas under Mayor Annette Strauss, I had the highest-level access. Thus, I was able to read all the papers in our City Archives written by Lee Harvey Oswald and collected by police from his residence when he was arrested. His words left me with no doubt that he assassinated the President to gain fame. I included his written documents in my 2000 book *The Mind of Oswald*.

That book was used by authors who wrote about the JFK assassination, such as Vincent Bugliosi (2007) *Reclaiming History.* W.W. Norton & Co., and Bill O'Reilly (2012) *Killing Kennedy: The End of Camelot.* Henry Holt & Co.

The goal of this book is to describe what became of the primary people and groups involved with President Kennedy and how they went on with their lives. We also want to understand this tragedy well enough to prevent other such acts in the future.

In addition, we will consider the character of our leader. President Kennedy's death is not as important as his life; thus, we will try to understand his life and character. As Russian author Fyodor Dostoyevski said, "It is not the brains that matter most, but that which guides them—the character, the heart, generous qualities, progressive ideas."

THE KENNEDY ASSASSINATION AND FUNERALS

November 22-25, 1963

CHAPTER ONE

Shots Fired at President John F. Kennedy

"A man may die, nations may rise and fall, but an idea lives on. Ideas have endurance without death."

John F. Kennedy: Remarks at the Opening of a USIA Transmitter at Greenville, North Carolina, February 8th, 1963.

On November 22nd, 1963, President Kennedy and his wife, and Texas Governor John Connally and his wife were riding through Dallas, Texas, on a motorcade to show the President to potential voters for the next election.

One bullet was fired from the 6th floor of the Texas School Book Depository, hit a signal light post, and veered off in another direction, striking cement on the street that shot up to the cheek of bystander James Tague. The car salesman had encountered such traffic due to the presidential motorcade that he had gotten out of his car in Dealey Plaza. Deputy Sheriff Eddie "Buddy" Walters saw Tague and said, "You have blood there on your cheek." Tague testified about this to the Warren Commission and went on to write various books about the assassination over the years.[1]

---

1 "President Kennedy's Third Man at Shooting" The Sydney Morning Herald, May 2, 2014. https://www.smh.com/au/national/president-kennedys-third-man-at-shooting-20140502-zr31l.html

The second bullet hit the President between his shoulders and exited through his neck, nicking the knot of his tie. President Kennedy can be seen on Abraham Zapruder's videotape clutching his throat. The bullet, having hit only flesh, did not stop in mid-air and continued forward into the back of Governor John Connally, seated in a small lower jump seat in front of the President.

That bullet was fired using a four-power scope to enlarge the target seen from the sixth floor of the Depository, some 80 yards away from the President. The third and fatal shot that hit the President's head was measured 88 yards from that sixth-floor window.

Lee Oswald was arrested later that day for killing a policeman and the President. He was working on the 6th floor of that Depository on that day.

Three years earlier, he had been tested in the U.S. Marine Corps for marksmanship, with his rifle firing slowly from 200, 300, and 500 yards and firing rapidly from 200 and 300 yards. The Marine scoring system was this: over 190 points was a marksman, over 210 was a sharpshooter, and over 220 was considered an expert. On December 21st, 1956, Oswald scored 212 and was designated as a sharpshooter. On his 200-yard rapid-fire test, he hit 8 of 10 bullseyes and scored 48 out of 50. On his 300-yard rapid fire, he hit 7 of 10 bullseyes, scoring 46 out of 50. These scores are found on Warren Commission Exhibit 239.

At the time of the assassination, several people had seen someone holding a rifle standing in the sixth-floor window of the Depository. Four people immediately reported that they saw the assassin fire: A. L. Euins, H. L. Brennan, reporter Bob Jackson, and J. R. Worrell, Jr. Brennan had watched him the most and immediately gave the police an identification.

Brennan had awaited the motorcade, standing and sitting below that sixth floor window to watch the parade as the limousine moved at 11 mph to enable people to clearly see the President. Brennan looked up to see Oswald fire the two last shots. Within minutes, police began to broadcast his description to officers: "Slender white male, about 30 years old, 5 feet 10 inches and weighing about 165 pounds."

Policeman Marrion Baker ran into the Texas Schoolbook Depository and up the stairs to the sniper's nest and found the sniper had pushed boxes around that window to hide himself from any employee who came onto the sixth floor that morning.

There were three spent shells found by the window. The rifle, having been tossed between boxes, had one shell left in the firing chamber. Lee Oswald's book orders for the day were hanging on a hook and had been untouched during the morning, so he had not done any depository work that day.

Lee had plenty of time to reflect on what might take place as he awaited the motorcade that morning. What did he think about? Did he imagine that this was the most important moment in his life? Did he think that he might escape from the police? Did he figure that he would become famous and that his name would be mentioned for decades? He knew he would be talked about. An adage comes to mind about Oswald: "There is only one thing in the world worse than being talked about and that is not being talked about!"

After Brennan gave police a description of the shooter, they ordered Depository foreman Roy Truly to do a roll call of employees going back to work after the shooting. Truly did this within the hour, and only Lee Oswald was missing. His address was given to the police. That turned out to be his wife's address where she was staying with Mrs. Ruth Paine in Irving, Texas. He lived in a rooming house in Dallas across the Trinity River in a suburb called Oak Cliff.

Lee could have been caught right away. That policeman climbing the stairs toward the sniper's site encountered Oswald coming down the stairs but dismissed him when someone said he was an employee. Lee had grabbed a drink and looked as if he was part of the crew, but once the policeman continued ascending the stairs, Lee set down the drink and left the building.

There was chaos in the street. Abraham Zapruder, a women's clothing lines salesman, had just gotten a new projector and had walked downstairs to the street to photograph the motorcade. He took an assistant because he felt a bit unsteady holding up the projector, and she helped him stand on the cement step where he filmed everything. He was standing in front of the area, which someone called a "grassy knoll." Zapruder's videotape of the assassination would later help solve many questions about the timing of the bullets, who was injured, when, and the President's final seconds of life.

After the shooting, the limousine began to speed to Parkland Hospital. Zapruder was mounting the stairs to his office in the Dal-Tex building across the street from the Book Depository. He ran into his office building, hollering to people, "I've got it, I got it all. They killed him." Another man, a photographer, was following Zapruder up the stairs because they saw him filming the parade and wanted to get the films processed and published. The Zapruder film information did not come out for many months.

CHAPTER TWO

Parkland Hospital Reactions

"Do not pray for easy lives. Pray to be stronger men."
John F. Kennedy quoting Rev. Phillips Brooks
during a Presidential Prayer

Meanwhile, the presidential limousine sped to Parkland Hospital as Mrs. Kennedy was crying to her husband, telling him that she loved him.

The author was working as a nurse in the locked psychiatric unit on the 8th floor of Parkland Hospital. After an early career running a travel agency in Europe, a return to the U.S. to take up health studies began with psychiatric nursing and progressed to psychology later. Suddenly, the patients were creating a commotion.

"The president's been shot, and they're bringing him here," screamed one of our patients watching television. Our patients began running around to look through windows as the nursing staff was caught by surprise. One lady ran to the locked doors and banged on them, saying, "Let me out, let me out." Another lady hollered at her, "No, we'll be safe. They won't get us locked in here." Still another got down on the floor and seemed to be praying to God to save the President or to save herself. It was chaos.

We began giving some patients sedatives to restore order and relieve their stress and their ravings. Meanwhile, we called the head of our unit in an outer office, Dr. A. W. DeLoach, and told him of our conditions in the unit. He had not heard about the shooting of the President. We asked if we should turn off the television set. He said to leave it on since the patients might be more anxious about the unknown rather than the known news emerging. The usual incoming shift of nurses could not arrive due to the commotion and blocked doorways. We all worked beyond our shift time.

Before this nursing work, my first job at Southwestern Medical School was as a secretary for the chairmen of three surgical departments. Two of those chairmen went to the emergency room to tend to President Kennedy.

One was Dr. Kemp Clark, the chairman of the Department of Neurosurgery, who would announce the death of President Kennedy having occurred about 1:00 Dallas time. The other doctor for whom I worked was Dr. Robert Walker, who chaired the Oral and Maxillofacial Surgery programs. He had stepped into the emergency room to examine the face and neck in case the President would need help with repairs but quickly saw that the President could not be helped in any way.

Later, Dr. Kemp Clark was asked to describe events in the emergency room to the Warren Commission. The President was a patient whom physicians had followed his entire life due to a variety of illnesses. He had been given last rites five times before they were given on this day. Now, it was no longer necessary for doctors to maintain a watchful eye over a man who had just lost track of where else he might go in life. His health battles were over.

CHAPTER THREE

Dr. Kemp Clark's Description of the President's Death

"A nation reveals itself not only by the men it produces, but also by the men it honors, the men it remembers."

John F. Kennedy on October 26th, 1963, at Amherst College upon receiving an honorary degree.

Here is Dr. Clark's account to the Warren Commission of how the President died:

Mr. Specter: At approximately what time did you arrive in the emergency room?

Dr. Clark: I would guess that I arrived at approximately 12:30.

Mr. Specter: And who was present if anyone, upon your arrival, tending to the President?

Dr. Clark: Dr. Jenkins, that is M. T. Jenkins, Dr. Ronald Jones, Dr. Malcolm Perry, Dr. James Carrico; arriving with me or immediately thereafter Dr. Robert McClelland, Dr. Paul Peters, and Dr. Charles Baxter.

Mr. Specter: What did you observe the President's condition to be on your arrival there?

Dr. Clark: The President was lying on his back on the emergency cart. Dr. Perry was performing a tracheotomy. There were chest tubes being inserted. Dr. Jenkins was assisting the President's respirations through a tube in his trachea. Dr. Jones and Dr. Carrico were administering fluids and blood intravenously.

The President was making a few spasmodic respiratory efforts. I assisted in withdrawing the endotracheal tube from the throat as Dr. Perry was then ready to insert the tracheostomy tube. I then examined the President briefly.

My findings showed his pupils were widely dilated, did not react to light, and his eyes were deviated outward with a slight skew deviation. I then examined the wound on the back of the President's head. This was a large gaping wound in the right posterior part, with cerebral and cerebellar tissue being damaged and exposed. There was considerable blood loss evident on the carriage, the floor, and the clothing of some of the people present. I would estimate 1500 cc. of blood being present.

As I was examining the President's wound, I felt for the carotid pulse and felt none. Therefore, I began external cardiac massage and asked that a cardiotachioscope be connected. Because of my position it was difficult to administer cardiac massage. However, Dr. Jones stated that he felt a femoral pulse.

Mr. Specter: What is a femoral pulse?

Dr. Clark: A femoral artery is the main artery going to the legs, and at the junction of the leg and the trunk you can feel the arterial pulsation in this artery. Because of my position, cardiac massage was taken over by Dr. Malcolm Perry, who was more advantageously situated.

Mr. Specter: What did the cardiotachioscope show at that time?

Dr. Clark: The caradiotachioscope had been attached and Dr. Faoud Bashour had arrived. There was transient electrical activity of the President's heart of an undefined type. Approximately, at this time the external cardiac massage became ineffectual, and no pulsations could be felt. At this time, it was decided to pronounce the President dead.

Mr. Specter: At what time was this fixed?

Dr. Clark: Death was fixed at one o'clock. This was an approximation as it is, first, extremely difficult to state precisely when death occurs. Secondly, no one was monitoring the clock, so an approximation of 1 o'clock was chosen.

Mr. Specter: And did you have any part in the filling out of the death certificate?

Dr. Clark: Yes. I filled out the death certificate at the request of Dr. George Burkley, the President's physician at the White House, signed the death certificate as a registered physician in the State of Texas, and gave this to him to accompany the body to Washington.

Mr. Specter: Did you advise anyone else in the Presidential party of the death of the President?

Dr. Clark: Yes, I told Mrs. Kennedy, the President's wife, of his death.

Mr. Specter: And what, if anything, did she respond to you?

Dr. Clark: She told me she knew it and thanked me for our efforts… May I add something to what I said in the first press conference?

Mr. Specter: Yes, please do.

Dr. Clark: I remember what Dr. Perry said at the first press conference. He was asked if the neck wound could be a wound of entrance or appeared to be a wound of exit and Dr. Perry said something like "possibly or conceivably" or something of this sort….

Well, this would mean that the missile would have had to be fired from below upward or that the President was hanging upside down. [The doctors had not turned the President's body over and did not know of a wound in the back, so they were considering whether the wound in the throat and the head were somehow connected.]

Mr. Specter: Did Dr. Perry discuss anything with you prior to that second conference about a phone call from Washington, DC?

Dr. Clark: Yes, he did.

Mr. Specter: Would you relate briefly what Dr. Perry told you about that subject.

Dr. Clark: Yes. Dr. Perry stated that he had talked to the Bethesda Naval Hospital on two occasions that morning and that he knew what the autopsy findings had shown and that he did not wish to be questioned by the press, as he had been asked by Bethesda to confine his remarks to that which he knew from having examined the President, and suggested that the major part of this press conference be conducted by me.

In later years, my old friend and former boss, Dr. Clark, gave the watch he used to tell the time of Kennedy's death to charity. In 1949, his mother had bought a special Patek Philippe ref. 1463 chronograph with pulsometer 18-carat gold watch during a visit to Switzerland when Kemp was in medical school. He showed it to me and others many times and was quite proud of it. The watch was unique, and on the 50th anniversary of President Kennedy's death, he donated it to Christie's auction house to benefit charities such as the American Red Cross. A watch such as that recently sold for $242,000.[2]

---

2 https://www.hodinkee.com/articles/found-on-the-50th-anniversary-of-the-jfks-assassination-his-doctors-watch

Kemp Clark was a very thoughtful man who had seen so many terrible head injuries by young people that he began a program called *Think First* to help youth avoid risky behavior. Other physicians picked up that program and kept it going for many years.

CHAPTER FOUR

Dr. Robert Walker's Account of the President's Death

*"When at some future date the high court of history
sits in judgment on each of us, our success or failure will be
measured by the answers to four questions:
First were we truly men of courage? Secondly, were we truly men
of judgment? Third, were we truly men of integrity?
Finally, were we truly men of dedication?"*

**John F. Kennedy before the Massachusetts State Legislature
January 9th, 1961**

My other earlier boss, Dr. Robert V. Walker, described what happened and what he saw on that fateful day. Dr. Walker talked with me some weeks after the assassination. He had a way with words, which I admired in the letters I had typed for him. He said something like this: "Sickly John Kennedy, the great hope and despair of his father after losing an older son, succumbed to the bullets of a brooding introvert."

Chairman of Oral Surgery, Robert V. Walker, M.D., whom I had served as secretary in earlier years, had played baseball for the Tulsa Oilers before opting for his surgical career. His career was ending because he was dying of pancreatic cancer. He decided to do a video about the day the President was assassinated because he and only one other physician who attended the President were still alive. This video was made six months before he died on October 11th, 2010. Here are some of his comments:

Head nurse Doris Nelson protected Jackie. When I saw Jackie standing in front of me with her skirt and legs covered with blood, I just didn't know what to say. I went into the Trauma Room where anesthesiologist "Pepper" Jenkins was trying to set up his anesthesia machine. The President was a big man and his feet stuck out from the bed. I checked for wounds to the mouth, face, or jaw, and I saw the wound to the head—a big hole, and we all knew he wouldn't make it. Dr. Curtis came in and said, "I'll take care of his Addison's disease" and gave him fluids through the cutdowns. Dr. McClelland came in. The President was there only twenty minutes before they put him in a casket and tried to exit.

The doctors all went on to help Governor John Connally who would have died from his wounds without resuscitation and immediate care. The way we got to the Emergency Room was strange. A call went out for Chief of Surgery Tom Shires to come "stat" but we in the lunchroom knew he was in Galveston delivering a paper, so we showed up to help. Once Shires learned of the situation, NASA flew him to Dallas, and he was there to help Connally within 45 minutes. Pepper was in the Trauma Room when Jackie came in and kissed the President's legs and body and placed her ring on his finger. The priest did the last rites. As they were ready to take the casket to Love Field, City coroner Earl Rose objected and said, "In Texas, when you have a murder, you must have an autopsy in this state." The Secret Service was having none of that and an ugly scene developed. I was repulsed by that scene.

Jackie went on later to describe her time with President Kennedy as "that brief moment in Camelot." Malcolm Perry who had attended the President and performed the tracheotomy to open the throat for air had to enlarge the bullet hole in his neck to do so. He was asked by reporters just as he was leaving the Trauma Room whether the bullet hole was an entry or exit wound. He said, "It had clean edges, so I think it was an entry wound."

The story propelled much speculation about where the bullets came from—front or back. He was so very sorry that he nor the other doctors had not looked at the whole body and reached a verdict on where the entry and exit wounds were. He became so upset over all the criticisms and allegations his statement caused that he left practice for quite some time before he returned.

Two other doctors were involved in the Trauma Room scene: Dr. Red Duke, a training surgeon who became famous for his funny comments and had a T.V. show and Dr. Ron Jones. Well, as I said at the beginning of this address, I have no joy in telling about that terrible day.

I am the next to the last one alive, however, of those who were there that day. Dr. McClelland is still alive. [He died in 2019.] Many of the physicians who attended the President participated in the effort to save Lee Harvey Oswald's life when he was shot by Jack Ruby two days later.

Judge Joe B. Brown Jr., whom the author would come to know later after his father conducted the Jack Ruby trial, was called to go to the hospital and conduct the inquest. However, a Garland Justice of the Peace arrived first and insisted the autopsy be done here in Texas. There is a law requiring an autopsy to be done in the state where a murder took place. The Secret Service overrode that law on November 22nd, 1963.

However, Judge Brown, Jr. did do the inquest for the murder of Officer J. D. Tippit, whom Oswald shot later that day, and ordered the Medical Examiner to do that autopsy. Brown later asked the author to do a book about his father's trial of Jack Ruby for killing Lee Harvey Oswald. It is called *Dallas and the Jack Ruby Trial,* published in 2001.

CHAPTER FIVE

U.S. Government Reactions

"Change is the law of life. And those who look only to the past or the present are certain to miss the future."
John F. Kennedy in Frankfurt, June 26th, 1963

The transfer of power from one President to the next required a swearing-in of the new President. That took place in the rear of *Air Force One* right after Judge Sarah Hughes administered the oath of office to Lyndon Johnson, who said these words:

I do solemnly swear (or affirm) that I will faithfully execute the Office of President of the United States, and will to the best of my ability, preserve, protect, and defend the Constitution of the United States.

After the oath, Johnson called John Kennedy's mother, Rose Kennedy, around 2:30 or 3:00 pm to express his condolences. He said, "Mrs. Kennedy, I wish to God that there was something that I could say to you, and I want to tell you that we're grieving with you."

Mrs. Kennedy answered, "Thank you very much. That's very nice. I know you loved Jack, and he loved you."

"Here's Lady Bird," Lyndon said as he handed her the phone.

She said, "Mrs. Kennedy, we feel like our hearts have been cut out of us. We must remember how fortunate our country was to have your son as long as it did. Our love and our prayers are with you."

In a few minutes, Johnson put in a call for Nellie, the wife of injured Governor John Connally. He said, "We are praying for you, darling, and I know that everything is going to be all right, isn't it? Give him a hug and a kiss for me."

Then Air Force One took off with John Kennedy's body in a casket, and Jacqueline sat near him. Upon arrival, reporters greeted the plane, the new President, and his wife. When Lyndon Johnson came gravely down the steps and was given a microphone to speak, he said:

This is a sad time for all people. We have suffered a loss that cannot be weighed. For me, it is a deep personal tragedy. I know the world shares the sorrow that Mrs. Kennedy and her family bear. I will do my best. That is all I can do. I ask for your help and God's.

CHAPTER SIX

Central Intelligence Agency Reactions

*"We are not afraid to entrust the American people
with unpleasant facts, foreign ideas, alien philosophies, and
competitive values. For a nation that is afraid to let its people
judge the truth and falsehood in an open market
is a nation that is afraid of its people."*

**John F. Kennedy remarks February 26th, 1962, on the 20th anniversary
of the Voice of America**

On November 22nd, 1963, upon learning of the arrest of Lee Harvey Oswald in connection with President Kennedy's death, the Mexico City Station contacted CIA headquarters at Langley, Virginia. They said that Oswald had visited the Cuban Consulate in Mexico City the previous month and talked with a clerk named Silvia Duran.

That lady heard the news, remembered that Oswald came seeking a visa for Cuba, and described how he was involved with the Fair Play for Cuba Committee. He was in Mexico City from September 26th through October 2nd, after which he returned to Dallas having had no luck at all in getting a visa.

Duran said the young man came in seeking a visa to Cuba and to the Soviet Union. She had also learned that Oswald had a Russian wife, as the news reports were saying. She said his plan was to pass through Cuba to perhaps help Fidel Castro and then wind up in Russia again where he had defected after serving in the Marine Corps. He showed her a set of papers with his experience on subjects that might impress communists: Military and Far East, Photographer, Organizer, Russian Language, Resident of the USSR, Radio Speaker and Lecturer, Street Agitation, Marxist.

In Mexico City, he had been denied visas after talking with three men. He had argued with Eusebio Azcue, Obyedkov Kostikov, and Oleg Nechiporenko. The latter wrote a book in 1993 called *Passport to Assassination.* Nechiporenko said that Oswald told them in the Mexico City Soviet Embassy that the Washington, DC Soviet Embassy had put him off or turned down his request to return to the Soviet Union. Thus, he had come to Mexico in hopes of a better response.

He claimed that he had been followed by the FBI since his return to the U.S., was unable to get a job, and wanted to leave America. However, he wanted to visit Cuba on the way back to the Soviet Union. He was told that permission would have to be requested from Moscow and that even if he was granted a visa, it might take some four months.[3]

Oswald was refused a Cuban visa and got into a heated discussion with the Cuban consul, Eusebio Azcue, who told Oswald that a person like him was hurting the Cuban cause, not helping it.

He talked with Soviet KGB consuls Kostikov and Nechiporenko. In frustration, he pulled out his pistol, saying that he had to carry it to protect himself from the FBI. They took his weapon and extracted the bullets. The consul made little jokes. After trying to console Oswald, his gun was returned to him. He put the bullets in his pocket and left, with no promise of a quick Cuban or Soviet passport. He bought a return bus ticket under the name of H. O. Lee, matching his Tourist Card, and returned to Dallas on October 2nd, 1963.[4]

---

3 https://www.latimes.com/archives/la-xpm-1992-01-10-mn-1596-story.html
4 https://www.tpaak.com/tpaak-blog/2020/2/5/other-men-in-mexico-city-ii

As things happened on the day of the assassination, John McCone, the head of the Central Intelligence Agency (CIA), was meeting with its chief comptroller on the morning of November 22nd, 1963. They discussed the CIA's image problems. While having lunch, they heard the news about the Kennedy assassination. McCone phoned Bobby Kennedy, who lived nearby. He then told his people, "I'm going to Hickory Hill to be with Bobby."

He arrived at the Kennedy estate and was talking with Robert, the brother of the President, and wife Ethel, when the phone rang. Robert answered the phone, listened briefly, and then hung up. Robert said, "He's dead." It had been J. Edgar Hoover, head of the FBI.

A few minutes later, McCone and Robert walked around the lawn speaking privately. Lyndon Johnson called and told Robert he felt he should be sworn in right away. Robert was taken aback but then agreed. When Robert wanted to fly there right away, McCone said the slain President's body could be brought to Washington as soon as possible.

Air Force One landed at Andrews Air Force Base that evening and John Kennedy's body was taken to Bethesda Naval Medical Center for an autopsy.

McCone returned to the headquarters where the agency's first reaction was to suspect that a foreign, probably communist-directed, effort to destabilize the United States might be underway.

By the next day, information from the Mexico City meeting with the KGB officer at the Soviet Embassy was clarified. It was speculated that Oswald only wanted a change of residence to the Soviet Union rather than making a quick escape after assassinating the President.

However, the Soviets' inability to locate Nikita Khrushchev right after the assassination especially alarmed McCone and his deputies. The premier's absence from Moscow could have meant that he was in a secret command center, hunkering down for an American reprisal or preparing to strike at the United States. However, it became clear within 24 to 48 hours that this was not the case. News of the assassination deeply shocked Russian leaders and made them fear U.S. retaliation if Russia was implicated in any way.

McCone briefed President Johnson, McGeorge Bundy, and Dean Rusk concerning the Oswald-Cuba connection during the coming days. McCone went to the White House on November 23rd to pay last respects to the fallen President. Many world leaders notified the White House that they would send their highest officials to the funeral.

On Monday, November 25th, 1963, McCone attended the state funeral at St. Matthew's Cathedral in Washington. He personally told French President de Gaulle about the threats against him and the danger of marching in the open down the street. In addition to his many intellectual gifts, de Gaulle was exemplary of haughtiness, being both an aristocrat and a revolutionary. He was damned if he was going to fear the funeral processional walk to the burial site. Fifty-eight CIA security officers joined the procession at the funeral, walking along with the leaders to Arlington Cemetery.

Robert Kennedy had overseen the CIA's anti-Castro covert actions, so his dealings with McCone about his brother's murder had a special gravity. Did Castro kill the President because the President had tried to kill Castro?

McCone said he felt there was something troubling Kennedy that he was not disclosing. McCone later said that Kennedy worried about a connection between the assassination plans against Castro and the assassination of President Kennedy. He also felt that Robert Kennedy felt some guilt because he was directly or indirectly involved with the anti-Castro assassination planning.

A flustered Robert Kennedy asked McCone to affirm that the CIA itself was not involved in the assassination. When Kennedy began the question "if they [CIA] had killed my brother," he was quickly assured by MCone that they hadn't.[5]

---

5 DCI John McCone and the Assassination of President John F. Kennedy" by David Robarge, Studies in Intelligence, Vol. 57, No. 3 (September 2013).

CHAPTER SEVEN

Federal Bureau of Investigation Reactions

"If we cannot end now our differences, at least we can help make the world safe for diversity."

John F. Kennedy at the American University, June 10th, 1963

The Special Agent in Charge of the North Texas branch of the FBI, Gordon Shanklin, was told by his secretary: "Some shots were fired at the president's car." He dialed J. Edgar Hoover, director of the FBI. Hoover told Shanklin, "Offer the full services of our laboratory and fingerprint division. Find out how badly he's hurt and call me back."

Shanklin sent Agent Doyle Williams to Parkland Hospital, and he was roughed up by two Secret Service men until he could get out his government ID.[6] Cartha "Deke" DeLoach had also been the liaison between the FBI and the CIA.

Shanklin gathered his top North Texas FBI agents together. Unfortunately, special agent James Hosty sat in silence on the morning of November 22nd, 1963, when Shanklin asked if they had any information that might be useful to the Secret Service. One of Hosty's cases was a disgruntled defector to the Soviet Union who had returned to live in the Dallas-Ft. Worth area. He had

---

6 Hoover's FBI: The Inside Story by Hoover's Trusted Lieutenant. Cartha D. "Deke" DeLoach., Regnery Publishing, Inc. Washington, D.C., 1995, p. 115.

recently left Hosty an allegedly threatening note not to bother his Russian wife with questions that they should only ask her husband, Lee Harvey Oswald.[7]

FBI secretary Nanny Fenner said the note left by Oswald on November 12th, 1963, said something like this: "Let this be a warning. I will blow up the FBI and the Dallas Police Department if you don't stop bothering my wife." Someone at the FBI told Hosty to destroy this note.

Cartha DeLoach had been working as assistant director of the FBI's Domestic Intelligence Division since June 1961 and now was to be the intelligence end of the assassination investigation. Hoover wanted to see a few of his men right away. He was all business without a trace of sadness or sorrow. In fact, Deke DeLoach commented that Hoover seemed to take glee in calling Robert Kennedy to tell him of his brother's death.

According to DeLoach, Hoover told his men, "We want to go all out on this investigation, and we want to move fast." DeLoach thought all Hoover was thinking about was protecting the bureau and avoiding criticism.

Hoover must have liked Western movies, for he and John Wayne always had compliments for each other. In Hoover's eyes, he was similar to Wayne in movies as a good guy against the bad guys. He surrounded himself with very ambitious agents, determined to make their mark in the world if it was in accordance with Hoover's goals for the FBI.

Hoover's dislike of the Kennedys began years earlier, according to books by DeLoach and William Sullivan. In 1942, the FBI was investigating a beautiful young Scandinavian woman whom they suspected of spying for the Nazis in Washington while working as a journalist. Agents had a microphone planted in her apartment and a tap on her telephone. Hoover could hardly contain his delight when he saw Lt. John F. Kennedy's voice reported on those tapes. Hoover immediately reported Lt. Kennedy's liaison with the

---

7 DeLoach, p. 114

Danish woman to the White House along with a suggestion that Kennedy be transferred "for security reasons."[8]

Bill Sullivan was Hoover's right-hand man for several years, but he began to offer criticisms to Hoover, even suggesting that the old director was losing it and should resign. At the point where Sullivan resigned from the FBI, he had just finished writing his memoirs for *The Bureau: My Thirty Years in Hoover's FBI*. He was suddenly shot outside his home by a young man who said he mistook the man for a deer. Many have wondered about a possible assassination.

Hoover ordered his agents to enter Sullivan's house and scour it for any negative information about Hoover and the FBI.

As regards Lt. John Kennedy and his Danish mistress, DeLoach wrote that Kennedy never knew what hit him. One day he was dating glamorous women, and the next day he was on his way to command a P.T. boat in the middle of the Pacific.

While Hoover tried to sabotage Jack Kennedy's presidential election campaign, he later quietly helped Richard Nixon, according to DeLoach. Until the 1940s, Catholics were kept out of the bureau along with blacks, Jews, Hispanics, and female agents. It was called the "lily-white agency".[9]

When John Kennedy was President, he was asked why he didn't fire Hoover. The President said, "You don't fire God!" In fact, *Newsweek* writer Evan Thomas wrote an article about Hoover on September 22nd, 1991, entitled: "Mr. God Goes to Washington."

On November 22nd, 1963, Hoover sent two FBI agents, Francis O'Neill and James Sibert, to accompany the casket and observe the autopsy of the dead President. At Bethesda Naval Hospital, doctors found no single bullet

---

8 The Bureau: My Thirty Years in Hoover's FBI, William C. Sullivan, W.W. Norton & Co., New York, 1979, pg. 47-57
9 DeLoach, p. 48

for the entry wound in the right strap muscle where the bullet traversed the neck of the President. William Geer, the Secret Service agent who had driven the automobile and who attended the autopsy, told the doctors that a bullet was found on wounded Governor John Connally's gurney.[10]

That bullet that had passed through the President's neck and the Governor's chest was found at the hospital. A recent book by Secret Service agent Paul Landis, according to an interview with him in 2023, said that he had found the bullet in the car and placed it where it could be seen by those caring for the President at Parkland Hospital.

Clint Hill, the Secret Service agent who threw himself over the body of Jacqueline and John Kennedy did not endorse Landis' book about this, saying that he found discrepancies in the details. For example, Landis said he put the bullet on the gurney where the President lay but he was never in that ER room with the President. Some believe that Landis, at age 88, taking credit for this act was questionable.11[11] However, somebody placed the nearly pristine bullet where the Parkland medical staff could see it and analysis of bullet scratch marks fit the rifle that was found.

The two FBI agents present at the autopsy brought back two of the many tiny metal fragments found in the President's brain: 1.65 grams and 0.15 of a grain. FBI special agent Vincent Drain, Dallas Police Lt. J. C. Day, and Secret Service agent Winston Lawson recorded the evidence of the assassination:

1. A live 6.5 mm. rifle shell was found in a 6.5 Mannlicher-Carcano rifle on the sixth floor of the Texas Book Depository building.
2. Three spent 6.5 mm. shells were found on the sixth floor of the Depository inside the northeast window.
3. One blanket where the rifle had been stored in the garage of Mrs. Ruth Paine in Irving, Texas.

---

10 DeLoach, p. 131

11 Jacqueline Cutler, "I Buried It Bad" in USA Today, November 5, 2023.

4. The shirt was taken from Lee H. Oswald at police headquarters.

5. Brown wrapping paper was found on the sixth floor near the rifle, believed to have been used to wrap the weapon.

6. Sample of brown paper was used by the Book Depository, and a sample of paper tape used for mailing books.

7. Fragment of the nearly pristine bullet found in the wrist of Governor John Connally.

8. Smith and Wesson .38 revolver, taken from Lee H. Oswald at Texas Theater.

9. 3 bullets recovered from the body of Officer J. D. Tippit.

10. One 6.5 mm. bolt action rifle, inscribed "1940, Made in Italy." On the four-power scope of the gun was inscribed "Ordnance Optics Inc., Hollywood, California."

11. At the autopsy, X-rays showed 30-40 metal fragments lodged in the skull and embedded in the brain of President Kennedy.

John Kennedy's Brain

[Note: After the autopsy and examination of metal in the brain, the remnants of the brain were placed in a stainless-steel container with a screw-top lid. First, the container was stored in a file cabinet in the office of the Secret Service. In later days, it was then taken to the National Archives in a secure room used by Kennedy's secretary, Evelyn Lincoln, while she organized his presidential papers. When it was reported missing some years later, an investigation was ordered by Attorney General Ramsey Clark. It was learned that former Attorney General Robert Kennedy and his assistant Angie Novello had taken the container to prevent it from being put on view.][12]

---

12 James Swanson, End of Days: The Assassination of John F. Kennedy, 2013

Deke DeLoach's book about his FBI career described studies with the following findings:

A May 1992 *Journal of the American Medical Association* stated that the physicians who performed the autopsy on the night of November 22nd, 1963, established beyond a reasonable doubt that the President was struck by only two bullets, which hit him from above and behind his head and neck.

Some say a sniper was firing from the grassy knoll but a photograph by Mary Moorman at the moment the President was shot clearly showed the grassy knoll and all the people waiting there with no gunman or suspicious figure. In addition, Abraham Zapruder was standing on the cement walkway at the grassy knoll and no bullets whizzed by him as he videotaped the President putting his hands to his throat and then his head exploding with the last bullet.

Some say more should have been done at the autopsy. However, the physicians doing the autopsy had been told that Jacqueline Kennedy requested a limited autopsy, so their main attention was on the head and neck of the President.

Deke DeLoach wrote that later in the day after Oswald's arrest, Dallas Police Chief Jesse Curry said on television that the FBI had Lee Harvey Oswald under surveillance. The Dallas Agent in Charge, Gordon Shanklin, said they had a file on Oswald. As always, Director Hoover was concerned with his own reputation and that of his bureau. If they were following Oswald, why didn't they let the Secret Service know about his job at the Texas Schoolbook Depository on the motorcade route? This indicated sloppy work by FBI agents. For agent Hosty, he lived with depression and self-reproach for the rest of his life according to various local news reports.

Hoover told Deke DeLoach to call Chief Curry to make a public retraction about having Oswald under surveillance as soon as possible. He added that if the chief didn't offer the retraction, Hoover would cut off all privileges. Within minutes, Curry was back on television with a correction of sorts. But Hoover thought it was insufficient and did cut off Curry's Dallas Police Department privileges.[13]

---

13 DeLoach, p. 133

CHAPTER EIGHT

Jacqueline Kennedy's Reactions

*"I believe in an America that is officially neither Catholic,
Protestant nor Jewish—where no public official either requests or
accepts instructions on public policy from the Pope,
the National Council of Churches, or any other ecclesiastical source—
where no religious body seeks to impose its will directly or indirectly
upon the general populace or the public acts of its officials—and
where religious liberty is so indivisible that an act against
one church is treated as an act against all."*

**John F. Kennedy, presidential candidate, September 12th, 1960,
at the Greater Houston Ministerial Association**

Jacqueline sat quietly on a chair just outside Trauma Room 1 at Parkland Hospital and asked someone for a cigarette. She had handed a doctor a large piece of her husband's skull upon arrival. She watched everybody go by as doctors came and went. Finally, Dr. Kemp Clark came out and told her that the President was dead. She said, "I know."

From the emergency room at Parkland Hospital, Jacqueline Kennedy asked that a priest be called to administer last rites to the President. It was the parish of Father Oscar Huber, C.M., who arrived within thirty minutes. A sheet covered the President and Huber stood next to Jacqueline to carry out last rites as he anointed the body. He said over the President's body words such as: "I absolve you from your sins in the name of the Father, and of the Son, and of the Holy Ghost. Amen." Jackie then asked Father Huber to pray for her husband.[14]

Huber explained later in an interview that anointing is to be done before the soul has left the body. Huber said the time of the soul leaving the body might be two to three hours after a sudden death. Thus, last rites could guarantee salvation if the deceased had sorrow for his sins. Father Huber thought that John Kennedy was a good man from what he had read and would have sorrow for his sins. Father Huber donated that interview to the JFK Library some months after Kennedy's death.[15]

Some may wonder about this issue of anointing after death. There is the Catechism of the Catholic Church 1514: "The anointing of the sick is not a sacrament for those only who are at the point of death. Hence, as soon as any of the faithful begins to be in danger of death from sickness or old age, the fitting time for him to receive this sacrament has certainly already arrived." The three parts of the anointing are the prayer for God's help for the sick person, the laying of hands on the sick person, and the anointing with oil on the forehead and hands, signifying healing and the presence of God.

There is also thought to be a judgment at death according to Catholicism such as this: You will stand before God and your entire life will be laid bare. It will be determined if you died in God's friendship or not. After your judgment, there are three options: heaven, purgatory, or hell.

There had never been a Catholic president before. It was the convention of 1776 that declared the exercise of religion to be free in the United States. Many thought it really didn't matter what religious denomination a president

---

14 https://parade.com/232133/parade/priest-who-gave-jfk-his-last-rites-i-assured-mrs-kenedy-i-would -pray-for-the-president/

15 https://www.jfklibrary.org/sites/default/files/archives/JFKOH/Huber%2C%20Oscar%20L/ JFKOH-OLH-01/JFKOH-OLH-01-TR.pdf) Source: "The Strange Saga of JFK and the Original 'Dr. Feelgood'" Peter Keating, November 22, 2013

claimed. As Thomas Jefferson said, "It does me no injury for my neighbor to say there are twenty gods or no god. It neither picks my pocket nor breaks my leg. The way to silence religious disputes is to take no notice of them."[16]

Jacqueline Kennedy spent the two days after the death of her husband arranging a funeral based on the funeral of President Abraham Lincoln. Some have said she should not have placed him in the same category as Lincoln, but there was nothing to stop her from asking for this special service.

She instructed chief usher J. B. West to follow the details of Lincoln's 1865 state funeral. She trained little John to salute the flag at the appropriate time. She prepared Carolyn to kneel and kiss the flag-draped coffin of her father.

Various officials and heads of state were received and viewed the coffin. The public was not admitted at the outset. On November 24th, the coffin was taken to the Capitol Rotunda. There, the public was admitted, and more than 240,000 people filed past Kennedy's flag-draped coffin. On November 25th, 1963, the day of the funeral, a horse-drawn caisson carried the casket down Pennsylvania Avenue to the White House. That is where Mrs. Kennedy, her children, and the mourners, official and personal, all waited.

They walked with the procession—military escort, band, and the symbolic riderless horse with boots reversed in the stirrups—eight blocks to St. Matthew's Cathedral, where the funeral service was held.

Even though Mrs. Kennedy was warned that there were threats against the heads of state, she insisted on this walk to the church by leaders and the others in the procession. De Gaulle's determination (despite an offer that he could ride in a truck, tank, or vehicle) dared unknown forces to be unsuccessful in any assassination attempts. The leaders and the widow were resolute in their actions as the band played Chopin's *Sonata #3 Funeral March* and the crowd proceeded at a slow pace.

---

16 Thomas Jefferson. Notes on the State of Virginia, Query XVII, "Religion."

Near the head of the marching mourners were 6'4" President Lyndon Johnson and 6'3" President Charles de Gaulle, looming tall targets for assassins. Johnson was warned by the Secret Service and others that there would be little protection available. Despite being extremely nervous, he proudly strode along with the others.

Prince Philip represented the Queen of England, who was pregnant with Edward, who was born four months later. The Prince Consort played with little John Jr., making him laugh during the long wait. Jaqueline was very beholden to him for distracting the little fellow.

After the church service, the caisson carried the President's remains to their final resting place in Arlington Memorial Cemetery. John and Jacqueline Kennedy had been impressed by the eternal flame at the Tomb of the Unknown Soldier at the Arch of Triumph in Paris. She had asked for such a flame to be constructed, and she lit the flame with a taper when they arrived at that site in the cemetery.

On that day, November 25th, 1963, she strode along with the procession. She behaved as if she was beautiful and reverent. Perhaps that was the secret of Jackie's charm, her gentle behavior and respect for people.

Since she believed that all the heads of state walked with little protection, risking their lives. She wrote President Johnson the following letter the next day.[17]

Dear Mr. President,

Thank you for walking yesterday behind my husband. You did not have to do that. I am sure many people forbade you to take such a risk, but you did it anyway.

Thank you for your letters to my children. What those letters will mean to them later—you can only imagine. The touching thing is

---

17 https://newscut.mprnews.org/2013/11/a-letter-from-jackie/index.htm

they have always loved you so much. They were most moved to have a letter from you now.

And most of all, Mr. President. Thank you for the way you have always treated me, the way you and the first lady have always been to me, before, when my husband was alive, and now as President.

I think the relationship of the presidential and vice-presidential families could be a rather strained one. From the history I've been reading ever since I was in the White House, I gather it often was in the past.

But you were my husband's right arm, and I always thought the greatest act of a gentleman that I had seen on earth was how you, the Majority Leader when he came to the Senate as just another little freshman who looked up to you and took orders from you, could then serve as Vice President to a man who had served under you and been taught by you.

But more than that we were friends, all four of us. All you did for me as a friend and the happy times we had.

I always thought way before the nomination that your wife should be First Lady, but I don't need to tell you here what I think of her qualities, her extraordinary grace of character, her willingness to assume every burden. She assumed so many for me and I love her so much. And I love your two daughters.

It was so strange. Last night, I was wandering through this house. There in the Treaty Room is your chandelier, and I had framed the page we all signed. Underneath, I had written, "The day the Vice President brought the East Room chandelier back from the Capitol."

It mustn't be very much help to your first day in office to hear children on the lawn at recess. It is just one more example of your kindness that you let them stay. I promise they will soon be gone.

Thank you, Mr. President.

The new President telephoned the former first lady the day after the funeral.

He said: "I just wanted you to know you were loved by so many and so much."

She said: "Oh, Mr. President!"

He said: "I'm one of them. Listen, sweetie, now first thing you've got to learn some things and one of them is that you don't bother me. You give me strength. Don't send me anything. You just come over here and put your arm around me. That's all you do. When you haven't got anything else to do, let's take a walk. Let's walk around the backyard and just let me tell you how much you mean to all of us and how we can carry on if you give us a little strength. I want you to know this I told my Mama a long time ago when everybody gave up about my election in 1948."

She said: "Yes?"

He said: "My mother and my wife and my sisters and you females got a lot of courage that we men don't have. And so, we have to rely on you and depend on you, and you've got something to do. You've got the President relying on you."

She said: "Okay. Any time. Thank you for calling, Mr. President. Goodbye."

He said: "Bye, sweetie. Do come by."

She said: "I will."[18]

On December 1st, 1963, Jacqueline Kennedy sent this letter to Chairman Nikita Khrushchev.[19]

18 https://americanradioworks.publicradio.org/features/prestapes/jklbj.html
19 https://history.state.gov/historicaldocuments/frus1961-63v06/d120

Dear Mr. Chairman President,

I would like to thank you for sending your representative to my husband's funeral. He looked so upset when he came through the line, and I was very moved. I tried to give him a message for you that day, but it was such a terrible day for me, I do not know if my words came out as I meant them to.

So now, in one of the last nights I will spend in the White House, in one of the last letters I will write on this paper at the White House, I would like to write you my message.

I send it only because I know how much my husband cared about peace, and how the relation between you and him was central to this care in his mind. He used to quote your words in some of his speeches—"The next war the survivors will envy the dead."

You and he were adversaries, but you were allied in a determination that the world should not be blown up. You respected each other and could deal with each other. I know that the new President will make every effort to establish the same relationship with you.

The danger which troubled my husband was the war might be started not so much by the big men as by the little ones.

While big men know the need for self-control and restraint—little men are sometimes moved more by fear and pride. If only in the future the big men can continue to make the little ones sit down and talk before they start to fight.

I know that the new President will continue the policy in which my husband so deeply believed—a policy of control and restraint—and he will need your help.

I send this letter because I know so deeply the importance of the relationship which existed between you and my husband, and also because of your kindness, and that of your wife in Vienna.

I read that she had tears in her eyes when she left the American Embassy in Moscow, after signing the book of mourning. Please thank her for that.

Jacqueline Kennedy hand-wrote this note shortly after the assassination to Mrs. J.D. Tippit, whose husband was killed by Oswald:

What can I say to you—my husband's death is responsible for you losing your husband. Wasn't one life enough to take on that day?

I lit a flame for Jack at Arlington Cemetery that will burn forever. I consider that it burns for your husband too and so will everyone who ever sees it.

With my inexpressible sympathy, Jacqueline Kennedy[20]

Apparently, Mrs. Kennedy reached out to Khrushchev and to Mrs. Tippit because she understood that all humans have similar emotions and goals for themselves.

---

20 https://www.huffpost.com/entry/jackie-kennedy-letter-widow_n_4311773

CHAPTER NINE

Lyndon and Lady Bird Johnson's Reactions

"When I ran for Presidency of the United States, I knew that this country faced serious challenges, but I could not realize the burdens of this office—how heavy and constant would be those burdens."

John F. Kennedy, July 25th, 1961, Radio and Television Report to the American People on the Berlin Crisis

Soon after the assassination of President John Kennedy, Mrs. Lady Bird Johnson wrote down an account of what happened. She continued to write a diary that was over 800 pages and which was made available to the public.

It all began so beautifully. After a drizzle in the morning, the sun came out bright and clear. We were driving into Dallas. In the lead car were the President and Mrs. Kennedy. John and Nellie Connally, a Secret Service car full of men, and then our car with Lyndon and me and Senator Ralph Yarborough...

Suddenly, there was a sharp, loud report. It sounded like a shot. The sound seemed to me to come from a building on the right above my shoulder. A moment passed and then two more shots rang out in rapid succession.... I thought the noise must come from firecrackers...

Over the car radio system, I heard "Let's get out of here!" and our Secret Service man, Rufus Youngblood, vaulted over the front seat on top of Lyndon, threw him to the floor, and said, "Get down."

Senator Yarborough and I ducked our heads. The car accelerated terrifically—faster and faster… We pulled up to a building. I looked up and saw a sign, "HOSPITAL." Only then did I believe this might be what it was. Senator Yarborough kept saying in an excited voice, "Have they shot the President?" I said something like, "No, it can't be." We were still the third car. Secret Service men began to pull, lead, guide, and hustle us out. I cast one last look over my shoulder and saw in the President's car a bundle of pink, just like a drift of blossoms, lying in the back seat. It was Mrs. Kennedy lying over the President's body.

The Secret Service men rushed us to the right, then to the left, and then onward into a quiet room in the hospital—a very small room… People came and went. There was talk about where we would go—to the plane, to our house, back to Washington…

Lyndon said, "You had better try and see Jackie and Nellie." We didn't know what had happened to John [Connally]… Suddenly, I found myself face to face with Jackie in a small hallway… She was quite alone. I don't think I ever saw anyone so much alone in my life. I went up to her, put my arms around her, and said something like "God help us all."

And then I went to see Nellie… I hugged her tight and we both cried, and I said, "Nellie, John's going to be all right."

I think it was Kenny O'Donnell's face that I first knew the truth and from Kenny's voice that I first heard the words "The President is dead." Mr. Kilduff entered and said to Lyndon, "Mr. President."

Our departure from the hospital and approach to the cars was one of the swiftest walks I ever made… We entered Air Force One for the first time. There was a TV set on, and the commentator was saying, "Lyndon B. Johnson, now President of the United States."

We heard that we were going to wait for Mrs. Kennedy and the coffin. There was a telephone call to Washington. I believe to the Attorney General [Robert Kennedy]. It was decided that Lyndon should be sworn in here as quickly as possible because of national and world implications and because we did not know how widespread this was as to intended victims...

Mrs. Kennedy had arrived by this time, as had the coffin. With Jackie standing by Lyndon, her hair falling in her face but very composed, with me beside him. Lyndon took the oath of office.

We all sat around the plane. The casket was in the corridor. I went into the small private room to see Mrs. Kennedy, and though it was a very hard thing to do, she made it as easy as possible. She said things like, "Oh Lady Bird, we've liked you two so much... Oh, what if I had not been there. I'm so glad I was there."

I looked at her. Mrs. Kennedy's dress was stained with blood. One leg was almost entirely covered with it and her right glove was caked. It was caked with blood, her husband's blood. That immaculate woman, exquisitely dressed and caked in blood. I asked her if I couldn't get someone in to help her change and she said, "I want them to see what they have done to Jack."

I tried to express how we felt. I said, "Oh, Mrs. Kennedy, you know we never even wanted to be Vice President and now, dear God, it's come to this." The flight to Washington was silent... I remember one little thing Lyndon had said in the hospital room—"Tell the children to get a Secret Service man with them." [The Johnson daughters were teenagers 16 and 19.]

Finally, we got to Washington. The casket went off first, then Mrs. Kennedy, and then we followed. The family had come to join her. Lyndon made a very simple, very brief, and I think strong statement to the people there. Only about four sentences. We got in helicopters, dropped him off at the White House, and I came home with Liz Carpenter.

At 9 p.m. the night of the assassination, Johnson was back in his office and called his old friend, Supreme Court Justice Arthur Goldberg. After Goldberg expressed his confidence in Lyndon, the new President had a request.

LBJ: I want you to be thinking about what I ought to do to try to bring all these elements together and unite this country. And the main thing is to preserve our system in the world because if it starts falling to pieces and some of the extremes are going to—proceed on the wrong assumption, why we could deteriorate pretty quickly.

AG: It won't. I have no doubt about that…

LBJ: I want to give some thought, by the way, whether we ought to have a joint session of Congress—after, and what would I say to them? Think about it… I want you to think about who I talk to on the delivery side and how I ought to do it without—I mean with dignity and reserve and without being down on my knees, but at the same time, men who'll have respect and confidence. There's nobody in town I believe in more than you and I have just got to have your help.

AG: Well, it is there for the asking and we wish you every good fortune in the world. You'll do well. We have complete confidence.

[Johnson did speak to a joint session of Congress on November 27th, 1963.]

On November 25th, after Kennedy's funeral, Johnson phoned Larry O'Brien, one of Kennedy's close aides. Ken O'Donnell, a long-time friend of Kennedy, was with Larry when the phone call occurred.

LBJ: Needless to say, I'm most anxious for you to continue just like you have been because I need you a lot more than he did.

LO'B: Mr. President, Ken is here with me. Do you have an immediate problem?

LBJ: No, no, I just wanted you to know how strongly I felt about you and Ken and all the rest of the staff, and I had talked to some of them individually, but I hadn't had a chance to run into you, and I think you know the confidence and admiration I have for you.

LO'B: I know that Mr. President.

LBJ: I don't expect you to love me as much as you did him, but I expect you will after you've been around awhile.

LO'B: Right, Mr. President.

CHAPTER TEN

The New President's Reactions

"Mankind must put an end to war or war
will put an end to mankind."
John F. Kennedy address to United Nations September 26, 1961

On November 28, 1962, Johnson appointed Supreme Court Chief Justice Earl Warren to chair a Commission to investigate the murder of President Kennedy. He also wanted his long-time mentor, Senator Richard Russell, to serve on the committee but knew Russell didn't like Warren. Thus, he simply announced Russell's appointment and then phoned him.

Johnson used the fear of nuclear war with the Soviet Union to coerce national leaders to investigate the assassination and work with each other, whether they liked them or not.

Transcripts of his phone calls show how he persuaded people by saying that a war could "kill 40 million Americans in an hour." He would say, "We've got to save our country." He often would add a little sweetness to his requests. He said things like, "Just come and sit in the warm water of the White House swimming pool and have a little sherry and a good hamburger. A car will be over to pick you up in 20 minutes."

Some people were resistant to his requests so that he had to issue commands. Here is an example of that with Richard Russell when he discussed the creation of the Warren Commission to investigate the assassination:

LBJ: Dick, it has already been announced and you can serve with anybody for the good of America. We've got to take this out of the arena where they're testifying that Khrushchev and Castro did this and did that and kicking us into a war that can kill 40 million Americans in an hour.

Russell: I have never...

LBJ: You're my man on that commission. And you're going to do it. And don't tell me what you can do and what you can't because I can't arrest you and I'm not going to put the FBI on you, but you're god dammed sure going to serve. I'll tell you that.

Russell: Mr. President, you ought to have told me you were gonna name me.

LBJ: I told you. I told you today I was gonna name the chief justice when I called you.

Russell: You did not...

LBJ: I did...

Russell: You didn't tell me you were gonna name him...

LBJ: I told you I was gonna name Warren and you said it would be better to name Harlan.

Russell: Well, you ought not to be so persuasive.

LBJ: Well, I think I ought to.

Russell: I think you did wrong getting Warren and I know damned well you did wrong in getting me. But we'll both do the best we can.

LBJ: No, I think that's what you'll do. That's the kind of American both of you are. Good night.

There was something terribly enthralling in the exercise of influence. Johnson knew how to persuade the older men but was especially proud when he could convince younger people to tell his story. To project one's soul onto some gracious person, to hear one's own intellectual views echoed back to one with the added music of passion and youth was a real joy to President Johnson.

Chief Justice Earl Warren was reluctant to lead this investigation. However, he consented, and the Warren Commission was created on November 29, 1963, just seven days after the assassination. The President directed the Commission to evaluate all the facts and report its findings and conclusions to him.

Once the Warren Commission finished its study, Warren said he never saw any convincing evidence to disprove the finding that Lee Harvey Oswald was solely responsible for assassinating President Kennedy.

In a call with J. Edgar Hoover who was investigating Kennedy's assassination, Hoover told Johnson that Lee Harvey Oswald was the lone gunman.

LBJ: Well, your conclusion is a. he's the one that did it; b. the man he was after was the President. He would have hit him three times, except the Governor turned.

JEH: I think that is correct.

LBJ: That there is no connection between him and Ruby that you can detect now. And e. whether he was connected with the Cuban operation with money, you're trying to...

JEH: That's what we're trying to nail down now because he was strongly pro-Castro, he was strongly anti-American, and he had been in correspondence, which we have, with the Soviet embassy here in Washington and with the American Civil Liberties Union and with this Committee for Fair Play to Cuba. None of those letters, however, dealt with any indication of violence or contemplated assassination...

It seems to me that the President ought to always be in a bulletproof car. It certainly would prevent anything like this from ever happening again. It doesn't mean you could have a thousand Secret Service men on guard and still a sniper can snipe you from up on the window if you are exposed, like the President was. But you can't do it if you have a solid top, bulletproof top to it, as it should be...

LBJ: You mean, if I ride around my ranch, I ought to be in a bulletproof car?

JEH: Well, I would certainly think so Mr. President. It seems to me that the car down on your ranch there... the little car that we rode around in when I was down there. I think it ought to be bulletproof. I think it ought to be done very quietly... I think you ought to take precautions because on that ranch, it is perfectly easy for somebody to get on the ranch.

LBJ: Think those entrances all ought to be guarded though, don't you?

JEH: Oh, I think by all means. I think you've got to recognize the capacity of a so-called prisoner because without that security, anything can be done.

Lyndon Johnson began the business of meeting with people who would serve him serve the country and invite important leaders of other countries to visit him. On

December 29, 1963, he welcomed West German Chancellor Ludwig Erhard for an official state visit. Rather than hosting it in Washington, D.C., he invited the chancellor and his companions for a barbecue at the LBJ ranch.

Bad weather caused them to move the dinner into the local high school gymnasium. A local broadcast personality emceed the event, and Texas pianist

Van Cliburn played classical music. The food was served buffet style on paper plates and included pinto beans, spareribs, coleslaw, and fried apricot pies.

The Johnsons continued to incorporate the arts even within their own family. Their daughter, Luci Baines Johnson, recited "Peter and the Wolf" at the National Music Camp on July 23, 1964. Van Cliburn was invited to direct the Interlochen Youth Symphony and perform the music to accompany Luci. All performed in the casual attire of a camp uniform to an audience of almost 4,000. It is quite likely that Johnson wanted to copy the elegant cultural contributions inspired by Jacqueline Kennedy at the White House.

Howard Brennan's Reactions

"One person can make a difference,
and everyone should try."

John F. Kennedy at City Hall, New Orleans, Louisiana, on May 4, 1962

A total of five people observed someone with a rifle moving and poking it in and out of the window on the sixth floor of the Texas Schoolbook Depository where Oswald worked. They assumed it was security personnel of some sort with the presidential motorcade about to arrive. However, it was the description given by Howard Brennan that was broadcast to police officers after the assassination. He knew what the sniper looked like, and he felt he had to give this information to law enforcement personnel. Here is the statement by Howard Leslie Brennan on November 22, 1963:

> I am presently employed by the Wallace and Beard Construction Company as a steam fitter and have been so employed for about the past 7 weeks. I am working on a pipeline in the Katy Railroad yards at the west end of Pacific Street near the railroad tracks. We had knocked off for lunch and I had dinner at the cafeteria at Record and Main Street and had come back to see the President of the United States.
>
> I was sitting on a ledge or wall near the intersection of Houston Street and Elm Street near the red-light pole. I was facing in a northerly direction looking across the street from where I was sitting. I take

. 49 .

this building across the street to be about 7 stories anyway in the east end of the building and the second row of windows from the top I saw a man in this window. I had seen him before the President's car arrived. He was just sitting up there looking down apparently waiting for the same thing I was to see the President. I did not notice anything unusual about this man.

He was a white man in his early 30's, slender, nice looking, and would weigh about 165 to 175 pounds. He had on light colored clothing but definitely not a suit. I proceeded to watch the President's car as it turned left at the corner where I was and about 50 yards from the intersection of Elm and Houston and to a point, I would say the President's back was in line with the last window I have previously described. I heard what I thought was a backfire.

It ran in my mind that it might be someone throwing a firecracker out the window of the red brick building and I looked up at the building. I then saw this man I had described in the window, and he was taking aim with a high-powered rifle. I could see all of the barrel of the gun. I do not know if it had a scope on it or not. I was looking at the man in this window at the time of the last explosion.

Then, this man let the gun down to his side and stepped out of sight. He did not seem to be in any hurry. I could see this man from about his belt up. There was nothing unusual about him at all in appearance. I believe that I could identify this man if I ever saw him again.[21]

A description of the suspect was broadcast to all Dallas police at 12:45 a.m. Brennan later at the line-up of Lee Harvey Oswald said, "He looks like him. But the man I saw wasn't disheveled like this fella… I just can't be positive."

---

21 https://texashistory.unt.edu/ark:/67531/metapth339901/n1/1/

During extensive questioning, Brennan said that if he could identify the shooter, and in case there was a conspiracy, he was afraid for the safety of himself and his family. But after Oswald was killed, he no longer felt it was dangerous to identify him.

The first shot hit the arm of a traffic signal light and street name that hung out over the street of the motorcade route. A later photograph of that street sign showed a bullet hole. The bullet trajectory was redirected, and the bullet hit a concrete curb where the cement flew up and cut the cheek of a parade observer, James T. Tague mentioned earlier.

The second shot caused Mrs. Kennedy to reach over to her husband's throat which he clutched. The third and fatal shot was fired some 88 yards from the 6th floor window into the back part of the head, and brain matter splattered everywhere. The skull blast made it clear to Mrs. Kennedy that an assassin was shooting people in the limousine, and she was scared. Fearing for her life, she jumped onto the back of the limousine, but Secret Service Agent Clint Hill running forward behind the limousine, pushed her back into the seat and laid his body over both Kennedys as they sped off to Parkland Hospital.

Mr. Brennan ran to a policeman to describe the man he saw. Mr. Brennan was a man with an ulcer, a family, and had deep religious convictions. He discussed this experience with his pastor, J. Edward Cherry Holmes. He was coaxed by Cherry Holmes to write a book about his experience, and the two produced *Eyewitness to History: The Kennedy Assassination as Seen by Howard L. Brennan,* produced in 1987 by Texian Press.

CHAPTER TWELVE

Lee Harvey Oswald's Reactions

*"All men are created equal, and the rights of every man
are diminished when the rights of one man are threatened."*

John F. Kennedy, June 11, 1963, Report to the American People on Civil Rights

After the assassination, Oswald left the Depository and got on a bus to go to his boarding house. However, the bus was caught in traffic from the motorcade and did not move. In addition, a former landlady, Mary Bledsoe, was on the bus and she had evicted Lee from her premises three weeks earlier when she heard him speaking Russian on the telephone.

He got up from his seat, asked for a transfer, and got off the bus. He walked over to the Greyhound bus station where a cab was waiting. He got in the cab and gave the driver the destination of an intersection two blocks from his rooming house at 1026 Beckley across the Trinity River. He had the driver let him out and he walked the rest of the way to his lodging.

When he entered, his landlady was watching television and tried to tell him about the assassination. He rudely paid her no attention. He went to his room where we know from police reports that he picked up his pistol and a jacket, probably intended to cover his pistol. Then, without a word, he walked out the front door. She was surprised that he had come home in the middle of a workday. She wondered if he expected someone to pick him up but saw nobody when she looked out.

Anxious as he must have been, he couldn't stay still. He kept moving and walked a few blocks further across the street near the Oak Cliff Christian Church at Tenth Street and Patton. Suddenly, a Dallas police patrol car pulled over to Oswald, probably in response to the description sent out by headquarters about the presidential assassin.

Oswald had made up cards in his billfold using other names like A. J. Hidell in addition to cards with his own name. He had no driver's license because he never learned to drive nor had the money for a vehicle. He may have been afraid the officer would make a fuss over his I.D. cards and the two names on the cards.

The officer was getting out of the car to come over and examine him and his identification cards more closely. Then, Oswald shot Officer J. D. Tippit four times.

He was seen shooting the officer by four witnesses. Oswald then slowly jogged off, discarding his spent cartridges and saying something like "poor damn cop" or "poor dumb cop." He would shortly pull off his jacket and drop it, probably thinking it would be described by the witnesses to the shooting.

Within a minute, he was on Jefferson Street, where there were stores and the Texas movie theater. Jefferson was the main thorough for this Dallas suburb called Oak Cliff. The movie theater was showing a 1961 Audie Murphy narrated movie called *War Is Hell* about Korea. So many people in Dallas had met Texan Murphy, including the author, that he was not only a war hero but our Dallas hero. Murphy was the most decorated soldier of WWII and had been injured three times. His movie directors knew he had trouble sleeping, having suffered post-traumatic stress symptoms, and could only rest if he had a gun under his pillow. Somehow, that extraordinary ex-GI contrasted with the ex-GI who would enter this theater with a gun.

The other movie in this double-feature cinema was the 1963 *Cry of Battle* starring Van Heflin, Rita Moreno, and James MacArthur, about Filipino soldiers fighting Japanese soldiers.

Witnesses who saw Oswald kill Officer Tippit got on the dead officer's radio phone and reported the murder. So, police cars were racing up and down Jefferson Street. As Oswald turned away from the street to look in the window of a shoe store, manager Johnny Brewer saw him moving furtively. Brewer had the radio on and knew about the murder of the president and the murder of a policeman only three blocks away. Oswald had been a customer at his store sometime in the past, so Brewer paid attention.

He stepped outside his store to watch Oswald walk a few steps and then duck into the movie theater without paying the lady in the outer ticket booth. Brewer then walked over to that lady, Julia Postal, who was also listening to the news on the radio. When asked if she had sold a ticket to a man in a brown shirt just now, she said, "No."

Brewer told her to call the police. He then went inside to speak with the concessions manager who had not noticed anyone enter. Brewer told him the police were on their way and he wanted to take the police to the back door and have the house lights turned on. They agreed to do this.

The police quickly arrived and were taken to the back door. They entered with Brewer. Standing on the stage with the lights up, Brewer pointed to Oswald toward the back of the theater, where only 7 or 8 people were attending the movie.

Some wrestling with police officers which will be described shortly occurred. Oswald was taken out the front door and placed in a police car to be driven to headquarters downtown. Officers examined his wallet and weren't sure what his name was because of his fake cards.

He was taken to the fourth floor of Dallas Police Headquarters for questioning by Captain Will Fritz.

CHAPTER THIRTEEN

Dallas Police Department Reactions

"I hope that all of you who are students here will recognize the great opportunity that lies before you in this decade to be of service to our country... I congratulate you on what you have done, and most of all I congratulate you on what you are going to do."

John F. Kennedy, November 15, 1963, National Convention of the Catholic Youth Organization

Let us go back to the moment of the assassination of Officer J. D. Tippit to better understand the actions of the police department. Police officers are justified in stopping people if they have a close match to the description of a wanted suspect or if they display furtive movements, as well as other behaviors such as loitering, acting fearful or overly emotional, or being out of place for an area or time of day. The author has written about such things as this in the November 2020 *Criminal Justice in America: The Encyclopedia of Crime, Law Enforcement, Courts, and Corrections,* produced by ABC-CLIO, Santa Barbara, California.

Chances are that Officer Tippit asked Oswald what he was doing and to show some identification like a driver's license. Lee had made a Selective Service card with his picture and the name Alek James Hidell at a print shop job where he worked for a short time. He knew that his cards would raise suspicion if the officer saw them.

One observer of Oswald ran to the slain officer's car and figured out how to call the police department. He gave the description at 1:22 p.m. of the man who shot Patrolman J. D. Tippit. The suspect was described as "a white male about 30, 5'8", black hair, slender." That was very close to the description police had for the president's assassin.

Officer Tippit had served in the Dallas Police Department for eleven years and had Army service receiving a Bronze Star. His funeral was held the same day as Oswald's and Kennedy's, and some 2,000 people came to the service—many of whom were policemen. After Abraham Zapruder sold his film of the assassination, he donated $25,000 to Mrs. Tippit. Donations poured in from the public and she had enough money to raise their three children. She would later marry. She received some $650,000 from sympathetic people. She died at age 92 on March 2, 2021.[22]

The next report of Lee Oswald's whereabouts came from Johnny Calvin Brewer, assistant manager of the Hardy Shoe Store on Jefferson Avenue, two doors down from the Texas Theater. He gave this affidavit to the police authorities.

Friday, November 22, 1963, I was at work at Hardy's Shoe Store, 213 W. Jefferson. I had heard on the radio that the President had been shot and also that a policeman had been shot in Oak Cliff. About 1:30 pm, I saw a man standing in the lobby of the shoe store. This man was wearing a brown sports shirt. He also acted as if he was scared. About this time, a police car came up the street going west on Jefferson. After the police car passed, the man in the lobby walked up Jefferson toward the Texas Theater. I followed this man up the street and he went into the theater.

I asked the girl in the box office if she sold the man a ticket and she replied that she did not think so. I went into the show and asked

---

22 https://www.pulpinternational.com/pulp/keyword/Abraham+Zapruder.html

Dutch, the concession man if he had seen a man come in. Dutch said that he had been busy and did not notice. Dutch and I then checked the exits to see if any of them had been opened. The exits were all closed and did not appear to have been opened.

I went back to the box office and told Julie to call the police. When the police arrived, the show was stopped, and the lights were turned on. A man in the middle section and about five or six rows of seats from the back stood up when the lights were turned on. An officer approached him, he said something, and they struggled to get his gun as he hit the officer and knocked him back. Several other officers then joined the fight, and the man was taken out of the theater. This was the same man I had seen in front of the shoe store where I work. The reason I noticed the man in front of the store was because he acted so nervous, and I thought at the time he might be the man who had shot the policeman.[23]

Johnny Brewer also testified at the President's Commission on the Assassination of President Kennedy on April 2, 1964. He explained that those inside his store were listening to a transistor radio and heard about the President being shot and the police officer being shot. These are interesting excerpts from his testimony:

Mr. Belin: Why did you happen to watch this particular man?

Mr. Brewer: He just looked funny to me. Well, in the first place, I had seen him some place before. I think he had been in my store before. And when you wait on somebody, you recognize them, and he just seemed funny. His hair was sort of messed up and he looked like he had been running, and he looked scared, and he looked funny.[24]

---

23 https://www.govinfo.gov/app/details/GPO-WARRENCOMMISSIONHEARINGS-7
24 https://www.govinfo.gov/app/details/GPO-WARRENCOMMISSIONHEARINGS-7

Brewer was helpful to police at the Texas Theater, identified Oswald in a line-up, and he was cited as a local hero for years to come.

The Texas Theater also had some fame in later years with special films. In an interesting aside, the Texas Theater was opened in 1931 by millionaire Howard Hughes (1905-1976) who produced many movies and married movie star Jean Peters.

Here are the movies Hughes produced: *Seven Sinners* 1925, *Two Arabian Knights* 1927, *The Mating Call* 1928, *The Racket* 1928, *Hell's Angels* 1930, *The Front Page* 1931, *The Age for Love* 1931, *Cock of the Air* 1932, *Sky Devils* 1932, *Scarface* 1932, *The Outlaw* 1943, *The Sin of Harold Diddleboch* 1947, *Vendetta* 1950, *Two Tickets to Broadway* 1951, *Macao* 1952, *The Las Vegas Story* 1952, *The French Line* 1953, *The Conqueror* 1956, and *Jet Pilot* 1957.

Howard Hughes starred in 1942 *Pardon My Stripes* as a college boy. In fact, Howard bought RKO for actress Ingrid Bergman, but she declined to marry him. She chose to make movies with and marry Roberto Rossellini but talked Hughes into financing their first movie together called *Stromboli.* When shown in the United States, Howard reduced the Italian movie by some 20 minutes and changed the ending which was provided in voice narration at the end of the movie.

Policeman Sgt. Gerald Hill was one of three officers who searched the sixth floor and found three spent shells by the window and the rifle that had been tossed between boxes. His unit was then directed to go to the area where police officer J.D. Tippit had been shot, searching for the villain who did in one of their own.

When they arrived at the Texas Theater and Brewer pointed toward Oswald, Hill and two other officers approached. Oswald stood up and said, "This is it!" and began to pull out his pistol and fired but a policeman had his finger or thumb on the trigger of the weapon so that it was a misfire.[25]

25 https://www.dallasnews.com/news/2011/08/10/jerry-hill-dallas-officer-who-found-jfk-evi-
dence-and-handcuffed-oswald-dies-at-81/

That was our dear friend Gerry Hill, who had attended Adamson High School with the author's husband, Bob Cheney. Gerry told us about how he felt sure that Oswald was a "loner" and there was no conspiracy. He said he thought Oswald's phrase "This is it!" was important because it showed he was expecting to have some big showdown after what he had done.

Gerry told us years later that he had been approached by Oliver Stone who was making the movie about the JFK assassination with Kevin Costner. Hill told us he declined to work with Stone's people because: "They didn't want the facts. They had some story to tell that they had made up."

Meanwhile, policemen learned from foreman Roy Truly of the Texas School Book Depository that Oswald was the only employee who did not return to their post, Lee Oswald. The police asked for the home address of Oswald, but he had given the foreman his wife's address where she was staying in the home of Quaker woman Ruth Paine in Irving, Texas. Lee had never listed his actual boarding house room on Beckley Avenue in Dallas. So, the police went to the home where Marina Oswald and her two baby daughters were living.

After his arrest, Oswald was interviewed by Captain Will Fritz. Fritz had learned that Lee Oswald had not returned to work at the Depository after the assassination and that Lee Oswald was arrested at the Texas Theater for killing Officer J. D. Tippett.

That officer did not have a recording device and had only a very small office with his desk and three or four chairs. Thus, he asked the other officials who sat in on interviews to record their own versions of the interviews to check against his. Here are some of the more important parts of the captain's report.

Captain Will Fritz Interviews with Lee Oswald
11/22-24/635

I asked him why he left the [Depository] building, and he said there was so much excitement he didn't think there would be any more work done that day. I asked him if he owned a rifle, and he said that he did not. I asked him where he went when he left work, and he told me that he had a room on 1026 North Beckley, that he went over there and changed his trousers and got his pistol and went to the picture show. I asked him why he carried his pistol and he remarked, "You know how boys do when they have a gun, they just carry it."

Mr. Hosty (FBI agent) was sitting in on the interview and asked Oswald if he had been in Russia. He told him, "Yes, he had been in Russia for three years." Hosty asked him if he had written to the Russian Embassy, and he said he had.

This man [Oswald] became very upset and arrogant with Agent Hosty when he questioned him and accused him of accosting his wife two different times. When Agent Hosty attempted to talk to this man, he [Lee] would hit his fist on the desk. I asked Oswald what he meant by accosting his wife when he was talking to Mr. Hosty. He said Mr. Hosty mistreated his wife two different times when he talked with her…

[The police department had learned from the CIA and FBI that Oswald went to Mexico City in October 1963.] FBI Special Agent Mr. Hosty asked Oswald if he had been to Mexico City, which he denied. I [Fritz] asked him what his political beliefs were, and he said he had none but that he belonged to the Fair Play for Cuba Committee and told me that they had headquarters in New York and that he had been secretary for the organization in New Orleans.

Saturday, the next day, Captain Fritz interviewed Oswald further. Lee denied bringing a package to work except to say he brought a sack lunch. He denied telling Frazier (his co-worker who drove him to work) that he was fixing up his room with curtain rods. [He had told Wesley Frazier that morning that his long package wrapped in brown paper was curtain rods for his apartment.]

He said he ate lunch at the company lunchroom but the people he cited as being there and seeing him had already denied his presence. He denied ever ordering a gun or a rifle but then admitted that he purchased the gun which was taken from him at the time of arrest. He stated that he would not take a polygraph examination without the advice of counsel. [He had requested an ACLU lawyer, but the man declined to defend Oswald and they had been unable to find anyone who would take his case. Perhaps no lawyer wanted his resume to contain defending a man who killed the president.]

Oswald admitted he carried a Selective Service card with the name Hidell as well as one with his name, but declined to state that he wrote the signature of Alek J. Hidell and declined to say why he carried it.

Fritz questioned him again that evening. One photograph of Oswald with his gun, rifle, and two radical newspapers (taken in the backyard by Marina according to what she told police and her testimony) was found when they took Oswald's possessions from Ruth Paine's house. The photograph was enlarged in the police lab to see the details better. It was shown to Oswald who sneered and said he had never seen the picture before. Of course, he had not seen the enlargement before. Then he said they were false photographs and said that they apparently superimposed his face on the photograph with a rifle and put a gun in his pocket.

The police department had learned of threats to kill Oswald and believed he would be safer in the Dallas County Jail some six blocks away. Plans were made to transfer Oswald once he finished with the authorities who were scheduled to question him.

Sunday morning, November 24, 1963, Oswald was being questioned about his post office boxes because he and A. J. Hidell were listed for one box. He said, "I don't recall anything about that." When asked about his most recent box and that mail was to be delivered to the ACLU (American Civil Liberties Union) and FPCC (Fair Play for Cuba) there, he shrugged his shoulders and said he didn't recall that. When asked if he was a communist, he denied it but admitted that he was a Marxist. When questioned about his undesirable discharge, he bristled and explained that his discharge was changed due to his defection to Russia, not because of his behavior during his enlistment period.

When asked about the name A. J. Hidell found on his ID cards, he said, "I've told you all I'm going to about that card. You took notes. Just read them for yourself if you want to refresh your memory. You have the card. Now you know as much about it as I do." He admitted his arrest in New Orleans for his activities with the FPCC where he fought with some Cubans who were against Castro.[26]

Captain Fritz made some phone calls to see if the transfer to the county jail was ready. Everything was ready to transport him to the county jail but the unexpected happened. Oswald would be fatally shot by Jack Ruby within minutes when he was taken downstairs to a police vehicle. He died within the hour. This was the first live murder ever televised as it happened and was seen by millions of viewers.

President Kennedy's funeral on Monday was declared a National Day of Mourning and he was buried at Arlington Cemetery. Officer Tippit's funeral

---

26 https://www.archives.gov/research/jfk/finding-aids/fritz-papers.html

in Dallas on Monday had a huge turnout of law enforcement personnel and others. Lee Oswald's funeral on Monday had only family and reporters who attended. Those reporters helped carry the casket to the empty hole where he was buried. The minister had not shown up.

CHAPTER FOURTEEN

Marina Oswald's Reactions

"In the final analysis, our most basic common link is that we all inhabit this small planet. We all breathe the same air. We all cherish our children's future. And we are all mortal."

John F. Kennedy, American University commencement, June 10, 1963

Police were questioning Marina Oswald and her landlady, Ruth Paine, to learn about her husband's recent behavior. With help from a Russian-speaking policeman, Marina told how Oswald returned from his fruitless attempt to get a visa to Cuba in Mexico City. Lee let Marina know he was back in Dallas, had no luck at the embassies, and was looking for a job.

She let her landlady, Mrs. Paine, know only that Lee was looking for work. Ruth mentioned this to a neighbor who said that her son had just gotten a job at the Texas Schoolbook Depository. Marina felt inadequate with her Russian language to call someone, so she asked Ruth to call and see if there were any openings at the Depository.

Ruth Paine talked to foreman Roy Truly, explaining that Lee had served in the Marines and now had to support a wife and child. Truly set an appointment for Lee and was impressed that he was quite polite. Thus, he hired the lad to fill book orders from 8 am to 4:45 pm for which he would receive $1.25 per hour. Lee began work on October 16, 1963. Four days later, little Audrey

Rachel Oswald (named after actress Audrey Hepburn) was born at Parkland Hospital.

Ruth's neighbor, who had gotten the job at the Book Depository, had a car, so he drove Oswald to Ruth Paine's house on weekends so Lee could be together with his girls.

The *Dallas Morning News* and the *Daily Times Herald* both published the President's parade route on November 19, 1963, three days before the event. The Trade Mart was selected for the luncheon where the President would address the city's upper echelon. Thus, the motorcade would wind through Dallas from Love Field Airport through many tall buildings to the Trade Mart. Pictures and names of people who caused problems at Adlai Stevenson's event were distributed at the Trade Mart personnel so they could be spotted and watched. But nobody was able to spot troublemakers on the motorcade route.

Oswald usually rode home with his co-worker on Friday evenings but had seen the route of the motorcade for Friday. So, he told his workmate that he wanted to ride to see his family on Thursday evening, adding that he needed to get some curtain rods for his apartment. Thus, he had already decided that he was going to get his rifle and would carry it to work on Friday morning unless his wife wanted to get back together.

Thus, he rode home to see his wife on 11/21/63, a day earlier than they usually planned to spend their weekends together. Though shocked, Marina was glad to see him, and Ruth Paine re-arranged things to allow him to spend this night with his family.

Oswald pled with his wife to return to him, saying he could now afford to get an apartment for them to live together again. Three times, he asked her, and three times, she declined to live with him. He promised things like a clothing washer/dryer for her mounting diaper problems with the two little ones. She was determined to avoid living with him any time soon. He had insulted and hit his wife numerous times, according to several of their friends who spoke with police in the coming days.

The Oswalds dined with Ruth Paine and her children Friday evening, November 21, and they talked of the President's trip to Dallas. The ladies seemed to look forward to seeing it on television the next day. Lee played with the children outside for a bit, and then all went to bed. He tried to snuggle, but Marina pushed him away. If she had responded to his advances and left the door open to return to him, things might have turned out differently for the world.

He got up in the morning and went into the garage to wrap his rifle in some packing paper he had brought home from his work site. He left the garage light on. He had less than twelve dollars, having left his wife $170 and his wedding ring as he said his goodbye to Marina that morning. She did not realize until the police came that he had left his wedding ring and so much money for her. That little money in his pocket suggested that he had no particular plans for escape.

When Mrs. Paine rose that Friday morning and went about her tasks, she noted the light and assumed Lee had gotten something out of the garage.

That Friday morning, he met his co-worker and placed the wrapped package in the back seat. He did not want to talk as they drove in through sprinkles on the way to work.

At work, he had three book orders hanging on his rack, but he did not work on them. They hung just where they were put. Instead, he re-arranged book boxes to devise a hidden nook by the 6th-floor window where he could not be seen by others coming up to that floor without some effort. While waiting for the presidential motorcade, did he imagine that he was going to be a somebody whose name would be on the lips of people for years to come? Was he excited with an intoxication of ideas to spice up his morning plot?

CHAPTER FIFTEEN

Bernard Weissman's Reactions

"Goethe tells us in his greatest poem that Faust lost
the liberty of his soul when he said to the passing moment:
'Stay, thou art so fair.' And our liberty, too, is endangered if we pause
for the passing moment, if we rest on our achievements
if we resist the pace of progress. And those who look only to the past
or the present are certain to miss the future."

John F. Kennedy, Frankfurt, June 25, 1963

An ad ran in the *Dallas Morning News* on the day of the assassination. The ad is quoted here, and readers will see that it is an anti-Kennedy ad. The name posted at the bottom of the ad is Bernard Weissman, chairman of the American Fact-Finding Committee. Weissman came to Dallas on November 4, 1963, to join his ex-military buddy Larrie Schmidt, who was working with John Birch Society members. Those included Joseph P. Grinnan, Harvey Bright, Edgar R. Crissey, Nelson Bunker Hunt, and retired Major General Edwin Walker. Weissman was asked to take the ad to the Dallas Morning Newspaper and given $1,465 to pay for the full-page document.

Schmidt invited Weissman to join the John Birch Society, but he declined when he discovered that too many of them were anti-Semitic. Weissman was Jewish and, while in Dallas, found some temporary work as a carpet salesman for a few days.

These two men were shocked that the assassination occurred and worried that they might be blamed because of their ads critical of Kennedy. Bernard Weissman and Larrie Schmidt left town together as quickly as they could. Walker also feared retribution and flew to Shreveport, Louisiana, for a few days. That information was gathered by our old friend, local Dallas newsman Hugh Aynesworth, who covered the assassination in 1963. Hugh just died on December 23, 2023.

The full-page anti-Kennedy ad began with large letters saying, "Welcome Mr. Kennedy to Dallas" and continued thusly:

… A city so disgraced by a recent liberal smear attempt that its citizens have just elected two more Conservative Americans to public office.

…A city that is an economic "boom town," not because of Federal handouts, but through conservative economic and business practices.

…A city that will continue to grow and prosper despite efforts by you and your administration to penalize it for its non-conformity to New Frontierism.

…A city that rejected your philosophy and policies in 1960 and will do so again in 1965—even more emphatically than before.

MR. KENNEDY, despite contentions on the part of your administration, the State Department, the Mayor of Dallas, the Dallas City Council, and members of your party, we free-thinking and America-thinking citizens of Dallas still have, through a constitution largely ignored by you, the right to address our grievances, to question you, to disagree with you, and to criticize you.

In asserting this constitutional right, we ask you publicly the following questions—indeed, questions of paramount importance and interest to all free peoples everywhere—which we trust you will answer…in public, without sophistry.

Those questions are:

WHY is Latin America turning either anti-American or Communistic, or both, despite increased U.S. foreign aid, State Department police, and your own Ivy-Tower pronouncements?

WHY do you say we have built a "wall of freedom" around Cuba when there is no freedom in Cuba today? Because of your policy, thousands of Cubans have been imprisoned, are starving, and being persecuted—with thousands already murdered and thousands more awaiting execution and, in addition, the entire population of almost 7,000,000 Cubans is living in slavery.

WHY have you approved the sale of wheat and corn to our enemies when you know the Communist soldiers "travel on their stomachs" just as ours do? Communist soldiers are daily wounding or killing American soldiers in South Vietnam.

WHY did you host and entertain Tito—Moscow's Trojan Horse—just a short time after our sworn enemy, Khrushchev, embraced the Yugoslav dictator as a great hero and leader of Communism?

WHY have you urged great aid, comfort, recognition, and understanding for Yugoslavia? Poland, Hungary, and other Communist countries, while turning your back on the pleas of Hungarian, East German, Cuban, and other anti-Communist freedom fighters?

WHY did Cambodia kick the U.S. out of its country after we poured nearly 400 million dollars of aid into its ultra-leftist government?

WHY has Gus Hall, head of the U.S. Communist Party, praised almost every one of your policies and announced that the party would endorse and support your re-election in 1964?

WHY have you banned the showing at U.S. military bases of the film "Operation Abolition"—the movie by the House Committee on Un-American Activities exposing Communism in America?

WHY have you ordered or permitted your brother, Bobby, the Attorney General, to go soft on Communists, fellow travelers, and ultra-leftists in America while permitting him to persecute loyal Americans who criticize you, your administration, and your leadership?

WHY are you in favor of the U.S. continuing to give economic aid to Argentina, in spite of the fact that Argentina has just seized almost 400 million dollars of American private property?

WHY has the Foreign Policy of the United States degenerated to the point that the CIA is arranging coups and having staunch Anti-Communist Allies of the U.S. bloodily exterminated?

WHY have you scrapped the Monroe Doctrine in favor of the "Spirit of Moscow"?

MR. KENNEDY, as citizens of the United States of America, we DEMAND answers to these questions, and we want them NOW.

THE AMERICAN FACT-FINDING COMMITTEE

"An unaffiliated and non-partisan group of citizens who wish truth."

Bernard Weissman,

Chairman

P.O. Box 1792—Dallas 21, Texas

The last sentence is obviously false because they are affiliated and partisan through the John Birch Society.

That morning, John Kennedy awoke in the Fort Worth hotel, where he spoke to an audience before flying to Love Field Airport in Dallas. That very morning, he had read this *Dallas Morning News* article and told Jackie they were heading into "nut country."

He added, "If somebody wants to shoot me from a window with a rifle, nobody can stop it, so why worry about it?" Mr. Kennedy had often told Dave Powers, one of his top aides, that it would be so easy for someone to shoot him with a rifle from a tall building. This statement can be found at:theglobeandmail.com/news/world/jfkassassination-three-hours-that-changed-the-world/article15558304 by James Swanson in 2013.

There was also a handbill given out on the streets of Dallas on the morning of the assassination. It showed front and side views of the head of John Kennedy with a title under the pictures saying, "Wanted for Treason."[27] This handbill was also the work of retired Major General Edwin Walker and his friend Robert Surrey, according to research by the Warren Commission. The text under this title reads: This man is wanted for treasonous activities against the United States:

- Betraying the Constitution (which he swore to uphold): He is turning the sovereignty of the U.S. over to the communist-controlled United Nations. He is betraying our friends [Cuba, Katanga, Portugal] and befriending our enemies [Russia, Yugoslavia, Poland].
- He has been WRONG on innumerable issues affecting the security of the U.S. [United Nations-Berlin Wall-Missile removal-Cuba-Wheat deals-Test Ban Treaty, etc.]
- He has been lax in enforcing Communist Registration laws.
- He has given support and encouragement to the Communist-inspired racial riots.
- He has illegally invaded a sovereign State with federal troops.
- He has consistently appointed Anti-Christians to Federal offices, Upholds the Supreme Court in its Anti-Christian rulings, and Aliens and known Communists abound in Federal offices.
- He has been caught in fantastic LIES to the American people [including personal ones like his previous marriage and divorce].[28]

---

27 https://www.orwelltoday.com/jfkadtreason.jpg
28 https://www.yahoo.com/video/2015-07-21-was-jfk-secretly-married-to-another-woman-before-jackie-21212108.html

The last statement referred to a rumor that John Kennedy had married socialite Duri Malcolm after a drunken party in Palm Beach in 1947. According to many researchers, this information was not true.

One of the articles that denied the rumor was a story carried in the *Time Magazine* on September 28, 1962, entitled "The Press: An American Genealogy."[29] Here is a short quotation from that article:

"Absolutely False." Just a few days ago, Durie Shevlin herself, for the first time, denied the whole story in detail. Vacationing with her husband at the Grand Hotel in Montecatini, Italy, she said: "It's absolutely false and ridiculous. I'm not even sure how the story began. I've been married to Mr. Shevlin for 15 or 16 years, and previously I was married for a short time to John Bersbach and then to Firmin Desloge, by whom I had a daughter who's 20 now. I know the President's family well and have known him for a long time and saw him years ago at Palm Beach and once went with him and his family to an Orange Bowl game in Miami. I've rarely seen him since." She said that she has never discussed the Jack-and-Durie matter with the Kennedys because "it's too embarrassing."

---

29 Content.time.com/time/subscriber/article10,3309,940088-55.00.html

CHAPTER SIXTEEN

Jack Ruby's First Reactions

"Forgive your enemies, but never forget their names."
John F. Kennedy from his book Profiles in Courage

The morning of November 22, 1963, was a day when Jack Ruby was setting up his weekend ads for his nightclub at the *Dallas Morning News* office two blocks from the site of the assassination. A couple of his checks for ads bounced, so the newspaper required that he come into the office to pay for ads with cash.

On this morning, he was unhappy and puzzled by a *Dallas Morning Newspaper* page with a black border and a picture of President Kennedy's front and side views of his head just described in the previous chapter. Ruby was asking questions about the black-bordered ad signed with a Jewish name.

He was quite upset with this anti-Kennedy ad and was surprised to find someone of his own race involved. He was not immediately told who paid for these ads, but it was later traced to retired Major General Edwin Walker and John Birch Society members, who were opposed to communism and the United Nations. These people included Nelson Bunker Hunt, H. R. (Bum) Bright, Edgar Crissey, and others.[30]

---

30 Warren Commission, V. 1, pp. 489, 504, 506-509, 514; V. 5. Pp.487-514.

Walker had organized an October 24, 1963, United Nations Day attack on Adlai Stevenson, American ambassador to the United Nations. Crowds were invited by Walker and his associates to rebel against Stevenson, and they did so, spitting and hitting him on the head with signs. Stevenson had warned the President not to visit Dallas during his campaign because of the rabble-rousers in Dallas.

Suddenly, while Ruby was complaining about that Kennedy ad, news of the shots fired at the President was on a television set. Employees and Ruby ran to look at the TV screen. They followed the news and left business aside as events unfolded. As the story developed, it was finally announced that the President was dead.

Ruby called his sister, who had recently come out of the hospital following a "nervous breakdown," according to what he told newspaper employees. He told her of this terrible news, and she began to cry. Ruby held the phone to the ear of the ad man he was talking with. He said, "Listen to my sister crying."

The newspaper employees realized that Ruby was quite distraught. Jack sat and stared for a while. Such was indeed some vague yet compelling power that caused him to stare. Before he left the newspaper office, he changed his ad for Saturday night to inform the public that his club would be closed in honor of the President's death. He then went to the other newspaper *(Times Herald)* to give them the same information about his club closure.

Jack Ruby's Carousel Club was located at 1312 ½ Commerce Street, Dallas, Texas. His nightclub billboard advertised "Continuous shows. Glamourous girls. Open to 2 am nitely."

Ruby continued to obsess over the ad with a black border entitled "Welcome Mr. Kennedy to Dallas." It claimed to want the answers to questions that accused Kennedy of befriending enemies, being soft on Communism, being supported by the American Communist Party, and being lax in protecting

U.S. security. Who was this Jew, and did the black border symbolize death as Ruby thought it did?

Ruby finally left the newspaper offices but learned that the President had died, and his body was to be flown elsewhere for autopsy. President Lyndon Johnson had been advised to leave Dallas as soon as possible since there was the possibility this was a conspiracy of some sort. He would not leave without Jacqueline Kennedy, and she would not leave without her husband's body.

Governor John Connally was hospitalized because the bullet that exited from Kennedy's throat penetrated his chest and hit his arm, so he needed an operation quickly. District Attorney Henry Wade visited Connally, his former college roommate and Navy buddy. The hospital room was declared a government office of sorts since Connally read and signed various important papers during his days of hospitalization after surgery.

In later years, when Nellie Connally was the only person still alive who rode in the fateful limousine, she wrote a book in 2003 entitled: *From Love Field: Our Final Hours with President John F. Kennedy.* She had shielded her husband from bullets as he fell into her lap. She donated her notes of that infamous day and her blood-spattered dress to the LBJ Library.

Jack Ruby was too agitated to stay still during these hours, but his whereabouts are a bit unclear in the hustle and bustle of events. He was an Alfred Hitchcock character and loved to be where the action was. He was the product of a Chicago West Side gang, a food faddist, and a hypochondriac who regularly exercised at the YMCA. He liked to walk into the strip girls' dressing room without a shirt to show off his muscles.

Jack Ruby never married. He kept four dachshunds in a room near his nightclub kitchen. He called them "my children" and called his favorite, Sheba, his "wife." He considered himself a minor celebrity and passed out cards and invitations to his club. He liked to be in the news and kept up a rapport with various press figures, drumming up patronage for his nightclub. He was something of an unpaid pimp putting his strippers together with policemen or customers.

His quick temper got him into trouble with the police, but his special offers and free drinks for police officers rarely had him facing charges. He shared his apartment at this time with salesman George Senator, a down-on-his-luck old friend, but there was no evidence that they were having a homosexual relationship.

Shortly after 1:30 pm on the day of the assassination, Judge Joe B. Brown, Jr. was asked to prepare two search warrants for police officers. One was for the house address Oswald had given his employer at the Texas Schoolbook Depository, where his wife and two daughters roomed with Ruth Paine. The other was for Lee's boarding house on Beckley Street where the landlady tended rental rooms. These search warrants were given to the officers who went to those two sites.

Other happenings that afternoon included Oswald's mother, Marguerite. That afternoon, she heard her son's name mentioned as the one arrested for the President's murder. Thus, she called a Fort Worth newspaper to say she needed a ride to see her son, Lee Oswald, who was jailed after his arrest. Reporter Bob Schieffer volunteered to transport her so he could cover the story. He later worked for CBS. He was shocked by the selfish Marguerite Oswald, who spent their time together telling him of her need for money.

Dallas police officers took Marina, her two daughters, and Marguerite to see Oswald and to stay in a hotel in-between visits. After this terrible weekend, which ended in the death of Lee Oswald, except for collecting her belongings, Marina did not stay in touch with Ruth Paine. The separated Paines stayed in contact with each other, but Michael died in 2018. Ruth is often contacted for interviews about her house (now a museum) and other issues.

Upon hearing of the assassination, Soviet premier Nikita Khrushchev went to the American Embassy in Moscow to signify his condolences on the death of the President. He soon learned that there was fear that the assassination grew from a Russian conspiracy since Oswald had lived in Russia. Many of these events were broadcast on the radio, and Ruby was an avid news collector from radio tidbits. He would use some of what he learned when he entered the main police department where Oswald was being held and interviewed.

Jack Ruby was next seen Saturday, November 23, around 6 pm by a police reporter for the *Dallas Morning News,* John Rutledge. Ruby, police detectives, and reporters jammed the third-floor corridor of the police station where the Homicide Bureau was located. There were blinding TV cameras and lights, and Ruby was between two out-of-town newspapermen. It was supposedly a corridor closed to all but accredited press people. Ruby had no badge like they did, but he bent his head and scribbled on a piece of paper, acting like a reporter. He was assisting out-of-town reporters with the spelling of the sheriff's name, the police chief's name, and directions.

Rutledge knew Ruby wasn't supposed to be there. He hollered, "Hey, Jack, what are you doing here?" "I'm helping these fellows," Ruby shouted. And apparently, he was.

At about 7 pm, Oswald was brought down this corridor to the room where he was charged with murdering Officer Tippit. Assistant District Attorney Bill Alexander, Captain Will Fritz, and Justice of the Peace David Johnston took Oswald into a side room where some reporters were peeking through blinds. Oswald questioned whether this was a court or a judge, and Alexander told him to shut up, and the charge was read.

As Oswald was taken from the room, reporters shouted questions to him. A reporter said, "Did you shoot the President?" "I didn't shoot anybody, no sir. I'm just a patsy." A patsy is like a scapegoat whom people blame for something they did not do. And thus, began the ruse that many later believed involved other people who participated in the President's assassination.

That evening, Ruby went to his synagogue, where they were having a memorial service for the President. He shook hands with the rabbi and thanked him briefly for some help he had given Ruby's sister during her hospitalization a few days earlier.

Ruby then went to a delicatessen and bought a lot of sandwiches and soft drinks with high caffeine. He telephoned the Homicide and Robbery Bureau and offered food and drinks for men working around the clock. The officer answered that everyone had eaten and didn't need any sandwiches.

Despite learning that he would not be welcome for his food, he went to the police department again. He was in the room with press people sitting on a desk. Lt. T. B. Leonard yelled, asking Ruby why he was there. "I brought the sandwiches," he said. "Where are they?" Ruby pointed, "They're in the car." "Go get them."

Ruby said, "No," and held up his notebook and pencil, "I'm a reporter tonight." What would have happened if the police had followed their orders and permitted only legitimate reporters into the room that night? If Ruby had not been permitted to enter an area where Oswald was, the young man would have been tried and punished for his crime by execution. He would undoubtedly have lied a lot because it was his nature to lie, as we now know from studies of his life.

By the end of the questions and Oswald's answers, Ruby had worked his way up toward the front of the room. District Attorney Henry Wade was standing on a platform answering questions. Some reporter asked whether Oswald had a connection with supporters of Cuba. Wade made some vague reference to a Free Cuba movement. Ruby had been following the news on radio and TV about Oswald and said, "The Fair Play for Cuba Committee," correcting the District Attorney.

Police reporter John Rutledge held up a telephone line to ask Wade a question. Ruby got the idea to call up a newscaster he knew at KLIF radio station to ask if he'd like to do a phone interview with the District Attorney. He did so, and then Ruby, whom District Attorney Wade did not know, said, "Henry, Henry, come over here." The D.A. then spoke with KLIF newsman William Duncan.

Ruby had suggested that the KLIF newscaster ask Wade whether Oswald was insane or not. Duncan did ask, and Wade responded that Oswald was sane. As an aside, this is the very Wade from the Wade vs. Roe attorney trial case who would argue a decade later that abortion was a constitutional right. Several decades later, that decision was overruled by the Supreme Court of the United States.

Later that night, around 1:30 am, Ruby carried his bag of sandwiches and colas to KLIF station newscaster William Duncan, who had talked with Henry Wade and later testified before the Warren Commission. Duncan said that Ruby seemed pleased that he was being in on something that was important to everyone. He quoted Ruby, "There I was, standing there looking up, and he [Oswald] was right in front of me."

Ruby left the news station at about 2 am and ran into a Dallas police officer and a former stripper from his club. They were talking about Oswald and said if this had happened in England, Oswald would have been dragged through the streets by the people and hung. Ruby bragged about arranging a telephone interview by Henry Wade about Oswald. He told them and others that he had "*scooped*" his competitors by closing his club as a "memorial to the President."

Ruby wanted to do even more in this great tragedy. So, he went to his apartment at about 4 am and woke his roommate, George Senator. He discussed the full-page anti-Kennedy ad in the *Dallas Morning News* on the day of the assassination. Ruby told Senator and later policemen that he thought the ad, billboard, and assassination were the work of either Communists or the John Birch Society.

He talked about the dead President's wife and children because he saw some information about them in the paper. He had also seen an anti-government billboard calling for the impeachment of Chief Justice Earl Warren of the Supreme Court. But here was the new President saying that Warren would head up a committee of seven people to analyze the assassination.

He wanted Mr. Senator to come with him while he drove to the billboard and snapped three pictures of it with his Polaroid camera. He had those three pictures in his pocket when he was arrested 29 hours later.

Then, he wanted to drive to the post office in hopes of locating the box number listed by the Jewish man's name on the anti-Kennedy newspaper ad. He pressed the button for the night clerk, who told him that only the Postmaster could give out that information.

Then Ruby and Senator had a cup of coffee and returned to their apartment to get some sleep. Ruby had barely gone to bed when the nightclub employee who was to tend the dachshunds called to say they were out of dog food. Ruby bawled him out with such anger that the employee decided to leave town. He left the nightclub right after the call, unbeknownst to Ruby.

CHAPTER SEVENTEEN

Jack Ruby's Second Reactions

"A good lawyer is going to try to protect his or her client."

**John F. Kennedy, as Senator, addressed the legal fraternity
at the University of Florida on October 19, 1957**

During Friday and Saturday, Oswald was visited by his wife and mother. He reassured them that he would be fine and had requested a good attorney. After they left the jail, the police took them to a hotel where they would be available to answer questions.

Marina tried to give Marguerite some pictures that Lee had her take. She pulled out a snapshot she had taken of Oswald holding his rifle and gun. He had inscribed the backside of the photo, "To my daughter." Marina wanted Marguerite to keep it because she thought it was incriminating, but Oswald's mother declined. Marguerite later testified that Marina tore up the pictures of Oswald and struck a match to burn the pictures.

Officials were desperately searching for some lawyer who would take the case and go to see Oswald. It was his right to have an attorney, but none wanted to take his case. Meanwhile, there were death threats against Oswald, and police officials decided the city jail was inadequate for safety.

Plans were being made to get a few more interviews with Oswald before the transfer with the FBI and the Postmaster about his various P.O. boxes where rifles and pistols were sent.

Meanwhile, people began leaving huge flower assortments on the main motorcade route. Ruby stopped to look at these and talked to people at these sites. He talked to one newscaster who later became Mayor of Dallas, Wes Wise. They talked a few minutes and Wise told of having been at the Trade Mart lunch where the President was to speak. He mentioned seeing presents to be given to the President, including a rocking chair and two Western saddles. Ruby also took some pictures of people bringing flowers to the assassination site.

Ruby had heard the night before that Oswald's transfer to the county jail would take place sometime the next morning, around 10 am, possibly. That evening, a stripteaser who lived in Fort Worth came over, unaware that Ruby had closed the club. She called, bereft of funds to get back home, and Ruby had his man on duty give her $5 to get back to Ft. Worth. He told her to call the next morning if she still needed money.

At some point in the middle of the night, he called a friend, entertainer Breck Wall, who had a nightclub show in Galveston, Texas, and they talked about the assassination and closing the club. Ruby said, "This guy who killed our President. Someone needs to do the same to him."

When Ruby awoke Sunday morning, he read the newspaper while breakfasting. He saw a letter to Caroline Kennedy about her father's death and saw a letter wondering if Mrs. Kennedy might have to come back for the trial of Lee Harvey Oswald.

Ruby Had to Go Downtown to Send Money

Sunday, November 24, 1963, Jack Ruby got a call from the Fort Worth stripper at about 9:15 am. She reminded him that he promised to send her $25 as soon as possible. He said he would go downtown and send the money by

Western Union. He took some amphetamines to keep him from being sleepy. He got in his car with his favorite dog, Sheba.

Ruby had $2,015.33 on him when arrested, plus a traveler's check for $50. He also put his gun, a Colt Cobra, into his pocket as he always did when carrying a lot of money. He drove downtown, past the assassination site, to the Western Union office. It was located a half block from the police building. He parked and left Sheba in the unlocked car. He went in to send the $25 and got a receipt.

He walked the half block back toward his car and saw some people near the police ramp going down into the basement. The guard was apparently talking to someone, and Ruby walked by the police car parked on the exit ramp. He wondered what was going on. He assumed the transfer of Oswald from city to county jail had already taken place, unaware of its delay. He walked down the ramp and saw the photographers awaiting Oswald, who was being brought down to a police car for the transfer to the county jail.

The policeman, James Leavelle, to whom Oswald was handcuffed, had said only moments earlier, "Lee, I hope if somebody tries to shoot you, they're as good a shot as you were," meaning that the person would hit Oswald instead of Leavelle. Oswald smiled and said, "You're being melodramatic. Nobody's going to shoot at me." Those were his last words.

CHAPTER EIGHTEEN

Jack Ruby Shot Lee Oswald

*"We must demonstrate that we are able to make
this society work and progress."*
**John F. Kennedy National Convention of Catholic Youth Organization,
November 15, 1963**

As Oswald and Leavelle advanced, Ruby took out his pistol. His bullet ripped into Oswald's mid-abdomen, hitting his spleen, stomach, kidney, liver, diaphragm, and aorta. Oswald said, "Oh," as he fell. He seemed to be unconscious and lay bleeding on the floor with arms splayed out akimbo.

About half a dozen policemen grabbed hold of Ruby. They dragged him inside the door to the jail office. Captain Glen King heard Ruby telling his captors, "You know me. I'm Jack Ruby. You didn't think I was going to let him get by with it, did you?"

Meanwhile, Leavelle had to get another officer to help him carry Oswald to the jail office. There, he took off the handcuffs and asked him whether he wanted to say anything, but Oswald did not answer. An ambulance was summoned, and he was attended by an on-the-scene medical student, who also noted that Oswald appeared too unconscious to speak.

Within a minute, said Leavelle, he heard Ruby cry out during his struggle, "I hope the son of a bitch dies."

Captain King rode up the elevator with Ruby. His captors, who knew Ruby shot a manacled man, said, "You dirty scum. You're the scum of the earth."

When the crowd outside heard that Oswald had been shot, cheers and applause broke out. Ruby began to receive hundreds of congratulatory telegrams and money for his defense immediately.

Ruby told Sgt. Patrick Dean, who was stripping him, "I wanted the world to know that the Jews had guts." Ruby added that he knew Oswald would get death for the killing but that he didn't see any point in a long trial or in subjecting Mrs. Kennedy to the strain of testifying.

When Jack Ruby shot Lee Oswald at the police station, Gordon Shanklin dispatched two agents to Parkland Hospital, the same place they had taken the president. "We're here to take any confession Oswald might make," they said. However, Oswald died on the operating table without regaining consciousness.[31]

Shanklin assigned Special Agents Manning Clements to research Jack Ruby and Bob Gemberling to research Lee Oswald. Gemberling retired from the FBI in 1976. The author has talked with Gemberling, and although he was certain that Oswald killed the president, he continued to follow leads about the assassination until his death.[32]

After Gemberling retired from the FBI, he wrote in 1997: "The hype and publicity promoting conspiracy theories about the JFK assassination has seriously prevented the young minds of those born shortly before and after the assassination from knowing the truth about this tragic event -- all for the sake of the almighty dollar."

---

31 p. 147 Hoover's FBI: The Inside Story by Hoover's Trusted Lieutenant. Cartha D. "Deke" DeLoach. 1995, Regnery Publishing, Inc. Washington, D.C.

32 p. 147 Hoover's FBI: The Inside Story by Hoover's Trusted Lieutenant. Cartha D. "Deke" DeLoach. 1995, Regnery Publishing, Inc. Washington, D.C.

CHAPTER NINETEEN

The Rat Pack or The Jack Pack Reactions

"Do you realize the responsibility I carry?
I'm the only person standing between Richard Nixon
and the White House."

John F. Kennedy, as a Senator in 1960, running for president

Lauren Bacall saw her husband, Humphrey Bogart, and his pals returning from a casino during the early 1940s and said, "You look like a pack of rats." She described the creation of the "Rat Pack" in her book, *By Myself*, on page 222:

> David and Hjordis Niven, Mike and Gloria Romanoff, Swifty Lazar (talent scout/agent), Frank Sinatra, Judy Garland and Sid Luft, Bogie and I formed a group known as the Rat Pack. In order to qualify, one had to be addicted to nonconformity, staying up late, drinking, laughing, and not caring what anyone thought or said about us. We held a dinner in a private room at Romanoff's to elect officials and draw up rules—Bogie's way of thumbing his nose at Hollywood. I was voted Den Mother. Bogie was in charge of public relations.
>
> No one could join without unanimous approval of the charter members. Nat Benchley, a visiting rat from New York, drew up an insignia for us—a large group of rats of all shapes and sized in all

positions. What fun we had with it all! We were an odd assortment, but we liked each other so much, and every one of us had a wild sense of the ridiculous. The press had a field day, but we had the upper hand.

Noel Coward was going to appear in Las Vegas for the first time at a nightclub in the Sands Hotel. The Sands was where Frank always played; he had an interest in it. Frank liked to fly his friends into Vegas, not a place most of us Rat Packers frequented…

No one was ever bothered with a bill for a hotel, for a meal—that was Frank's way. It made him feel good; it was his way of entertaining us—in his home as he had been in ours. And he had company—he wasn't alone. Then back to reality. Bogie enjoyed that convivial, crazy, party-holiday atmosphere for a while, but he wasn't one to pass his time aimlessly for very long. We were all good friends, but the Vegas-Palm Springs life was Frank's life, not ours.

At that time, the Rat Pack met at the Bogarts' house at 232 S. Mapleton Drive in Los Angeles. It had nearly 14,000 square feet, 6 bedrooms, 8 bathrooms and guest quarters for the help staff. Inside was a screening room to watch movies, an old Hollywood art deco bar, and there used to be a fake police car parked on the property. They all wanted to be associated with good movies, and Bogart had been in one of the best. *Casablanca* was about people who do the right thing. Good movies are about the example they set for those who watch them.

One of their less familiar members was Irving Paul "Swifty" Lazar (1907-1993). He had many clients including Bogart, Bacall, Cary Grant, Cole Porter, Ernest Hemingway, Gene Kelly, Ira Gershwin, Joan Collins, Larry McMurtry, Madonna, Moss Hart, Noël Coward, Richard Nixon, Tennessee Williams, Truman Capote, and Walter Matthau.

Gradually, some joined, and some left the Rat Pack, and they began to appear together in casinos and even movies. Later additions included Errol Flynn, Nat King Cole, Mickey Rooney, Sammy Davis Jr., Dean Martin, Joey Bishop, Bing Crosby, and Peter Lawford. With Lawford's inclusion, the group began to support President John Kennedy. They appeared on stage together and made movies such as *Ocean's 11, Sergeants 3,* and *Robin and the 7 Hoods.* Sinatra became the leader after Bogart's death.

During Sinatra's leadership, visiting members were Ava Gardner, Robert Mitchum, Elizabeth Taylor, Janet Leigh, Tony Curtis, Lena Horne, Jerry Lewis, Cesar Romero, Cary Grant, Rex Harrison, Angie Dickinson, Spencer Tracy, Katherine Hepburn, and Shirley MacLaine.

When the group supported John F. Kennedy, they were sometimes called the Jack Pack. However, there was a dreadful falling out between Lawford and Sinatra over John Kennedy. Lawford asked Sinatra if he could host the president at his Palm Springs house in March 1962. At the time, Lawford said the president agreed, so it was set up. Sinatra paid to have a helipad constructed and made great changes in his house.

Suddenly, Lawford had to tell Sinatra that the Attorney General Robert F. Kennedy advised his brother to sever ties with Sinatra because of his connections with Mafia figures, so the visit was canceled. Sinatra was terribly furious.

Instead, Kennedy stayed at Bing Crosby's estate (where he spent a night with Marilyn Monroe), and this infuriated Sinatra. Lawford's connections were severed, and he was written out of later Rat Pack movies. These details were described in James Spada's 1991 book *Peter Lawford: The Man Who Kept the Secrets,* published by Bantam Books in New York.

While the president probably enjoyed this tryst, he was not inclined to deal with temper tantrums and clashes that resulted when Monroe called his home and spoke with a shocked Jacqueline. She had some hard words for her husband after that call.

Patricia Kennedy, the sixth child of Rose and Joseph Kennedy, met and married British actor Peter Lawford.

Patricia had gone to a boarding school in London, then attended a convent school in Bronxville, New York, and graduated with a B.A. from Rosemont College in Pennsylvania in 1945. She was interested in theater and began working as an NBC assistant in producing Kate Smith's radio show, Father's Petyon's Family Theater, and Family Rosary Crusade.

Brother John Kennedy introduced her to Lawford in 1949, and they married in 1954. They had four children but divorced in 1965. She held tea parties during John's campaign for the U.S. Senate and later for the Presidency. She held fund-raisers for the arts and worked with the National Center on Addiction and the Kennedy Library on its museum exhibits. She died in 2006 at the age of 82, and Peter Lawford died in 1984, having had four marriages.

The Rat Pack members went on to entertain in Las Vegas. Those original pack members gradually died out in the 1970s, but that vain city continues to attract patrons and gamblers.

CHAPTER TWENTY

Police React to Oswald's Attempt to Kill Maj. Gen. Walker

"When we (Democrats) got into office, the thing that surprised me most was to find that things were just as bad as we'd been saying they were."

John F. Kennedy

General Walker had a letter in the newspaper two days after the assassination:
The death of Mr. Kennedy is not as surprising as it is tragic. The tragic events of yesterday demonstrate the internal threat that can never be underestimated. My sympathy for the Kennedy family is no less than it is for the millions of people who have sustained equal losses in the fight for freedom. The sacrifice of our leading American family is the sacrifice of every American for peace. There is ever need at this grave hour for strength and united without recrimination that only reflects differences in beliefs regarding an acceptable price for peace.

We all learned eight days after the assassination that Lee Oswald had tried to be somebody important by killing retired Major General Edwin Walker. Lee first tried to be important when he went to Russia after leaving the Marine Corps and wanted to become a citizen of that foreign country. However, he was only important in Russia for the first few weeks. People wanted to talk to him and learn about America.

When Oswald was no longer important, just another worker bored with his job, his disappointment with Russia grew. His favorite girlfriend laughed at his marriage proposal, and he was distraught. After a year, he began to make plans to return to the United States. While waiting for papers, he met and married a Russian wife to spite his earlier girlfriend, and they had a newborn daughter by the time he returned to America. He kept a diary of his life in Russia and even wrote a book about Russia for which he hoped to become famous. All this can be seen in my book *The Mind of Oswald,* published in 2000.

Upon returning to the U.S., Oswald was unable to find steady work. But he read newspapers and library books. He focused on news about Major General Edwin Walker since he and Walker both lived in Dallas, Texas. News about Walker gave Oswald a second chance to do something of importance since his Russian adventure proved fruitless.

He believed Walker was an extremist who was dangerous to the country. So, he decided to execute the retired military officer. He could then be seen as a hero in the minds of some.

How did Walker come to Oswald's attention? It was thanks to Attorney General Robert Kennedy, who ordered a psychological evaluation of Walker because he caused a riot over the integration of the University of Mississippi. The author did that psychological evaluation on November 9, 1962, and Oswald followed that and more about Walker, who was often in the news.

On April 10, 1963, six months before President Kennedy's assassination, Oswald tried to kill Walker. That evening, Walker was working on his income tax at a desk in his den when he bent down to pick up a paper that had dropped. At that second, Oswald fired his rifle through a window. Lee did not know whether he had hit Walker but quickly left the site, buried the rifle, and returned home by bus.

Lee had left his Russian wife, written instructions about what to do if he was arrested for shooting Walker. When he was late coming home that night, she found those instructions. Thus, she was upset when he got home. He explained his act to her, but she warned him that she hid those instructions and would turn them in if he repeated a similar deed again.

She told police who found the instructions that Lee claimed it would have been good if someone had shot Hitler before he became a dictator. Thus, he made himself out to be a hero by preventing Walker from hurting others.

Lee's instructions were found when police took Marina's belongings to the hotel where she stayed after Lee was killed. Everyone then realized that Oswald wanted to kill someone important, presumably so he would go down in history as an important person. He got his wish, of course, as he has gone down in history as a very important person. The police have a name for this kind of killing: "Fame through Assassination."

On November 22, 1963, Marina Oswald learned of the assassination of President John Kennedy on television and slightly later that afternoon, policemen came to the house where she was living with her two daughters. Policemen wanted to see if Lee owned a rifle. She led them to the garage where he had stored his rifle rolled up in a blanket. They picked it up, and the blanket sagged because there was no rifle there. Marina was stunned. Mrs. Payne commented that she had noticed the garage light was on when she got up in the morning and assumed Oswald had gone into the garage for something before he left for work that morning.

Marina, with her tiny girls, was taken downtown and questioned about her husband. By the time she arrived, Lee Oswald was accused of killing policeman J.D. Tippit, the President, and wounding the Texas governor. She was taken to the jail in the downtown Dallas Police Department. There, she was joined by Oswald's mother, who had heard news of the arrest and got a ride with a reporter to the jail.

There, Marina and Marguerite Oswald were permitted to talk to Lee in his cell. He talked of getting clothes and shoes for their two daughters, aged 1½ years and 33 days old. It is curious that he mentioned shoes since it was a shoe store manager who was responsible for locating him after the assassination. Lee assured Marina that everything would be all right but did not answer her questions about what he had done.

Two days later, Oswald was killed by Jack Ruby and lay dead at Parkland Hospital, where President Kennedy had died. Marina and Lee's mother took the children to see Lee's dead body. Marina shocked Marguerite when she lifted his eyelid and saw that he had wept.

Police and Secret Service were assigned to protect the Oswald family because they might be in peril, and much questioning was necessary to understand Oswald's past. Marina had her belongings brought to her hotel from Ruth Paine's house in Irving, Texas, by policemen.

On November 30, eight days after the assassination, Ruth sent along a Russian book Marina had left, and police found a note in Russian among the pages. It was translated, and Marina identified it as the letter Oswald left her on the night he went out to shoot Major General Edwin Walker on April 10, 1963. Here is the translation of that note:

1. This key is to the mailbox in the main post office in the city on Ervay Street; on the same street where is the drugstore where you always stood. Four blocks from the drugstore on that street is the post office, you will find there our mailbox. Last month I paid for the mail, so you don't worry about it.

2. Send to the Embassy the information as to what has happened to me, and clip from the newspapers (if there is something about me in the newspapers). I think that the Embassy will come quickly to your assistance when they learn everything.

3. I paid the house rent on the 2d so don't worry about it.

4. Recently I also paid for water and gas.

5. Possibly, the money from work will come. They send to our mailbox in the post office. You will go to the bank and (cash the check).

6. My clothing etc. You can throw out or give away. Do not keep these.

7. Certain of my documents are in the small blue valise. [This valise contained photos Oswald had taken of Major General Walker's house, garage, grounds, and car.]

8. The address book can be found on my table in the study should need same.

9. We have friends here. The Red Cross also will help you.

10. I left money as much as I could. $60 on the second of the month and you and June can live using $10 per week for another 2 months using it.

11. If I am alive and taken prisoner, the city jail is located at the end of the bridge through which we always passed on going to the city (right in the beginning go the city after crossing the bridge).

The police questioned Marina after seeing this translation and asked who Oswald had tried to kill. News reporters put this out for the public so that the world learned he had tried to kill another important person--Major General Edwin Walker six months earlier on April 10, 1963.

She testified that she talked with Oswald after he came home from shooting at Walker. She asked him why he wanted to kill Walker. She reported that he said, "Well, what would you say if somebody got rid of Hitler at the right time? So if you don't know about General Walker, how can you speak up on his behalf." She later claimed that he told her Walker was "something equal to a fascist."

When Oswald had her take his picture with his rifle, pistol, and newspapers with letters he had submitted criticizing Walker, Lee and Marina added a note on the picture they sent to family friends George and Jeanne de Mohrenschildt saying, "hunter of fascists ha ha ha" She described how Jeanne de Mohrenschildt had seen Oswald's rifle when they brought over a bunny on Easter day, April 14, 1963. They had seen the news about someone shooting at Walker. Marina said George de Mohrenschildt asked Oswald, "Did you take a potshot at Walker?" and laughed. Marina and Lee were shocked that the Mohrenschildt's correctly guessed what happened.

The Warren Commission asked Marina if she knew of others that he tried to kill. She recalled that he put on a good suit and picked up his pistol one day and she asked him where he was going. He said, "Nixon's coming to town, and I want to have a look." She cannot remember the date. She pushed and shoved him into the bathroom to stop him from going out. When he insisted on coming out of the bathroom, she pressed him to take off his clothes because she thought he could go nowhere undressed. Thus, he gave up the idea and undressed, she said.

However, there was another incident that she did not confess because it would have implicated her. Years after her testimony, she was working with author Priscilla Macmillan on the story of her life called *Marina and Lee*. She told of an amazing feat that Oswald wanted to do with her help.

Lee tried to be important by persuading his wife to join him in hijacking an airplane to fly to Cuba. He said he wanted to help Fidel Castro, so again, he tried to be valuable to someone. In late July, he insisted that his pregnant wife could hold her toddler's hand and hold a gun on passengers while he went to the cockpit to threaten pilots at gunpoint into changing course. Her resistance caused him to lay aside that plan.

Perhaps he had gotten the idea from a news story printed July 14, 1963, about a hijacked plane where a 33-year-old man, Leonard Bendicks, wanted to go to Havana, Cuba.

Marina had not told the Warren Commission about Oswald's plan to hijack an airplane and fly to Cuba with his wife and daughter. She apparently felt guilty about having discussed playing a part in the hijacking. She told not only McMillan but also testified to the 1979 House Select Committee on Assassinations, Commission Exhibit No. 1833:

Mrs. Oswald stated that while she and her husband resided in New Orleans on Magazine Street toward the end of August or early in September 1963, for a period of about two weeks, Oswald was making plans to hijack an airplane and force the pilot to take him to Cuba. She said he subsequently revised his plans to the extent that he included her as part of his planning. She said he told her that he was to sit at the front of the airplane with a pistol and that she was to sit at the back of the plane with a pistol. They were to be accompanied by their daughter June and were to attempt to force the crew to fly the plane to Cuba.

Mrs. Oswald stated that she refused to have anything to do with the plan and told Oswald, "Only a crazy man would think this up." She said Oswald told her he would buy a light-weight pistol for her and that he wanted her to at least learn how to hold it. She said she refused to do this. She said her husband told her that he had seen some lightweight pistols, but that she told him not to purchase one as she would not participate in the scheme. She said she recalled that

Oswald, during the period of time when he was planning to hijack the plane, studied a world map and figured out distances to various places. She said he told her it would be necessary to hijack a plane with sufficient gas to get them to Cuba.

She recalled that Oswald wrote out timetables of airlines on piece of paper. She does not know what happened to the map or the paper on which he wrote the timetables. During this period, she stated that Oswald began to do physical exercises to increase his physical strength.

She said that when she refused to take part in the scheme to hijack an airplane, she counseled Oswald to attempt to enter Cuba legally. Thereafter, her husband began planning to go to Mexico alone for the purpose of obtaining permission to enter Cuba.

LIVES OF PEOPLE
CONNECTED
WITH THE 1963
ASSASSINATION

1963-2024

President Johnson's Life
After the Assassination

The President planned to say this at his inaugural address:
"My fellow citizens of the world: ask not what America will do for you,
but what together we can do for the freedom of man. "
He changed it at the last minute to this:
"Ask not what your country can do for you, but what
you can do for your country."
John F. Kennedy Inaugural address January 20, 1961

President Lyndon Johnson went on to carry out programs begun or considered by President Kennedy. As he neared the end of the term he had filled, he wondered whether to run for the presidency or not. He trusted Lady Bird so completely that he asked her to make up a list of the pros and cons and give him a conclusion about what he should do. She took time off to go off by herself for a few days and prepared the following document, which was called the Huntland Strategy Memo.

Johnson wrote a 1971 memoir, published two years before his death. He wrote that he shared his anxiety and doubts over running with his wife. He wrote:

She and I went over it many times, from every viewpoint. That spring of 1964, I asked her to summarize and put down on paper the pros and cons and her own conclusions. This was the memo she gave me on May 14, written by hand on several sheets torn from a stenographer's notebook.

Lady Bird began with a draft announcement of his resignation so Lyndon could consider the emotional impact of such a letter. She not only wrote these words down but also read them into a dictating machine so they could be heard on the Internet.

I wish now to announce that I will not be a candidate for re-election. I wish to spend the rest of my life in my home state, in peace with my family, for whom the rigors of my duties have left me too little time for companionship. This decision is made easier by the fact that I can feel my conduct of the Presidency, which came in such a tragic hour of national rending, has not been without some solid accomplishments, thanks to the grace of God and the sturdy cooperation of the American people.

She sighed into the recorder, adding: "I hope he won't use it. That's that!" Next, she set forth the likely outcomes if he declined to run.

1. If you do get out, we will most probably return to the ranch to live. In the course of the next few months—or until we are forgotten—we will be criticized and our motives questioned—"what skeleton in the closet," what fear of what disclosure, cause you to make this decision? Etc. Etc.

That will be painful.

2. There will be a wave of feeling, national this time and not largely statewide—of "you let us down" –even bitter disappointment— similar to the wave of feeling after you accepted the Vice Presidency job with Kennedy.

This will be more painful.

3.   You may live longer, and certainly you will have more time for the Hill Country you love and for me and Lynda and Lucy. And that we'll all love! But Lynda and Lucy will in a year or so cease to be permanent residents of our life—only available for occasional companionship.

4.   You will have various ranch lands, small banking interests, and presumably the TV to use up your talents and your hours.

They are chicken feed compared to what you are used to.

That may be relaxing for a while. I think it is not enough for you at 56. And I dread seeing you semi-idle, frustrated looking back at what you left.

I dread seeing you look at Mr. X running the county and thinking you could have done it better. You may look around for a scapegoat. I do not want to be it. You may drink too much for lack of a higher calling.

She next set out what to anticipate if he ran for the Presidency and won. If you do not get out, you will most probably be elected President.

1.   In the course of the campaign and in the ensuing years, you and I and the children will certainly get criticized and cut up for things we have done, or maybe partly in a way have done, and for others that we never did at all.

That will be painful.

2.   You are bound to make some bad decisions, be unable to achieve some high vaulting ambitions, be disappointed at the inadequacies of helpers, or perhaps on your own.

That will be painful even more.

3.   You may die earlier than you would otherwise. Nobody can tell that—as the last 6 months show maybe Dr. Cain & Dr. Hurst can be helpful in advising here.

My Conclusion

Stay in.

Realize it's going to be rough—but remember we worry much in advance about troubles that never happen!

Pace yourself, within the limits of your personality.

If you lose in November—it's all settled anyway!

Then Lady Bird gave her husband a point in time, concluding, "If you win, let's do the best we can for three years and three or four months."

This remarkable argument demonstrated how important Lady Bird Johnson was to her husband, and she presented her White House diary, 783 pages, to the LBJ Presidential Library. They kept the diary and 123 hours of their original voice recordings.

Lyndon and Ladybird Johnson's Attempt to Copy the Kennedys

On September 7, 1966, Lyndon Johnson tried to more introduce cultural events at the White House. Lyndon made remarks at a reception at the White House honoring eleven American artists and winners in the Tchaikovsky International Music Competition in Moscow.[33] He spoke especially to Jane Marsh, who had taken musicians to the Soviet Union for that competition. Johnson said,

> It was about ten days ago that I spoke in the State of Idaho about the common feeling for life, love of song, and story which Americans share with the people of the Soviet Union. I said then that our compelling task is this: to seek every possible area of agreement,

---

33 https://libguides.tcu.edu/1962_vancliburn_competition/founding

to broaden in small ways and large cooperation between the United States and the Soviet Union... Last year, Congress established at our suggestion the National Endowment for the Arts, to enhance the place of the arts in our country.

Several members of the Arts Council have come to be with us tonight... And I am happy to present another national treasure: a distinguished American performer; winner of the 1958 Tchaikovsky competition, Mr. Van Cliburn of Longview, Texas.

The following year, on October 14, 1967, the White House got a call from the managing director of the Washington Performing Arts Society. He explained that Van Cliburn had come to town for a performance at the Society but left his clothing aboard a plane. They were called upon to help find someone's tuxedo who was a tall person.

Lyndon Johnson was the same height as Van Cliburn and he had a black tuxedo and black tie, but it was quite large. He offered it and Cliburn found the jacket was fine, but the pants were baggy and were pinned together. The white shirt front was very large, but the staff got him tucked in and ready to leave. Then, the president, who was in his swimming pool, wanted to see Van in the outfit.

Van Cliburn asked permission to tell the story of the suit, which President Johnson readily gave. When Van departed, he said, "Mr. President, I'll return this suit, but I will not return that stud. I hope you'll hold it for a minute, and then give it back to me—and it will be something for me to treasure the rest of my life." That was done, and he departed at 7:50, just in time for his performance. Studs were special black buttons that showed off the black bow and white shirt well. Think of Cary Grant and Sean Connery tuxedo scenes in movies to picture this.

Jacqueline Kennedy's Life After the Assassination

"I am the man who accompanied Jacqueline Kennedy to Paris, and I have enjoyed it."

John F. Kennedy, June 2, 1961

Jacqueline Kennedy's life was more impacted by the assassination than anybody else. Her immediate reaction was to plan the funeral and then to move herself and her children away from the White House two weeks after the president's death.

She was offered an ambassadorship to France as well as offers of ambassadorships to Mexico and Great Britain by President Johnson, which she refused to accept. At her request, he renamed the Florida Space Center the John F. Kennedy Space Center a week after the assassination.

Mrs. Kennedy spent 1964 in mourning and made few public appearances during that time. In the winter following the assassination, she and the children stayed at Averell Harriman's home in Georgetown. On January 14, 1964, Mrs. Kennedy made a televised appearance from the office of the Attorney General, thanking the public for the "hundreds of thousands of messages" she had received since the assassination and said she had been sustained by America's affection for her late husband.

She purchased a house for herself and the children in Georgetown but sold it later in 1964 and bought a 15th-floor apartment at 1040 Fifth Avenue in Manhattan in the hopes of having more privacy.

In January 1964, Jacqueline wrote her dear friend, Father Joseph Leonard, in Dublin, Ireland, about her husband's death. She had been raised in a Catholic family, but her parents divorced when she was ten, and she had to hide this fact from others because divorce was an anathema to Catholics. Thus, she had always been a very private person, hesitating to share herself with most other people.

However, Father Leonard was different. The two had been correspondents since she first met him in 1950. He was rendered deaf during war duty in Flanders, where he was awarded the British War Medal and the Victory Medal. He worked in London for a time and knew Irish playwright George Bernard Shaw and Henry James. Shaw sent Father Leonard his play, *Saint Joan,* and was happy to have his corrections.

The priest met Jacqueline's aunt, Annie Auchincloss, on her honeymoon with Wilmarth Sheldon Lewis and helped the Americans out because they were studying Horace Walpole and wrote of him at Yale. Father Leonard was able to provide much research about him. The couple told Jackie to look him up on her trip to Ireland.

Father Leonard, a St. Vincent de Paul priest, welcomed Jacqueline on her trip to Dublin. The 21-year-old was visiting Ireland with her stepbrother, Hugh Dudley Auchincloss III and she struck up a close friend with the beloved deaf priest. It was as if Father Leonard were conversant with God.

Father Leonard picked up Jacqueline and her stepbrother Hugh Auchincloss at the Dublin airport and took them around, telling Irish tales of castles and kings, and even included the Blarney Stone, where she lay down on the rocks and kissed it according to tradition. This cemented their relationship so that she used him as a father confessor from 1950 until his death in 1964.

She wrote him 33 letters, which were secreted in a safe at All Hallow's College for over fifty years after his death in 1964. They were accidentally found in 2014 and were considered for sale to raise church renovation funds. However, they were returned to the Kennedy family due to the personal comments by Jacqueline Bouvier Kennedy.

In her earliest letter, she signed off to the priest "Jacqueline, who really isn't a girouette." When they were together, Father Leonard knew of her knowledge of French and called her a "girouette." That is a French word for a weathervane that blows one way or the other according to the wind. Thus, the word means "fickle," and Jackie did not want to be described in that frivolous way.

They often sent books to each other and commented about them. Jackie Kennedy wrote about Father Leonard's Christmas gift for the couple in 1962:

> Your book *My Ireland,* by Kate O'Brien, brought the perfect Irish note to our Palm Beach Christmas. We will both enjoy reading it, because Kate O'Brien has made a great name for herself in this country with her charming style.

In her early letters, Jackie often ended them with terms of endearment such as "bushels, barrels, carts & lorry loads of love to you—Jacqueline XO" and "XXXOOO" She had to explain to him that Xs and Os meant hugs and kisses, then she told him: "Now you know what they mean so you don't have to reveal my indiscretions to other women!"

She suggested to the priest that their correspondence and friendship were similar to the 20th-century friendship between author Pincesse Bibesco and

Parisian abbe Mugnier, which resulted in a book of their letters entitled *La Vie d'une Amitie (A Life of Friendship).*2

Jacqueline Bouvier wrote the priest about her faith, a stockbroker she dated, and then her first date with John Kennedy, whom she met and began to date seriously. In 1951, when she was 22 years old, she wrote:

I suddenly realized this Christmas when my sister and I decided—after not going to church for a year—that we desperately wanted to change and get close to God again—that it must have been your little prayers that worked—all the way across the ocean.

In early 1952, she wrote:

I terribly want to be a good Catholic now and I know it's all because of you. I suppose I realized in the back of my mind you wanted that—you gave me the rosary as I left Ireland.

Jacqueline tried to be a good Christian and to live a life of moral virtue. She struggled to make the right choices, leaving her no regrets. She was not always able to achieve that, but it was apparently her goal.

She said in a July 1952 letter:

I think I'm in love with—and I think it would interest you—John Kennedy—he's the son of the ambassador to England—the second son—the older was killed. He's 35 and a congressman... Maybe it will end very happily—or maybe, since he's this old and set in his ways and cares so desperately about his career, he just won't want to give up that much time to extracurricular things like marrying.[3]

She additionally wrote that he might be like her father, who "loves the chase and is bored with the conquest—and once married needs proof he's still attractive so flirts with other women and resents you." At one point, she wrote, "It's so good in a way to write all this down and get it off your chest—because I never do really talk about it with anyone—but poor you has to read it."

After a year of marriage, she wrote, "I love being married much more than I did even in the beginning... Maybe I'm just dazzled and picture myself in a glittering world of crowned heads and Men of Destiny—and not just a sad little housewife... That can be very glamorous from the outside—but if you're in it—and you're lonely—it could be a hell."

She made a negative comment about Rose Kennedy, her mother-in-law. "I don't think Jack's mother is too bright-as she would rather say a rosary than read a book."

John Kennedy was becoming more influenced by culture as time passed. He gave a speech at Harvard on June 14, 1956, where he wanted to emphasize culture to these special students. He said, "If more politicians knew poetry, and more poets knew politics, I am convinced the world would be a little better place in which to live."

In 1956, she wrote to the priest after the birth of her stillborn daughter, Arabella, saying, "Don't think I would ever be bitter at God to see so many good things that come out of this—how sadness shared brings married people closer together.

Her entire letter is not available, but here are some of her comments in January 1964, less than two months after the assassination:

I am so bitter against God, but only he and you and I know that... [She did not want to] bring up my children in a bitter way [and was] trying to make my peace with God... I think God must have taken Jack to show the world how lost we would be without him—but that is a strange way of thinking to me.... God will have a bit of explaining to do to me if I ever see him.... I have to think there is a God—or I have no hope of finding Jack again.

Since this letter shows how Jacqueline still loved her husband, we must suppose that to love someone means to see them as God intended them, so she was able to overlook his frailties. This letter also reminded Father Leonard of the 1955 Irish visit with her husband when the priest took them to a little antique shop. There, she bought her husband a tiny silver pillbox and had it engraved. She wrote Father Leonard: "Though he lost everything—he never lost that—and always carried it with him—even when he died." Also included in the letters found at the church was a Christmas card signed by John and Jackie Kennedy from November 1963, sent just before the assassination.

In her January 1964 letter, she thanked Father Leonard for saying Mass and all his prayers. He had received permission from the Vatican to pray for President Kennedy even though he could no longer stand up and did all his final work while sitting.

She was comforted to learn that Father Huber, who pronounced last rites over Kennedy at Parkland Hospital, was of the same St. Vincent de Paul sect as Father Leonard. Her dear friend, the deaf priest, would die in 1964, and she sent flowers to his funeral.

When Jacqueline Kennedy and her children left the White House, she feared for herself and her children. For one year, she had the help of Clint Hill of the Secret Service. He was reassigned after that, and she had Secret Service protection until she remarried, and there was protection for her children up to age 16.

Robert Kennedy became a surrogate father for her children, but his own large family took up much more of his time. Jacqueline urged him to run for president but was worried about his safety. When he was shot to death on June 5, 1968, she suffered depression similar to that she suffered after her husband's assassination five years earlier. She feared for her life and those of her children, saying to Pierre Salinger, who had been Press Secretary for her husband, "If they're killing Kennedys, then my children are targets... I want to get out of this country."

Robert F. Kennedy
After the Assassination

"I nominate Robert F. Kennedy to be Attorney General."
President John F. Kennedy, July 21, 1961

Robert Francis Kennedy (November 20, 1925-June 6, 1968) served as a U.S. attorney general from January 1961 to September 1964 and as a U.S. senator from New York from January 1965 until his assassination. He was the 7th of the nine children of Joseph P. Kennedy, Sr., and his wife Rose. He said, "When you come from that far down, you have to struggle to survive." Robert, called "Bobby," was dismissed by his father, who favored Joseph Jr. and John. But Joe and Rose encouraged all their children to examine and discuss current events to propel them into public service.

As a child, he was quiet, gentle, and a poor student, so he had to repeat third grade. He was a stamp collector and saved a stamp from a handwritten letter from Franklin Roosevelt, who was also a philatelist. In 1938, Robert sailed to London with his mother and four youngest siblings to join his father, who began serving as U.S. Ambassador to the United Kingdom. He attended a private school for boys in London for the 7th grade. He returned to the U.S. just before the outbreak of WWII in Europe.

In 1939, he began the 8th grade at St. Paul's School, a Protestant prep school for boys in New Hampshire that his father favored. Rose took him out after two months and enrolled him in a Benedictine Catholic boarding school for boys, where he attended the 8th through 10th grades. Monks there thought him a poor to mediocre student except for history, a subject he liked.

Why did his mother want him to be in this Catholic school? Roman Catholics believe in the scriptures of the *New Testament* and holy tradition. Not only do Catholics believe in holy tradition, but they also believe that only the Roman Catholic church can decide what Catholics are to believe and prefer their own interpretations of the *Bible.* They also believe that Mary should be idolized and raised to the level of a goddess due to one phrase in Luke 1:28: "The angel said to her, 'Rejoice, highly favored one, the Lord is with you; blessed are you among women!'" So, Catholics believe we have access to God through Jesus and Mary.

Rose believed Robert appeared more loving to her, as he disliked bullying and dirty jokes. She saw him as trying to help others. So, she wanted to enhance those characteristics by going to the right school.

Robert eventually obtained a degree at Harvard University with a bachelor's degree in political science, and a law degree at the University of Virginia. He enlisted in the U.S. Naval Reserves at age 17 and served from 1944 to 1946 as a Seaman apprentice on the *USS Joseph P. Kennedy Jr.,* named for his deceased oldest brother. Robert broke his leg playing football but earned a varsity letter when his coach sent him in wearing a cast during the last minutes of a game against Yale.

Through 1945, Robert was active in brother John's campaign for the U.S. House seat. He sailed with a friend on a six-month tour of Europe and the Middle East, filing stories for the *Boston Post.* He submitted some stories from Palestine and praised the Jewish people he met for being "hardy and tough." He predicted that the Jewish people would soon be founding a state but worried that Arabs and Jews would soon be at war.

He married Ethel Skakel in 1950, having met her while skiing in Quebec in 1945. He continued with the *Boston Post* and covered the Treaty of Peace with Japan in 1951. He then took a trip through Asia with brother John, by then a U.S. Congressman from Massachusetts, and their sister Patricia. They met India's Prime Minister Nehru and Ali Khan just before his assassination.

In 1951, Robert started working as a lawyer in the Internal Security Division of the U.S. Department of Justice, where he prosecuted and prepared fraud cases against former officials of the Truman administration before a grand jury. He resigned in June 1952 to manage John's U.S. Senate campaign. He felt that his work had finally found favor with his father, who now saw him as having harder stuff. Robert was gradually becoming the echo of someone else's music, a common problem among the Kennedy boys.

Robert gained considerable notoriety when he became one of Senator Joseph McCarthy's investigators of people who might be communists. He had some run-ins with Roy Cohn and J. Edgar Hoover and wrote a book about corrupt practices called *The Enemy Within,* published in 1960 by Harper and Row.

He tried to mend fences with Hoover at the FBI, but the director was angry when he was made Attorney General under John Kennedy. He saw Robert as a threat and tried to get dirt on him from every possible source. Hoover even complained about his bringing his dog into the federal offices. The FBI files on Robert Kennedy focused mainly on a sexual affair with Marilyn Monroe during his marriage to Ethel.

The file can be found under the title "Marilyn Monroe—FBI File part two (1956) U.S. Department of Justice Publications and Materials and can be accessed at DigitalCommuns@University of Nebraska-Lincoln. Much has been blacked out under the Freedom of Information Act.

The first date with Monroe was arranged by Robert's sister, Patricia and brother-in-law, Peter Lawford, in late 1961 or early 1962. Robert was trying to make a film of his book dealing with criminal investigations and met with producer Jerry Wald. Perhaps he was jealous of the PT-109 movie about his brother, John.

The studio was upset with Marilyn's tardiness and decided to cancel her contract. Marilyn called Robert to tell him this bad news. He said he would take care of everything, but nothing was done. She called again; they had unpleasant words, and she threatened to make their affair public.

There are other sources of the affair between Robert Kennedy and Monroe in letters that have been sold by https://www.julienslive.com. A letter from Marilyn Monroe to Bobby, the son of Arthur Miller, sold for $1,280 and was dated February 2, 1961. Here are Marilyn's relevant comments:

Oh, Bobby, guess what: I had dinner last night with the Attorney General of the United States, Robert Kennedy, and I asked him what his department was going to do about Civil Rights and some other issues. He's very intelligent, and besides all that, he's got a terrific sense of humor. I think you would like him. Anyway, I had to go to this dinner last night as he was the guest of honor and when they asked him who he wanted to meet, he wanted to meet me. So, I went to the dinner, and I sat next to him, and he isn't a bad dancer either. He asked if I had been attending 'some kind of meetings.' I laughed and said 'no, but these are the kind of questions that the youth of America want answers to and want things done about.' Not that I'm so youthful, but I feel youthful. But he's an old 36 himself which astounded me because I'm 35. It was a pleasant evening, all in all."

Another letter was sold https://www.julienslive.com for $28,000 about the affair between Robert Kennedy and Marilyn Monroe. Both of these letters were owned by Lee Strasberg, Marilyn's favorite director. This short note was from Jean Kennedy Smith, Robert Kennedy's sister. Since Marilyn met

Robert in February 1961 and she died in March 1962, we might assume it was written during that year of their friendship. It was written to Marilyn Monroe by Robert's sister.

Dear Marilyn,

Mother asked me to write and thank you for your sweet note to Daddy.
He really enjoyed it and you were very cute to send it.
Understand that you and Bobby are the new item! We all think you
should come with him when he comes back east! Again, thanks for
the note.
Love, Jean Smith.

Marilyn's suicide and funeral were handled by her first husband, Joe DiMaggio. He banned three people from admission: Frank Sinatra, John Kennedy, and Robert Kennedy. Later, Robert saw Monroe as the union of sickness and stupidity that men like Frank Sinatra had found intellectually offensive. Robert was disappointed in himself, according to some reports. He wanted to be noble and had been when he helped Jacqueline Kennedy with her life and her children. He had saved his brother John's life when he was desperately ill in another country. He had a Christian reverence for misery, the sympathy that a healthy person feels for someone who is ill.

Many people encouraged Robert Kennedy to run for the presidency. Some believed he achieved power only because of his assassinated brother, John. Others thought he had become a crime fighter through his Senate Rackets Committee from 1957 to 1960. Many had read his 1960 book about that committee entitled *The Enemy Within.*

The FBI file on Robert F. Kennedy showed the earmarks of J. Edgar Hoover's special attention. Hoover considered him a political enemy. The materials in his file also contained details of his trip to Alabama to meet with Governor George C. Wallace. The second half of the file documents the public feud over wiretapping, with Hoover believing Kennedy had authorized wiretaps as early as 1961.

Although Robert Kennedy was a civil rights activist, his opponents stood out in that field. President Lyndon Johnson and Senator Eugene McCarthy inspired voters to act. The murder of Dr. Martin Luther King Jr. on April 27, 1968, spurred others like Hubert Humphrey to join the race for the Presidency.

Senator Robert Kennedy, aged 42, and his wife were expecting their 11th child. They were in a happy mood after Kennedy gave a speech after winning the California Democratic presidential primary. They were at the Ambassador Hotel in Los Angeles, which had been in various movies since 1935 with its elaborate nightclub, Cocoanut Grove. They had been told they could avoid crowds by exiting the ballroom through the kitchen pantry area.

Suddenly, just as Kennedy was shaking hands with a kitchen worker, shots were fired. Kennedy fell, and Paul Shrade, who was hit in the head with a shot, fell also. Four others were hit, and all five of the victims survived except Kennedy.

As the crowd of people passed by, 24-year-old Palestinian Sirhan Bishara Sirhan fired his eight-shot revolver at the senator, hitting him three times and wounding five other people. The shot that entered Kennedy's head behind his ear was a fatal shot. As he lay on the floor, he must have seen Paul Shrade bleeding and asked, "Is Paul all right?" He was reassured that Paul Schrade, a member of the executive board of the United Auto Workers and vice chairman of the Kennedy campaign for labor, was alive.

Kennedy lay on the floor, and as someone was about to pick him up to transport him to the hospital, he said, "Don't lift me." Kennedy then passed out and did not regain consciousness before his death the next morning.

Senator Kennedy was taken to two hospitals and died in the second one. Ethel Kennedy was pregnant with daughter Rory and was with her husband at the hospital. Robert Kennedy left ten children and one more on the way to be brought up by an overwhelmed mother in a home of loss.

Sirhan Sirhan was taken to the police department and arrested. The official report of DeWayne Wolfer stated that the first shot struck Kennedy behind his ear, the second passed through Kennedy's shoulder pad and hit Schrade, the third struck Kennedy (who had raised his arm to his head when he was shot) under the right armpit and lodged in his neck, and the fourth entered his back and came out through his chest.

When he was arrested, Sirhan said nothing about getting drunk or being drunk, but in later years, he told people that he could not remember the crime because he was drunk. Arresting officers made no mention of him being inebriated at the time of the shooting. At his trial, Dr. Edward H. Davis performed an EEG (electroencephalogram) after he was given six ounces of Gordon's Gin in eight minutes time. The doctor concluded that Mr. Sirhan did not become agitated, and the EEG failed to reveal any abnormalities before or after the administration of gin.

During the trial, Sirhan claimed to have amnesia about getting and firing the gun and even said he did not remember being interrogated.

Sirhan Sirhan was an unemployed college dropout who lived at home with his mother. He had some $400 in his pocket when he was arrested. His car needed repair, and he had been unable to get a job partly because he had not performed well as a jockey. He certainly felt that he was part of a different, more restricted society. He had a passionate need to move beyond the world of his origins.

We and our youths must develop a maturity and culture that does not depend upon guns and drugs.

When he was to testify about shooting Kennedy, he raised a clenched fist instead of raising his hand to take the oath. He told author Bob Kaiser in May 1969, "They can gas me. But I am famous. I achieved in a day what it took Kennedy all his life to do." Some thought another person did the shootings. Even though Sirhan occasionally said he did not shoot Senator Kennedy, he declined the offer of a polygraph to determine the truth, according to Dan E. Moldea's 1995 book *The Killing of Robert F. Kennedy.*

The 24-year-old assassin had written some pages saying such things as "I advocate the overthrow of the current president of the fucken [sic] United States of America. I have no absolute plans yet—but soon will compose some. I am poor—This country's propaganda says that she is the best country in the world—I have not experienced this yet."

Sirhan Sirhan was given a life sentence in prison for killing Senator Robert Kennedy. Various times since that trial, family and friends have come together to discuss whether Sirhan should be released. He has never clearly stated that he committed the crime and was sorry for it. Thus, the family has not been inclined to vote for a parole release.

In recent years, Sirhan has said that he was against Robert Kennedy's position on the Middle East. But his notebooks did not contain that information. Sirhan has said that in early years, he liked what he heard about Kennedy. But he has also told his mother that he does not remember killing the Senator or firing the gun. He has also added that he did this crime for his Arab brethren. But his own attorney, Emile Zola Berman, said,

> In his fantasies, he was often a hero and savior of his people. In the realities of life, however, he was small, helpless, isolated, confused, and bewildered by emotions over which he had no control.[34]

---

34 Dan E. Moldea, The Killing of Robert F. Kennedy. W. W. Norton & Company, New York, 1996.

Jumping years ahead, President Joe Biden called Ethel Kennedy on her 95th birthday, April 11, 2023, to wish her well. She had suffered the loss of her granddaughter Maeve Kennedy McKean, who was canoeing with her son in a Maryland boating disaster in 2020. While the 92-year-old Ethel Kennedy showed her typical strength and didn't shed a public tear when informed of the tragedy on Chesapeake Bay, her family realized how shaken she was by the latest family tragedy. Maeve, who had been a Peace Corps volunteer, took her little boy out in a canoe to shelter away from others during COVID-19. Swirling waters apparently upset the canoe and led to disaster.

That loss came less than a year after a granddaughter, 22-year-old Saoirse Kennedy Hill, died from an overdose of methadone, Prozac, Valium, and alcohol inside Ethel's large Hyannis Port compound in Massachusetts. Methadone was being used to wean her off opium. She had perhaps struggled with mental illness and wrote a high school essay that included these words:

People talk about cancer freely; why is it so difficult to discuss the effects of depression, anxiety, or schizophrenic disorders?... Just because the illness may not be outwardly visible doesn't mean the person suffering from it isn't struggling... Let's come together to make our community more inclusive and comfortable.

While the focus of loss has been mainly focused on John Kennedy and his family, his brother Robert and his family also suffered many losses.

Jacqueline Kennedy Married
Aristotle Onassis

"The first time you marry for love, the second for money,
and the third for companionship."

Jacqueline Kennedy

After the assassination of John Kennedy's brother on June 5, 1968, Mrs. Jacqueline Kennedy and her children were passengers on the 21-car train that traveled eight hours to transfer Robert Kennedy's body for burial. Seven-year-old John Kennedy, Jr. walked out on the open platform at one point. He didn't seem to know what to do with the noisy crowds who gathered to honor Robert Kennedy. Having visited Rome and the Pope with his mother two years earlier, the little boy seemed to bless the people as he had seen the Pope do with crowds.[35]

Onassis was named Aristotle Socrates by parents, who knew that Aristotle was a student of Socrates, the great Greek philosopher. Could their wisdom reside in the brain of their son? He was born to Greek parents who fled a terrible fire at Smyrna to Greece as refugees and had to rebuild a family and career. He was left with a vaunting ambition, an aching desire for more elegant surroundings such as his parents once had. He had become a multi-millionaire through shipbuilding.

---

35 https://www.history.com/news/robert-f-kennedy-death-funeral-train

Years earlier, Onassis had problems with the United States when he negotiated a deal to supply Saudi Arabian oil tankers. The American oil industry and the Saudi King had an agreement that he violated. Washington leaders learned of his deal and repossessed his tankers as they docked in America, seizing his profits. He pled guilty and paid $7 million, so the criminal charges against him were dropped.

Jacqueline appealed to her old friend, Aristotle Onassis, who had hosted the Kennedys on his yacht. In less than a year, they married on October 20, 1968, on his exclusive island of Scorpios, Greece. When Onassis married Jacqueline Kennedy, she said, "I do," surrounded by family. Her children, John and Caroline, participated by holding candles during the ceremony. Jackie's sister, Lee Radziwill, was the matron of honor. Around forty guests witnessed the 45-minute ceremony. They went to live on his private island of Skorpios.

The old Greek gentleman whose myasthenia gravis caused eyelids to be taped up since muscles did not work correctly was seen as a "joke" to young John, who was eight years old when Aristotle became his stepfather. Ari tried to spend some time with the children, which was hard on him. Quite often, the soul is healed by being with children. John Kennedy enjoyed his children playing around his desk. Onassis was an old man who had lost interest in playing with children who would have no meaningful conversations.

But the marriage served his purposes. He had been involved in a nine-year affair with Greek opera diva Maria Callas. However, Callas was a very emotional lady, demanding in certain ways. Ari had enjoyed her notoriety but did not intend to marry her. So, he ceased that affair to marry President Kennedy's widow and take on her children for their safety.

Onassis later took Jackie to Athens. As Onassis gazed at the beauty of his young wife, he worshipped her. He was the perfect Aladdin, making her dreams come true. And some of his own dreams came true through this union.

The Greek tycoon was much shorter than Jackie. Wife Jacqueline was angry at photographers and reporters who kept taking pictures of them, probing their differences and prying into her life. She decided to sue the paparazzi. Onassis didn't want her to, but she insisted. He was sent a bill for $400,000. He contacted Roy Cohn (a lawyer who was often helpful to Donald Trump) to represent him against the law firm, and Roy got them to cut that bill in half.

The shipping magnate had evened the score with the Kennedys by this marriage after Robert Kennedy had accused him of corruption in the shipping industry. He helped himself in other ways. The Onassis' yacht *"Christina"* had hosted Grace Kelly's honeymoon with Prince Rainier III of Monaco for an intimate wedding reception. In fact, it was Onassis who planted the idea in Rainier's mind to marry a movie star and have a male heir to keep France from taking over Monaco.

The little principality offered residents no taxes, no armies, a 12th-century palace, and a casino. Onassis had taken control of those who ran the casino, and it would benefit him to keep those investments. Since Rainier had been writing Grace Kelly for six months after her visit there, he proposed to the star. After the Rainier wedding, Monaco was then a place to see and be seen, and he had helped his own investments in that little principality. Their son, Albert, whose mother died when he was six, is now the prince of Monaco.

Onassis often had other prominent people on board his floating palace, the *Christina,* for rest and recuperation. For example, British Prime Minister Winston Church sailed with Onassis eight times between 1958 and 1963, and one of his hand-done paintings was hung in the yacht saloon.

During the marriage with Jacqueline, they lived in six places—her Manhattan apartment, her horse farm in New Jersey, his apartment in Paris, his private island of Skorpios, his house in Athens, and his yacht. Onassis invited Ted Kennedy to visit them often so the family connection could be maintained.

Jacqueline was free to do things without her ailing husband. One delightful surprise was an invitation to visit Richard and Patricia Nixon with her children at the White House.

Jacqueline's Secret Visit to the White House

Richard and Patricia Nixon flew Jacqueline and her children to the White House on February 3, 1971, to view the portraits of herself and President Kennedy by Aaron Shikler at the White House. They were invited to dinner as well as to tour the White House for the only time Jacqueline Kennedy visited after leaving in December 1963. She took 10-year-old John, Jr., and 13-year-old Caroline. The president and his two daughters and their dogs visited with Mrs. Kennedy and her children. Jacqueline Kennedy and her children wrote thanks to the Nixons, and the Nixons responded with their thoughts. All of these letters were handwritten.

Jacqueline Kennedy Onassis to President and Mrs. Nixon
February 4, 1971

You were so kind to us yesterday. Never have I seen such magnanimity and such tenderness.

Can you imagine the gift you gave me? To return to the White House privately with my little ones while they are still young enough to rediscover their childhood—with you both as guides—and with your daughters, such extraordinary young women.

What a tribute to have brought them up like that in the limelight. I pray I can do half the same with my Caroline. It was good to see her exposed to their example, and John to their charm!

You spoiled us beyond belief; the Jet Star, our tour, the superb dinner. Thank you, Mr. President, for opening one of your precious bottle of Bordeaux for us.

I have never seen the White House look so perfect. There is no hidden corner of it that is not beautiful now.

It was moving, when we left, to see that great house illuminated, with the fountains playing.

The way you have hung the portraits does them great honor—more than they deserve. They should not have been such trouble to you. You bent over backwards to be generous, and we are all deeply touched and grateful.

It made me happy to hear the children bursting with reminiscences all the way home.

Before John went to sleep, I could explain the photographs of Jack and him in his room, to him. "There you are with Daddy right where the President was describing the Great Seal; there, on the path where the President accompanied us to our car."

Your kindness made real memories of his shadowy ones.

Thank you with all my heart. A day I always dreaded turned out to be one of the most precious ones I have spent with my children.

May God bless you all,

Most gratefully,

Jackie

John Kennedy, Jr. to President and Mrs. Nixon
February 4, 1971

I can never thank you more for showing us the White House. I really liked everything about it. You were so nice to show us everything.

I don't think I could remember much about the White House but it was really nice seeing it all again.

When I sat on Lincolns bed and wish for something, my wish really came true. I wished that I would have good luck at school. I loved all the pictures of all the Presidents. I also really liked the old pistols. I really loved the dogs they were so funny as soon as I came home my dogs kept on sniffing me. Maybe they remember the white house. The food was the best I have ever had.

The shrimp was by far the best I have ever tasted.

And the steak with the sauce was really good.

And I have never tasted anything as good as the souffle was the best I have ever tasted.

I really liked seeing the Presidents office and the cabinet room a lot. Thank you so much again.

Sincerly John Kennedy

Caroline Kennedy to President and Mrs. Nixon
February 4, 1971

Thank you so much for the incredible tour you were so nice to do it and I just love everything about the house. All the rooms are so lively, and it was so sweet of you to take us around so specially. I Just love your dogs. King Timahoe is beautiful, and the others are so cute. The dinner was delicious. Your Swiss chef is the best thing that ever came out of Switzerland except maybe the chocolate.

Your daughters were so nice to me. I had such a good time, and it was so nice to see it all again.

The president was so nice to take so much time out of his schedule. Please thank him. The portraits were hung so nicely. You made them look so good. Everything was just perfect, and everyone was so nice. Please thank them all for me. Allen, John, the one who met us at the door, and everyone else. But thank you and your family most of all. I will really never forget it. Love Caroline.

P.S. The plane is fantastic, and the candy is wonderful. Sgt. Simmons is great and so is the pilot. All I seem to be saying is so nice, fantastic. Thank you, but it is all I can say.

President Richard Nixon to John Kennedy, Jr. February 28, 1971

Dear John,

We all greatly enjoyed your letter and we were particularly happy that your visit to the house when you lived as a very young boy left pleasant memories.

I will let you in on a little secret with regard to our dogs. Usually Mrs. Nixon, for obvious reasons, will not allow them to come to the second floor. So you can see that your visit was a special treat for them (and for me! I don't worry as much about what happens to the furniture.)

I was glad your wish which you made on the Lincoln bed came true. When you need another one like that, come back to see us. You will always be welcome in this house.

Sincerely, Richard Nixon

President Richard Nixon to Caroline Kennedy
February 28, 1971

Dear Caroline,

I want you to know how much we all appreciated your letter after our visit at the White House. We did not share the contents with anyone but our Swiss chef was deeply touched when I told him that you had written so generously about his culinary creations.

I recall that you told us your favorite subject was history but that a poor teacher this year had somewhat dampened your interest. I know a teacher can make a great difference, but I hope your enthusiasm for history continues.

History is the best foundation for almost any profession. But even more important you will find the really most fascinating reading as you grow older is in history and biography.

As far as the teacher is concerned, I recall that some of the teachers I thought at the time were the worst (because they graded so hard) were actually the best in retrospect. I would guess you are an exceptionally good student and I hope the teacher doesn't discourage you!

Mrs. Nixon, Tricia and Julie join me in sending our best. You will always be welcome in this house.

Richard Nixon

Onassis' son died in a plane crash in 1973. Jackie tried to help console him, but he was devastated and in deep depression. However, she had another concern during that year. She had maintained contact with John Kennedy's old friend, Chuck Spalding, who had introduced John Kennedy to Dr. Max Jacobson just before the Kennedy-Nixon debates. The president had used Dr.

Jacobson's methamphetamines extensively, beginning with the presidential debates before his election. On May 28, 1973, some ten years after the Kennedy assassination, Max Jacobson got a call from Spalding, who said he urgently needed to meet. The next day, the doctor was surprised to find Jacqueline Onassis waiting for him.

Jacqueline's Guilt About Using Dr. Max Jacobson's Drugs

Jacobson was to speak with a panel reviewing his license in two more days. Through the years, Jacobson had bragged about treating the president, and wore his PT-109 tie clasp as a badge of honor given him by President Kennedy. Jackie wanted to know what he would say if asked about the White House and her husband's treatment.

Dr. Jacobson assured her that there was no reason for concern. He mentioned that he had never taken money from Kennedy but was concerned about the hearing and had spent $35,000 on legal fees. She told him, "You don't have anything to worry about," suggesting that she might finance his legal help. He was discreet, and details about the treatment of the Kennedys did not emerge for many years.

What a strange adventure Jacqueline had shared with John Kennedy. She undoubtedly wondered how her actions would be seen and hoped that she would not be humiliated if news of their drug abuse surfaced. She also wanted to protect the president's reputation for her children's sake and for his own legacy.

Greeks Tried to Kidnap John Kennedy, Jr.

Although Jacqueline had married Onassis for her children's safety, a gang of eight Greeks tried to abduct 11-year-old John for ransom. On July 18, 1972, the *New York Times* reported that those Greek men planned a series of robberies and abductions of prominent people. The men were being indicted for conspiracy and were held in prison in Piraeus, the port of Athens.[36] No longer in danger, young John and sister Caroline, 13, were cruising peacefully with their mother on Aristotle Onassis' yacht. This close call illustrated to young John that his biking, jogging, and workouts required more caution.

Onassis, himself, was turning out to be a disappointment. Always interested in saving money, he talked to lawyer Roy Cohn about divorcing Jacqueline toward the end of his life so that he could leave all his money to his daughter. The divorce papers with Cohn were never completed, and Onassis died while still married to Jacqueline Kennedy.

Aristotle died in Paris during treatment for respiratory failure on March 15, 1975. Greek law ordered non-Greek surviving spouses a limited amount of assets, and after two years of legal dealings, Jacqueline accepted $26 million from Aristotle's daughter and sole heir.

When Onassis married Jacqueline Kennedy, he offered her $3 million to replace her Kennedy trust fund, which she would lose because she was remarrying. After Onassis's death, she was to receive $150,000 each year for the rest of her life. The whole marital contract was discussed with Ted Kennedy. However, after Onassis's death, Christina settled with Jackie Onassis for $25 million in exchange for Jackie not contesting Onassis's will.[37]

---

36 https://www.nytimes.com/1972/07/18/archives/athens-indicts-8-accused-of-plot-to-kidnap-a-kennedy.html

37 "Two Partisans of the Past: Into the '80s," Henry Allen, Washington Post, October 8, 1981.

Onassis died at age 69 and was buried on his island of Skorpios in Greece alongside his son, Alexander, and his sister, Artemis. Jacqueline Onassis also received her share of the estate, settling for a reported $10 million, which was negotiated by brother-in-law Ted Kennedy. This amount would reportedly grow to several hundred million under the financial stewardship of her companion, Maurice Tempelsman.[38]

38 McFadden, Robert D. (24 May 1994) "Death of A First Lady: The Companion; Quietly at Her Side, Public at the End," The New York Times.

Jacqueline Onassis' Life
After Aristotle's Death

> *"You look smashing in that pink suit."*
> *John F. Kennedy to Jacqueline on 11/22/63*
> **Friendship with Carly Simon**

After Ari's death, Jacqueline returned to Martha's Vineyard and Hyannis Port, Massachusetts. She made an interesting friend around this time. Carly Simon was the daughter of Richard L. Simon, co-founder of Simon & Schuster Publishers. Richard Simon (1899-1960) left a wife who died in 1994, but Carly was never very close to her. Jacqueline was 17 years older than Carly, but they hit it off.

Carly was a bundle of nerves when young. She stuttered and began to sing to handle that problem, just as country western singer Mel Tillis had done. Since her father was so involved in publishing, and she suffered from dyslexia, she constantly worried that he did not think well of her and saw her as a failure.

There may have been some consolation in talking with Jacqueline since young John Kennedy had inherited dyslexia and ADHD (attention deficit and hyperactivity disorder) from his father. Jacqueline had gotten some help from doctors who prescribed Ritalin for her son, who took it until his death. Jackie also tried to keep him occupied with active pastimes so that he constantly worked out. His inattention caused him to forget things and to have numerous little accidents that required minor or even major surgery. Did the two ladies talk about these things?

Carly did write about their friendship in 2019. She entitled the book *Touched by the Sun: My Friendship with Jackie.* The book is really about Carly and is certainly not a tell-all about Jacqueline, but it is very well-written and conveys good feelings between the women. They shared cigarettes, talked about love and life, and talked about movies. They had a special fondness for director Mike Nichols, for whom Carly had done music in one movie.

Jacqueline Onassis' Work as Editor

When Jacqueline became an editor for Viking, and then Doubleday later, Carly published some children's books through Doubleday. Carly Simon is an exceptional singer and sang "Nobody Does It Better" for the James Bond movie *The Spy Who Loved Me.*

In 1975, Jackie was hired as a consulting editor at Viking Press for two years at $200 a week. She resigned in 1977 because Viking insisted on printing an erroneous book about Ted Kennedy. She was then hired by Doubleday, where she was an associate editor. She also participated in the cultural and architectural preservation of Grand Central Terminal and other projects. During Jaqueline's publishing career, Caroline studied for a term in London, and John Jr. attended Collegiate School in New York.

Jackie acquired nearly 100 books over 19 years and helped many authors through her notes despite being ill and receiving treatment for cancer up to the last stages of the disease.[39]

---

39 https:www.townandcountrymag.com/society/a10334726/Jackie-kennedy-publishing-career/

Jacqueline Kennedy Onassis wrote three books. In 1964, she recorded seven historic interviews about her life with John F. Kennedy. It was re-published in 2011 entitled *Jacqueline Kennedy: Historic Conversations on Life with John F. Kennedy,* with 8 CDs to listen to her words. The book is 400 pages long and includes a foreword by Caroline Kennedy.

In 1974, she published a 63-page journal under Delacorte called *One Special Summer.* Jacqueline was 22 when she took her 18-year-old sister, Lee Bouvier Radziwill, to Europe. While traveling, they wrote and sketched to create this delightful little travelogue piece. Jackie had earlier spent a year in France, living with a French family while attending the Sorbonne. Her cards and letters had made Lee want to see the sights, and their enjoyment shows through their little journal.

In 1976, Jacqueline wrote *In the Russian Style* with the latest printing by Penguin Putnam. There is a great mixture of glorious pictures and text describing the royal court life of old Russia, stunning vintage clothing, and some details about the royal family. Descriptions of events like the Winter Palace ball are excellent.

Beginning in 1980, she spent much time with Maurice Tempelsman, a Jewish diamond merchant from Belgium, who also advised her on finances. In the early 1990s, she supported Bill Clinton and donated money toward his presidential campaign.

Jacqueline Onassis' Illness and Death

In November 1993, Jackie Onassis was thrown from her horse during a fox hunt in Middleburg, Virginia. The Red Fox Inn and Tavern dates back to 1728 and was built by a relative of George Washington named Joseph Chinn. Young George stopped in when he was doing survey work. There was a famous Civil War Battle near the inn in June 1863. The place was a favorite of the Kennedys. President Kennedy had Press Secretary Pierre Salinger set up a press conference there in February of 1961.

Mrs. Kennedy came back to visit after her marriage to Aristotle Onassis and wrote this note to owner Nancy Reuter, but the date is uncertain:

Dear Mrs. Reuter,

Not only are you the most generous person, but you must have the coziest, most enchanting house in Virginia. It just exudes happiness, all the warmth, love, and care that went into making such a home. I love your little girl's great wicker basket of cuddly toys and think how lucky she is to grow up in such a room—with such nice parents. I feel guilty and very grateful. Thank you more than I can possibly express.

Sincerely, Jacqueline Kennedy Onassis.

Jacqueline's fall from her horse on June 20, 1993, left her unconscious for some thirty minutes. Doctors examined her and helped her recover. However, they discovered a swollen lymph node in her groin. During the next month, she had a stomachache and swollen lymph nodes in her neck and was diagnosed with non-treatable non-Hodgkin's lymphoma, a blood cancer. She began chemotherapy in January 1994 and continued to work at Doubleday.

By March, the cancer had spread to her spinal cord, brain, and liver, and by May, it was deemed terminal. She left the hospital to die at home on May 18, 1994, surrounded by her children. President Bill Clinton read the eulogy at her funeral. Maurice Tempelsman read Jackie's favorite poem, *Ithaca*, written in 1911 by Greek poet C. P. Cavafy. It was about a trip that one can make toward a destination, but the goal is not the important thing. The things one learned along the way were of most importance. Thus, the longer it took to reach the destination, the better it was for the traveler.

She died at age 64 and was buried next to President John Kennedy and was laid to rest on May 23, 1994, at Arlington National Cemetery, next to the eternal flame she lit over the grave of her fallen husband 30 years earlier. Church bells tolled, and about 2,000 people lined the roadway as the hearse bore the body of the former First Lady to the cemetery. She was buried on a hillside overlooking the Potomac, alongside President John F. Kennedy and the two children they lost at birth.[5]

In his eulogy at Jacqueline Kennedy Onassis's funeral mass in New York, Senator Edward M. Kennedy, her brother-in-law, recalled her as "a blessing to us and to the nation - and a lesson to the world on how to do things right, how to be a mother, how to appreciate history, how to be courageous." Onassis died of lymphatic cancer in her Fifth Avenue apartment in New York.

Her two grown children and longtime companion, Maurice Templesman, were joined by about 100 relatives and a handful of close friends by her grave on the grassy slope at the cemetery. The cemetery was closed to the public for the day, but television cameras were permitted to film from a distance and brought the graveside service to an audience of millions. Stoic as their mother had been at the same place so many years earlier, John F. Kennedy Jr. and his sister, Caroline Kennedy Schlossberg, read from the Scriptures during the 20-minute service on the hot, still afternoon.

As they led the mourners away, Caroline placed a long-stemmed white flower on her mother's mahogany coffin while her brother knelt to kiss it before touching the black granite marker on his father's adjacent grave. They then paused for a moment of prayer at the grave of their uncle, Sen.

Robert F. Kennedy, assassinated just a few years after President Kennedy.

President Clinton bade Mrs. Onassis goodbye in his brief graveside remarks. "God gave her very great gifts and imposed upon her great burdens," Clinton said. "She bore them all with dignity and grace and uncommon

common sense... May the flame she lit so long ago burn ever brighter here and always brighter in our hearts. God bless you, friend, and farewell."

The little cousins who had played touch football at the family compound in Hyannis Port, Mass., were the somber young men serving as honorary pallbearers. Joining them was Jack Walsh, the Secret Service agent who guarded Caroline and John Jr. for 12 years after their father's death.

Marina Oswald's Life
After the Assassination

"The Russian pennant on the moon has shown us our task.
Mr. Khrushchev's confident boasts have outlined our challenge.
And I think we can live up to it I think we can make up for these years
of doubt and indecision. But together we can build a better nation –
and a better, happier, more peaceful world, where life is
good and men are free and freedom never falters."
Senator John Kennedy, November 28, 1959

Marina Oswald learned of the assassination of President John Kennedy on television, and slightly later that afternoon, policemen came to the house where she was living with her two daughters. Policemen wanted to see if Lee owned a rifle. She led them to the garage where he had stored his rifle rolled up in a blanket. They picked it up, and the blanket sagged because there was no rifle there. Marina was stunned. Mrs. Payne commented that she had noticed the garage light was on when she got up in the morning and assumed Oswald had gone into the garage for something before he left for work that morning.

Marina, with her tiny girls, was taken downtown and questioned about her husband. By the time she arrived, Lee Oswald was accused of killing policeman J.D. Tippit, the President, and wounding the Texas governor. She was taken to the jail in the downtown Dallas Police Department. There, she was joined by Oswald's mother, who had heard news of the arrest and got a ride with a reporter to the jail.

There, Marina and Marguerite Oswald were permitted to talk to Lee in his cell. He talked of getting clothes and shoes for their two daughters, aged 1½ years and 33 days old. It is curious that he mentioned shoes since it was a shoe store manager who was responsible for locating him after the assassination. Lee assured Marina that everything would be all right but did not answer her questions about what he had done.

Two days later, Oswald was killed by Jack Ruby and lay dead at Parkland Hospital, where President Kennedy had died. Marina and Lee's mother took the children to see Lee's dead body. Marina shocked Marguerite when she lifted his eyelid and saw that he had wept.

Police and Secret Service were assigned to protect the Oswald family because they might be in peril, and much questioning was necessary to understand Oswald's past. Marina had her belongings brought to her hotel from Ruth Paine's house in Irving, Texas, by policemen.

On November 30, eight days after the assassination, Ruth sent along a Russian book Marina had left, and police found a note in Russian among the pages. It was translated, and Marina identified it as the letter Oswald left her on the night he went out to shoot Major General Edwin Walker on April 10, 1963.

Marina was helped to find a place to stay for a short time in a hotel. She never returned to Ruth Paine's house in Irving, Texas, where she had stayed for some months. The police and Secret Service wanted to protect Marina because she was to testify at the Warren Commission hearings, which were just being organized by Chief Justice Earl Warren.

Finally, after Oswald's death, Marina found a life for herself and her daughters. She rented a house in Richardson, a Dallas suburb, for some time and worked as a drugstore clerk at Sun Rexall. She was sent donations of around $70,000. She sold Lee's Russian diary for $20,000 and a picture of him holding the rifle for $5,000.

She was criticized by many, and it was difficult for her to make friends. She met Anita and Albert Lang at some European Club in the area. She asked Anita if they could be friends, saying that she would understand if Anita did not want to be her friend. This was the kind of sadness that accompanied her life as the widow of a presidential assassin. Marina hired Anita to babysit her children. This was in the late 1960s and early 1970s.

She needed a good friend, and Anita was a good listener, so they got along quite well with each other. Marina quietly came across as gentle, but she could be very tough. When the babysitter's husband, Albert Lang, finally became a U.S. citizen, they all celebrated together. Lang went on to become involved in the home-building industry.

Marina and Kenneth Porter finally left Richardson and moved to Rockwall in the mid-1970s. In January 1965, Marina attended an eight-week course in English at the University of Michigan. In June 1965, she married electronics worker Kenneth Porter. They were married by a justice of the peace in Fate, Texas, a small town in Rockwall County. They had some problems in their marriage, causing her to file for domestic abuse once, but they obviously had special strains on their relationship. They have one son in addition to Marina's two daughters by Oswald.

Marina has lived many years in Rockwall, Texas, and for some time, she was a housekeeper for the author's friend, Dr. Barbara Montgomery (1925-2017). Barbara was a Fulbright scholar in China and Korea, taught history at El Centro College of the Dallas County Community College District from 1972 to 1997, served as a municipal judge, and was active in many organizations. She relayed to me and to my husband, Bob Cheney, how much she learned from Marina that was helpful to her work in organizations such as the Dallas Council on World Affairs.

In 1981, Marina gave permission to exhume Oswald's body to refute a claim that a look-alike Russian Soviet agent was buried in place of Oswald. In 1989, she became a naturalized U.S. citizen. On October 24, 2013, she sold Lee's wedding ring for $90,000. The gold ring he left in her cup with the $170 on the morning of the assassination had a tiny hammer and sickle stamped inside. Lee bought it in Minsk in 1961 for his marriage to Marina.

Jack Ruby's "Trial of the Century" for Killing Oswald

*"The ignorance of one voter in a democracy
impairs the security of all."*

President John Kennedy at Vanderbilt University convocation May 18, 1963

Jack Ruby killed Lee Oswald on November 24, 1963, and had to be tried for that crime. Judge Joe B. Brown found the trial would be in his docket. He had heart problems and was told that it might be too stressful for him. However, he said that he would handle it by getting help from some others.

He tried to make arrangements for the newspapers of the world and their TV and radio colleagues to cover the trial. That was the same kind of mistake that Police Chief Jesse Curry made when he tried to be decent to reporters by permitting them into the Dallas Police Department. That was how Ruby came to be in the police department, along with so many reporters. The chief was dealing with public opinion and was trying to show the world that the rumors of Oswald being beaten up during his arrest were not true. Oswald had tussled with the officers who arrested him at the Texas Theater earlier on the day of his arrest, so he had a black eye.

Judge Brown was also dealing with public opinion and had to contend with 568 members of the press seeking a seat at the trial. It was the largest collection of newspapermen ever to cover a trial in America. In Texas, a judge may allow cameras in his courtroom if he likes. The American Bar Association asked that Judge Brown keep them out. The judge decided against cameras because, as he said, "I wanted a dignified trial without people acting up for cameras."

He felt unable to handle the large number of admittance requests. So, he hired the Sam Bloom Agency, and they requested admittance requests by publishers rather than a reporter arriving at the door.

With Judge Brown's heart problems, he found the courtroom very hot and humid and required an injection by the doctor on the morning the trial began on March 4, 1964. Judge Brown would die one year later.

The main defense attorney for Jack Ruby was Melvin Belli. He was called the "Father of Demonstrative Evidence." His early use of pictures, movies, scale models, human skeletons, animals, and other devices was dramatic and highly effective. His high-profile clients included Mae West, Errol Flynn, Lenny Bruce, Zsa Zsa Gabor, Muhammad Ali, Alex Haley, Jim Bakker and Tammy Faye, The Rolling Stones, Chuck Berry, Martha Mitchell, Tony Curtis, and now Jack Ruby.

Despite his defense, on March 14, 1964, Ruby was convicted of "murder with malice" and received a death sentence. However, in late 1966, Ruby's conviction was overturned by the Texas Appellate Court, and he was granted a change of venue with a new trial to be in Wichita Falls, some 150 miles from Dallas. However, Ruby died of cancer before the second trial could take place. Belli wrote a book called *Dallas Justice* on his perspective of the Jack Ruby trial.

The defense attorneys opened the trial with plans for a mistrial for various reasons, such as how few people could attend the trial due to rules and lack of space. Quickly, Judge Brown was told by Ruby's lawyers that they were filing a motion of insanity at the time of the offense and at the present time. The jury of eight men and four women entered the jury box.

The charge was read to Jack Ruby, and then Judge Brown said, "Mr. Ruby, how do you plead?" He responded, "Not guilty, your Honor."

It became clear that the state meant to retrace Ruby's behavior over the period of two days and show that he made up his mind to kill Oswald hours before the shooting rather than it being an act with no forethought. Many believed Ruby's act was a last-minute choice rather than being planned hours ahead. The issue of whether Ruby could have killed Oswald earlier at the police station when they were very near each other came up.

The Western Union supervisor who accepted Ruby's $25 money order to the stripper had stamped the record only three minutes before Ruby shot Oswald. He was asked if there was anything different about his demeanor since he was a regular customer of the Western Union. The supervisor said, "No, sir, just a customer."

Ruby's lawyer, Marvin Belli, surprised everyone by arguing that Ruby's act of violence was not a last-minute action but was the result of a certain kind of epilepsy called "psychomotor epilepsy." He was relying on an electroencephalogram (EEG) brain wave test, which was rarely seen and little studied. Some of the details in descriptions by various doctors seemed to bore many in attendance and even some jurors. But these details were interrupted by occasional surprises.

For example, testimony was given about how Jack Ruby wanted people to call his dogs his "children." This would make him angry, just as he got angry when someone came into his bar with a gun. He took his own pistol and marched them out of his club when he learned a weapon was brought in.

His roommate, George Senator, described how Ruby was so upset by the assassination that he woke up Senator so they could drive around town and take pictures of billboards saying, "Impeach Earl Warren." Senator also described how Ruby tried to get a postal night clerk to give him information about the post office box number of a Jewish man whose name was on an advertisement insulting President Kennedy. Senator added that Ruby kept repeating that it was a shame that this had happened to Mrs. Kennedy and her children.

There was even a jailbreak during the trial. In the jail on the sixth floor above the courtroom, a deputy sheriff had been distributing soap to prisoners. Some of them had carved a mock knife and a mock gun, and the seven prisoners forced the deputy into an elevator, rode it down, and tried to make their way through the crowd. They jostled past one of the strippers who was waiting to testify for Ruby. She thought she was being attacked and went a little wild. The deputy sheriff ran over and took the soap gun away from that prisoner and hustled him back to his jail cell, and the rest were captured in a few minutes. A New York newspaper headed their story of this: "Oh, Dallas!"

Outside of the courthouse, a man and woman were picketing with a sign saying, "A Person Who Does Wrong Is Not Insane" and "Psychiatry Is Not the Hope of Killers." All these things were disturbing, but Judge Joe B. Brown was the most disturbed when he heard that Marguerite Oswald, the mother of Lee Harvey Oswald, was outside, intending to enter as a spectator. The judge felt that she would create a scene in the presence of the jury, which could cause a mistrial.

Thus, he sent a representative outside, where she was having an impromptu press conference and talking with reporters. She was given a subpoena, and Judge Brown went out of the courtroom to speak with her. She was always ready to pose for photographers, and they took pictures of the tete-a-tete with the judge.

She was told that since she would be called up during the trial, she was not to attend it other than for the moment when she was subpoenaed. She was quite willing to abide by the ruling but returned daily until she was called.

Dr. Manfred Guttmacher had spent a lifetime practicing psychiatry, and much of that was with the criminally insane. Two of his books lay on the counsel table as he testified. He said, "I don't think Ruby was capable of knowing right from wrong or of knowing the nature and quality of his acts at the time of the homicide."

He explained his view of Ruby's upbringing by a drunken immigrant father and an ineffectual mother who had become psychotic. Jack had been unstable, with siblings who had a mental illness and was often fired from jobs for fighting. He saw the President as the head of the ideal family group. Ruby had said about Kennedy, "I fell for that man," almost as if he fell in love with him. Ruby had always felt alone, unloved, and tried to fit in with any guys, even bad guys, until he just couldn't satisfy them anymore.

Judge Brown and the jury listened to various seeming experts describe some kind of brain problem that comes and goes called a "psychomotor variant," which they called a form of epilepsy. Brown trusted the Chief of Psychiatry at Southwestern Medical School, Dr. Robert Stubblefield. Dr. Stubblefield testified that he was not convinced of any kind of epilepsy seizure. Ruby did admit that he used Preludin, an amphetamine that suppresses sleep and appetite, after the assassination in order to stay awake.

Jack Ruby's rabbi, Hillel Silverman, was asked to testify because Ruby came to the synagogue for a brief service after the President's death. He told of times when Ruby's behavior had been bizarre, but on that evening, he seemed composed as he thanked Silverman for helping out his sister during her brief hospitalization.

An expert on epilepsy, Dr. Walter Bromberg, was called to testify about Ruby's mental health. He stated that Ruby showed a Messianic complex, a desire to be a martyr and a "savior of his race," and did not seem to know the nature and quality of his acts. Dr. Francis Michael Forrester, noted for examining President Eisenhower after he suffered a stroke during his second term, ridiculed the defenses' argument that Ruby was acting like a robot when he killed Oswald.

A final expert on EEGs, Dr. Gibbs, believed the EEG test was showing some form of epilepsy, but he could not tell from the tracing whether Ruby knew right from wrong when he killed Oswald.

Suddenly, everything stopped as all the lawyers looked tired, the jurors looked exhausted, and Ruby looked pale and haggard but continued chewing gum. Judge Brown sent the jury out. Prosecuting attorney Bill Alexander had made the case with these sentences:

"I tell you that Jack Ruby misjudged public temperament. He thought he could kill Oswald, that perhaps he would be a hero by doing it. He thought he could get away with it because of the condition of the public temperament at that time. Now that's the kind of a thing that the law seeks to deter. I tell you, that warrants the death penalty."

Another prosecuting attorney, Frank Watts, said,

"Ruby wanted the world to know 'that us Jews have some guts.' I happen to recall the words of a brilliant young leader, who could not be here today by any possibility, who said, "Ask not what your country can do for you, ask what you can do for your country.' I ask, 'What has Jack Ruby done for his country? What has he done for this country, after now professing the great love that he had for his President Kennedy?... I say to you that he was sane then and he is sane today. I say the blood is still red on the hands of Jack Ruby."

Melvin Belli wrapped up his closing statements to the jury.

"But let us think of who we are trying for this crime. Who would do a thing like this? The village clown, the village idiot? The man who is always around the police station bringing coffee, donuts, sandwiches? Publicity he wants, publicity he seeks. Ah, ladies and gentlemen, I suppose we'd all like to engrave our initials in some oak tree, or be in some column, or be sculpted into Mt. Rushmore. I think it's part of our craving to seek after some bit of immortality. But this poor sick fellow—and sick he is, and you know he's sick in your hearts."

When the defense finished, it took the jury 142 minutes to decide that Ruby was guilty of murder with malice and to affix his punishment at death, a verdict that shocked even Judge Brown.

The foreman of the jury kept a diary which his uncle edited and published. *The Jack Ruby Trial Revisited: The Diary of Jury Foreman Max Causey* was printed in 2000 by the University of Texas Press. Causey's 18-page diary was expanded to include letters from four other jurors about the trial. None of those five believed that Ruby was involved in a conspiracy to kill Oswald. They each thought Ruby killed Oswald to be publicized as a hero who slew the killer of the president.

They believed the defense should have dealt with Ruby's momentary loss of control brought on by emotions. Judge Brown had said of foreman Max Causey, "I don't think I have ever seen anyone temperamentally and intellectually better qualified to serve on a jury."

The jurors saw Attorney Belli as being critical of Dallas and jurors, claiming them all to be biased. Belli, in his 1964 *Dallas Justice: The Real Story of Jack Ruby and His Trial,* believed the jurors wanted to kill Ruby to appease their conscience after a president had been slain in their city. This little book also described how the jurors decided to carefully observe Ruby's demeanor when the verdict and sentence were read.[40][41]

---

40 "The Jack Ruby Trial Revisited: The Diary of Jury Foreman Max Cause" book review by Dr. Diane Holloway in International Social Science Revue, Volume 76, N. 3/4 (2001), pp 139-140.
41 https://alexhaley.com/2020/07/27/alex-haley-interviews-melvin-belli/

Alex Haley, author of *Roots* and former client of Melvin Belli, interviewed the lawyer. The interview was published in the June 1965 issue of *Playboy Magazine.41* Some interesting remarks are cited here:

Alex Haley: Despite the Warren Report, the belief persists in some circles that Oswald and Ruby were parties to a right-wing plot against the President's life. Do you feel that these suspicions have any substance?

Melvin Belli: They're hallucinatory and utterly preposterous... Now, I know as much about the assassination as any man alive, and I can tell you flatly that it was the barren, solitary act of Lee Oswald. He was a crazy man. And he and Ruby were strangers. Those are the facts. The most incredible thing to me is why the FBI didn't pass along to the Secret Service the lengthy file it had on Oswald. But as much as I detest the type of man that J. Edgar Hoover is, I can't make myself believe that the FBI or the CIA or anyone else suppressed knowledge of any plot. On the Warren Commission, we had seven wise and honorable men, some of the best. If they couldn't come up with the truth, then God pity us all.

On June 7, 1964, Jack Ruby was interrogated by members of the President's Commission on the Assassination of President Kennedy.[42] Here are some of the comments of Jack Ruby and Chief Justice Warren.

Warren: You wanted to ask something, did you, Mr. Ruby?

Ruby: I would like to be able to get a lie detector test or truth serum of what motivated me to do what I did at that particular time... Now, Mr. Warren, I don't know if you got any confidence in the lie detector test and the truth serum, and so on.

42 The Witnesses: The Highlights of Hearings Before the Warren Commission on the Assassination of President Kennedy, Bantam Books, New York City, 1964.

Warren: … If you want such a test, I will arrange for it.

Ruby: I do want it.

Ruby then went into details. Warren finally asked him this:

Warren: Did you know Lee Harvey Oswald prior to this shooting?

Ruby: That is why I want to take the lie detector test. Just saying no isn't sufficient. [Ruby had read in newspapers that some speculated that he and Oswald were involved in a conspiracy to kill and silence the killer of the president.]

Warren: I will afford you that opportunity.

Jack Ruby's Polygraph Interrogation by the F.B.I.

Jack Ruby's polygraph examination took place July 18, 1964, and the following people were present: Assistant Counsel Arlen Specter, one other representative of the Warren Commission, Assistant District Attorney William Alexander, Defense Attorneys Joe Tonahill and Clayton Fowler, two F.B.I. agents, Chief Jailer E. L. Holman, psychiatrist William Beavers, M.D., and the court reporter.

To minimize Ruby's distraction by those present, he faced a wall and could see only the examiner. F.B.I. special agent Bell P. Herndon conducted the polygraph into series. Only the most important questions will be mentioned here, but the public can read more of this in the Warren Commission Reports or in my book, *Dallas and the Jack Ruby Trial: Memoir of Judge Joe B. Brown, Sr.*, pp. 188-212.[43]

At the time of Ruby's polygraph examination, then FBI Director J. Edgar Hoover commented:

---

43 Dallas and the Jack Ruby Trial: Memoir of Judge Joe B. Brown, Sr. Dr. Diane Holloway, iUniverse, Lincoln, NE, pp. 188-212

"It should be pointed out that the polygraph, often referred to as 'lie detector,' is not in fact such a device. The instrument is designed to record, under proper stimuli, emotional responses in the form of physiological variations which may indicate and accompany deception. The FBI feels that the polygraph technique is not sufficiently precise to permit absolute judgments of deception or truth without qualifications. The polygraph technique has a number of limitations, one of which relates to the mental fitness and condition of the examinee to be tested."

Hoover knew the origin of the polygraph. It was developed by psychologist William Marston who additionally created the comic strip *Wonder Woman*. His wife had suggested that when she got upset, it seemed that her blood pressure went up. He took that idea and developed it into the polygraph used today. It is assumed that telling a lie makes a person physically anxious.

Herndon: Did you voluntarily request this test?

Ruby: Yes.

Hernon: Did you know Oswald before November 22, 1963?

Ruby: No.

Herndon: Are you now a member of the Communist Party?

Ruby: No.

Herndon: Have you ever been a member of any group that advocates the violent overthrow of the United States government?

Ruby: No.

Herndon: Between the assassination and the shooting, did anybody you know tell you they knew Oswald?

Ruby: No.

Herndon: Did you first decide to shoot Oswald on Friday night?

Ruby: No.

Herndon: Did you first decide to shoot Oswald on Saturday morning?

Ruby: No.

Herndon: Did you first decide to shoot Oswald on Saturday night?

Ruby: No.

Herndon: Did you first decide to shoot Oswald on Sunday morning?

Ruby: Yes.

Herndon: Did you enter the jail by walking through an alleyway?

Ruby: No.

Herndon: Did you walk past the guard at the time Lt. Pierce's car was parked on the ramp exit?

Ruby: Yes.

Ruby: The most important question, you haven't asked me yet, why did I shoot Oswald?

Alexander: Jack, they can't ask that kind of question for this machine. They can only ask you, was it for a certain purpose. It has to be a "yes" or "no" answer.

Ruby: At that particular moment, after watching television all that...

Fowler: Jack, let me interject right now, again as your attorney, I advise you not to answer this question.

Ruby: Clayton, I'm sorry, I've got to answer it. I've got to because, believe me, it means an awful lot to me. I didn't want, I felt so carried away, that at that particular time of the great tragedy, I felt somehow in my little bit of a way I could save Mrs. Kennedy the ordeal of coming back for trial here.

Specter: All right, fine, Mr. Ruby. That's the same answer to that general question that you gave when the Commission heard your testimony.

Herndon: Do you attend the synagogue regularly?

Ruby: How can I answer that one?

Herndon: Just relax. Did you go to the synagogue that Friday night?

Ruby: Yes.

Herndon: Did you see Oswald in the jail on Friday night?

Ruby: Yes.

Herndon: Did you have a gun with you when you went to the Friday night press conference at the jail?

Ruby: No.

Herndon: Did any foreign influence cause you to shoot Oswald?

Ruby: No.

Herndon: Did you shoot Oswald because of any influence of the underworld?

Ruby: No.

Herndon: Did you shoot Oswald in order to save Mrs. Kennedy the ordeal of a trial?

Ruby: Yes.

Herndon: Did you know the Tippit that was killed?

Ruby: No.

Herndon: Did you ever meet with Oswald and Officer Tippit at your club?

Ruby: No.

Herndon: Were you at the Parkland Hospital at any time on Friday?

Ruby: No.

Specter: Mr. Ruby, do you now have any other questions which you would like us to ask you on this polygraphy examination?

Ruby: They didn't ask me another question, "If I loved the President so much, why wasn't I at the parade?"

Specter: You may go on the record with any facet you think is important for the Commission to know about.

Ruby: And yet, it's strange that perhaps I didn't vote for President Kennedy, or didn't vote at all, that I should build up such a great affection for him, when everything points against me... What I'm trying to bring out is this: It's, and everyone was much surprised, why should I be carried away so emotionally to commit the act, and yet knowing how I felt and knowing I know I'm telling the truth, how can we bring that point out that I am not sincere in why I did it.

Alexander: Tell us what you had in mind and then we'll frame the question.

Ruby: Whether or not I am of criminal background or whether I'm an honest and sincere person, because all those things came out and suspicions came out that Jack Ruby was involved in this and that and leaves a lot of suspicion as to my background and character.

Alexander: Are you a law-abiding patriotic citizen?

Ruby: Yes... I became closely attached to our beloved President when he gave that wonderful speech when we had our problem in Cuba at that time. That was a very tremendous speech and then I followed him on television and in magazines wherever he went, to Ireland and different places... One more thing, should you ask me or isn't it necessary, why I suddenly was so carried away to get involved in this serious crime?

Alexander: Jack, that won't work on the machine.

Specter: We have to ask you a "Yes" or "No" question, and we've already covered that by asking you the question about Mrs. Kennedy, whether you didn't shoot Oswald to avoid having her come to trial.

Ruby: In other words, I can't answer truthfully and have another reason for doing it, is that correct? [Ruby knew somehow that there were more reasons for killing Oswald than helping Mrs. Kennedy. He sort of knew that he did it to increase his self-importance or for some selfish purpose, rather than just out of love or patriotism.]

Jack Ruby won a new trial to be set in a different location—Wichita Falls, Texas—where jurors were not so near the presidential assassination site. They were ready to move him on December 5, 1966, when he was found to have cancer that had spread to the liver, lungs, and brain. He died January 3, 1967, in the same Parkland Hospital where Kennedy and Oswald had died. Family members were with him when he died.

After an autopsy on February 1, 1967, Dallas County Medical Examiner Earl Rose sent a letter regarding the cause of death to Justice of the Peace Bill Richburg:

The autopsy studies on Jack Ruby have been completed. The protocol is closed to show the cause of death as follows: Pulmonary emboli as immediate cause of death secondary to bronchiolar carcinoma of the lungs.

How Did Oswald Select His First Assassination Target?

*"The greater our knowledge increases,
the more our ignorance unfolds."*

**President John F. Kennedy at Rice University in Houston
on September 12, 1962**

Lee Harvey Oswald was always looking for some way to become noticed, become important, and accomplish something that would attract attention. He was a great reader and read the lives and deaths of many famous people. If it was his aim to become famous, killing an important person might help him achieve his goal. So, he sought a target that was close enough for him to reach with his limited transportation. He relied on news coverage about how a supposedly good person, like a Major General, could be a bad person.

The psychiatric evaluation of Major General Edwin Walker was carried out as ordered by Attorney General Robert Kennedy on November 8-10, 1962, after Walker interfered with the integration of the University of Mississippi. Racism was the issue that stirred the General to rally people to fight integration. Since Walker was an extremist, Oswald may have thought that his death might be a good thing. He was nearby, living in the same town and only a few miles away.

What was the news about his target? In September 1962, black Air Force veteran James Meredith wanted to enter the University of Mississippi to earn a degree. Democratic Governor of Mississippi, Ross Barnett, declared, "No school will be integrated in Mississippi while I am your governor."

At his behest, the state legislature quickly created a plan. They passed a law that denied admission to any person "who has a crime of moral turpitude against him" or who had been convicted of any felony offense or not pardoned. The same day it became law, Meridith was accused and convicted of "false voter registration" in Jackson County. The conviction against Meredith was in error because Meredith met voter qualification by owning land in northern Mississippi and was registered to vote in Jackson, where he lived.

On September 20, Meredith was rebuffed again by Governor Barnett in his efforts to gain admission, though university officials were prepared to admit him.

On September 26, 1962, Walker broadcast this message on several radio stations:

> Mississippi, it is time to move. We have talked, listened, and been pushed around far too much by the anti-Christ Supreme Court! Rise to stand beside Governor Ross Barnett at Jackson, Mississippi! Now is the time to be heard! Thousands strong from every State in the Union! Rally to the cause of freedom! The battle cry of the republic! Barnett yes! Castro no! Bring your flag, your tent, and your skillet. It's now or never! The time is when the President of the United States commits or uses any troops, federal or state, in Mississippi! The last time in such a situation, I was on the wrong side. That was in Little Rock, Arkansas, in 1957-1958. This time—out of uniform—I am on the right side! I will be there!

Walker had resigned from the military, which meant that he did not receive a pension. He later asked for a pension, and it was finally restored. Incidentally, he was in trouble with the Internal Revenue Service because he did not pay $4,000 due on his 1961 income tax.

On September 28, 1962, the Court of Appeals found Governor Barnett in civil contempt and ordered that he be arrested and pay a fine of $10,000 for each day that he kept up the refusal unless he complied by October 2.

Attorney General Robert F. Kennedy had a series of phone calls with Governor Barnett between September 27 to October 1. Barnett reluctantly agreed to let Meredith enroll in the university but secretly bargained with Kennedy on a plan that would allow him to save face.

We do not know whether Barnett shared those plans with Walker or not. But we know this. On September 29, 1962, Walker issued a televised statement:

This is Edwin A. Walker. I am in Mississippi beside Governor Ross Barnett. I call for a national protest against the conspiracy from within. Rally to the cause of freedom in righteous indignation, violent vocal protests, and bitter silence under the flag of Mississippi at the use of federal troops. This today is a disgrace to the nation in 'dire peril,' a disgrace beyond the capacity of anyone except its enemies. This is the conspiracy of the crucifixion by anti-Christ conspirators of the Supreme Court in their denial of prayer and their betrayal of a nation.

Those comments seemed a little crazy to many people. However, Barnett promised to maintain civil order. Robert Kennedy ordered 127 US Marshals, as well as 316 deputized US Border Patrol and 97 Federal Bureau of Prisons officers to accompany Meredith during his arrival and registration.

On that day, September 29, President Kennedy issued a proclamation commanding all persons engaged in the obstruction of the laws and the orders of the courts to "cease and desist therefrom and to disperse and retire peaceably forthwith." He intended to use the militia or the armed forces to suppress any insurrection, domestic violence, unlawful combination, or conspiracy. This emergency proclamation seemed good but backfired.

That evening, after State Senator George Yarbrough withdrew the State Highway Police, a 15-hour riot broke out. Whites opposing integration had been gathering at the campus and began fighting with federal agents. Despite the Kennedy administration's reluctance to use force, it ordered the nationalized Mississippi National Guard and federal troops to the campus. In the violent clashes that followed, two civilians were killed by gunshot wounds. Six federal marshals were shot, along with hundreds who suffered injuries. White rioters burned cars, pelted federal agents and soldiers with rocks, bricks, small arms fire, and damaged university property.

Walker was arrested on October 1, 1962, in Oxford, Mississippi, on four federal charges. Those charges were surely read by Oswald:

Section III—for assault and resisting or otherwise opposing federal officers, including marshals, in the performance of their duty.

Section 372—for conspiracy to prevent a federal officer from discharging his duties.

Section 2383—for inciting or engaging in an insurrection against the United States.

Section 2384—for conspiracy to overthrow or oppose by force the execution of the laws of the United States.

When Walker was taken before the United States Commissioner, Omar D. Craig, fixed bond at $100,000, Mr. H. M. Ray, U.S. Attorney for the Norther District of Mississippi, said:

General Walker has been quoted in the newspapers as calling for twenty thousand citizens from each state to assemble in Oxford in protest. At the time the complaint against Walker was filed, nobody had any idea whether we were going to have that kind of Coxey's Army in Oxford. [Coxey's Army was a protest march by unemployed workers from the United States, led by Ohio businessman Jacob Coxey, when they marched on Washington, DC, in 1894.]

Walker was not immediately able to post bail, so a commitment began with the following sentence:

You are hereby commanded to take the custody of the above-named defendant and to commit him with a certified copy of this commitment to the custodian of a place of confinement within the Northern District of Mississippi approved by the Attorney General of the United States where the defendant shall be received and safely kept until discharged in due course of law.

Walker was flown on October 1, 1962, to an institution in Springfield, Missouri. On October 2, a motion was filed to cause Walker to have a psychiatric examination. A telegram from Dr. Charles Smith, Chief Psychiatrist of the United States Bureau of Prisons, read:

I, Charles E. Smith, Medical Director and Chief Psychiatrist of the Federal Bureau of Prisons, Department of Justice, having been duly sworn, do hereby certify that I have examined carefully various news reports concerning the actions and behavior of former Major General Edwin Walker, including his appearance before the Committee of the United States Senate on Armed Forces in April of this year and news reports of his appearances on the Campus of the University of Mississippi during the past several days.

Some of his reported behavior reflects sensitivity and essentially unpredictable and seemingly bizarre outbursts of the type often observed in individuals suffering with paranoid mental disorder. There are also indications in his medical history of function and psychosomatic disorders which could be precursors of the more serious disorder which his present behavior suggests.

From this and other information available to me I believe his recent behavior has been out of keeping with that of a person of his station, background, and training, and that as such it may be indicative of an underlying mental disturbance.

On October 6, 1962, Walker's bail was reduced to $50,000, which he posted on October 7, and he returned home to Dallas amidst 200 cheering supporters. They carried signs saying: "Welcome Home, General Walker," "Win with General Walker," and "President '64."

Walker was released under a stipulation between his lawyers and the government, which provided for a private psychiatric examination conducted by Dr. Robert Stubblefield, Chief of the Psychiatry Department of the Southwestern Medical Center, and not only by Dr. Stubblefield but by a psychiatrist engaged in private practice to be named by the United States.

Texas laws state that patients who are a danger to themselves and/or to others may be held up to ninety days for evaluation before release. Psychiatrists and patients attempt to shorten this as much as possible. Since the issue with retired Major General Edwin Walker was whether he was sane enough to work with his lawyers in a trial for his charges, his sanity could be evaluated rather quickly.

18 USC 4244 (1958) "Mental incompetency after arrest and before a trial."

Whenever... the United States Attorney [Robert Kennedy] has reasonable cause to believe that a person charged with an offense against the United States may be presently insane or otherwise so mentally incompetent as to be unable to understand the proceedings again him or properly to assist in his own defense... The court shall cause the accused to be examined as to his mental condition by at least one qualified psychiatrist, who shall report to the court. He shall file a motion for a judicial determination of such mental competency of the accused, setting forth the proof for such belief with the trial court in which proceedings are pending.

Dr. Manfred Guttmacher also shared with Dr. Charles Smith that there was a real possibility of deterioration in the mental processes of Mr. Walker over the past year or two from his study of Walker's past and his recent statements in Oxford, Mississippi. He thought Dr. Stubblefield's opinion that Walker was competent to stand trial for the alleged crimes would be sufficient if it could be accomplished. Also, there was great consternation among physicians through the American Medical Association, warning doctors that they should not become a tool for political purposes.

Walker, who told everyone that he was just "Mister" Walker due to his retirement from military service, was released from prison on his own recognizance and was required to submit to a psychiatric evaluation within five days.

He used those days to be with friends and advisors at Tanglewood-on-the-Lake, a resort near Lake Texoma between Texas and Oklahoma. He flew the plane there and back and joked with his attorney, Gen. Clyde Watts of Oklahoma City, and others.

He came with his attorney and advisor on November 8, 1962, to meet Drs. Robert Stubblefield, Chief of the Psychiatric Services at Southwestern Medical School and Parkland Hospital, and Dr. William DeLoach, Chief Psychiatrist of the Psychiatric locked Inpatient Unit on the 8th floor of Parkland Hospital, next door to the medical school. DeLoach was a distant cousin of FBI assistant to J. Edgar Hoover, Cartha (Deke) DeLoach, who is also mentioned in this book.

After Dr. Stubblefield had a private interview with Walker, they went over to the locked inpatient psychiatric unit at the hospital. Dr. DeLoach and the author of this book, as a nurse in training to become a psychologist, met him. He was accompanied by two men who went into Dr. DeLoach's office to talk for a few minutes.

Walker's lawyers had talked with Hungarian psychiatrist Thomas Szasz, who flew into town for the day. They wished to have him be the other psychiatrist for the defense of Mr. Walker. The psychiatrist said that in the South, with his thick accent and unfamiliarity with everything involved, he would not be received well. However, he had recommendations for the evaluation to which both Drs. Stubblefield and DeLoach agreed. These conditions were:

Walker would not speak with a man once he was under evaluation, would not speak with a psychiatrist, and would not write anything down.

Dr. Szasz flew out in the morning, and Walker spent the night in the hospital.

Dr. DeLoach had hired me in 1961 when he was made Chairman of the Psychiatric Inpatient Unit. He chose the author, he said, because I had worked for department chairmen at the medical school and had run a European travel agency in the British Isles and France where there were complicated problems with people, and had dealt with people like the American Ambassador to Great Britain, John "Jock" Hay Whitney, etc. I had studied nursing and psychology and would soon become a psychiatric nurse in this Psychiatric Unit and later become a psychologist.

When I arrived at work the morning of November 9, 1962, Drs Stubblefield and DeLoach met me at 8 a.m. and said something like this:

Walker is finally settled in here. He was instructed by lawyers and Dr. Szasz not to speak to men, or psychiatrists, or write anything down. So, you are going to handle him for this two-day evaluation. He does not want to eat with others. He said that since he is six feet three, he attracts a lot of attention; especially from the ladies. He does not want to interact with anyone on the ward. When we asked if he might speak with our secretary, they all agreed. That was fine so that is what we are calling you.

You will take him his meals and try to get him to do some psychological tests, but he won't write things down. You will. Please go in and try to learn as much as you can about him. Our mission is to see if he is able to work with his lawyers to defend himself or whether he is insane or psychotic.

On our unit, nobody wore uniforms. So, I knocked on his door, and he opened it with a smile. I said, "Hi, I'm Diane. I am Dr. DeLoach's secretary. I'm sure you are hungry for breakfast. May I bring it to you with some coffee?" He said, "Yes, and I would like some nice hot strong coffee."

I took in his meal and returned to take away the dishes later. Then I told him we were going to talk later, but for now, did he need anything. He said that he was going to smoke, and it didn't matter what our rules were. I said, you can smoke in this room but not outside where others might not like breathing your smoke. Then, I said something like this:

I'll come back later to ask you some questions about your life. I've heard some things about you, and you've served many interesting places and done such important work that I'm sure I will be hearing about." He did not object so I said, "Why don't you tell me when you would like to chat."

We set a time for about an hour later. In that interview, I asked him about his most interesting assignments, and he loved talking about himself. He made it clear that he was important and had great status. I responded with statements of admiration for his work, which were sincere. We spoke like this for an hour or so. I then asked questions for an approximate IQ score, and he could be scored at a bright average. There was not enough time for the next important evaluation tool, a personality inventory. But I was confident that he would let me ask him the questions, and I would mark his answers on my scale sheet.

When I arrived at his door the next morning, he said, "This is my birthday and I'm going out for a while. But I'll be back this afternoon."

I gave him my best wishes and said I would see him later. He called for me about 1:30 p.m., and I came in to sit with him and read him the statements in the Minnesota Multiphasic Personality Inventory (MMPI), a standard psychological evaluation of personality. If a person is psychotic, they will not understand the questions. I introduced it by explaining that I would read him a sentence, and he could choose an answer "yes" or "no" or "no answer." He agreed, which surprised me greatly. We then proceeded for some 3 ½ hours. He decided not to answer about 20 questions, but the test had 365 questions, and his answers were sufficient to score it properly.

When we finished, he had begun to sweat a bit and expressed regret that it had been a long and tiring ordeal. I was also worn out from the tension and told him to just relax. I did not tell him that I was the one who would score the test and would explain to Dr. DeLoach what it showed. I simply said to him, Dr. DeLoach will be coming to see you with the results a bit later. He said, "I will not talk to him. I will only talk to you."

He asked about me and knew that I was learning psychiatric nursing and psychology. He also learned that I had lived in London and Paris and had worked with Ambassador Whitney to arrange assemblies for some of our traveling choral groups. Jock had financed movies like *Gone with the Wind* and *Rebecca.* So, Edwin Walker said he had an aunt or some female relative who was in silent movies and then talkies later. Then he added, "I want to know what you found out on this test." I promised to come back in an hour or so to discuss this with him.

I returned after scoring the tests. Walker had a high average intelligence and some personality problems. I knew that he realized he was answering some questions that sent up red flags. So, I mentioned that he was rather anxious and seemed to feel that a lot of people were against him. That lit him up. He became angry and said something like, "Well, they are after me. That's why I'm here, damn it." I gradually calmed him down, but later, he mentioned that others criticized much of what he said and did.

In scoring his personality inventory, I could see answers showed a prominent paranoid personality but little evidence of a psychosis. (He did not hear or see things that were not real.) I shared this information with Dr. DeLoach, who said I should try to keep him calm. He said, "You go back in and tell him that these are good results, and he is capable of going through his trial and defending himself as he works with his lawyer. Tell him I will be in shortly, and he is going to be discharged this evening or tomorrow morning."

So, I returned knocked on his door; and he smiled when I entered so he appeared calm. I told him what Dr. DeLoach had said. I also told him that he was not psychotic or out of his head or in need of medicines such as anti-depressants or, anti-anxiety or psychotropic medications.

Then, I decided to try to get a little more information. I said, "I am so impressed with your past and your successes. I wish we could talk about what you are planning to do once you are home again."

That must have been the right thing to say because he responded, "So you want to know my future?"

He started off about how important it was for him to be able to help people understand the terrible influence of communism. He had all sorts of plans but added, "I'm not sure where you're coming from. You've probably been trained in some of those schools where you've been brainwashed to believe US propaganda."

I said something like, "When I lived in Europe, I heard many criticisms of the United States. We are not perfect, are we?"

He then said, "You are correct! I want to get out of here as soon as possible. I will be working with Christian leaders. There is so much I could be doing rather than sitting around here. You will be reading about me. Do you follow the news?"

I said, "Yes, sir. And every day when I drive to work, I drive right past your house on Turtle Creek Boulevard. I saw one day when you flew your flag upside down."

"Okay, you know about me. Now, see if you can get me out of here."

I then left to tell Dr. DeLoach about our conversation. I was asked to prepare a written report for Drs. DeLoach and Stubblefield, but since I was not yet a qualified psychologist, I was told that my name would not be mentioned in the report. It simply helped the psychiatrists complete their study about his ability to undergo a trial. While I don't remember the details, I remember most of the main conclusions:

There was no evidence of a psychotic illness; he was not hearing, seeing or believing in things that were not real, so he would be able to prepare for his own defense.

He had a deeply paranoid state of mind, believing others had it in for him.

There was a suggestion of homosexuality with many negative thoughts about women.

After Major General Walker was discharged to some friends who came to get him, Dr. DeLoach asked me to join him as he talked with Dr. Stubblefield about the test results.

Dr. Stubblefield, always the soul of diplomacy, said something like:

We have accomplished what we wanted to know—whether he is competent to stand trial. He will know what is going on while he works with his lawyers. I'm going to send this and explain that we were limited by the recommendations of his lawyers and Dr. Szasz and can do no more. I thank you both so much for your help.

His report was sent on to Claude F. Clayton, District Judge, who wrote these words, among other things, on December 6, 1962:

It is ordered: That said report shall be filed in the jacket file as a public record, and that a hearing for a judicial determination of the question of sanity or insanity, competency or incompetency is not required and shall not be held.

Walker continued to make news the following year. In 1963, when it was learned that Adlai Stevenson and later President Kennedy would be coming to Dallas, he worked with other John Birch Society members to undermine both men.

United Nations Ambassador Adlai Stevenson had come to speak in Dallas on UN Day, October 24, 1963. On the night just before he came to Dallas, Walker rented the same Dallas Memorial Auditorium in which Stevenson would speak. Walker advertised his opposing event as US Day. He invited members of the John Birch Society, the National Indignation Convention, the Minutemen, and other right-wing organizations that were fundamentally opposed to the existence of the United Nations.

Walker instructed his audience to buy all the tickets they could afford to the Stevenson speech and fill the auditorium with rightists. Then Walker told them to heckle Stevenson mercilessly and to bring Halloween noisemakers and their own prepared speeches to recite in the hallways and generally disrupt the speech in any way they could. Walker orchestrated verbal attacks on Adlai Stevenson on UN Day, October 24, 1963.

Walker also instructed his followers to hoist a banner on the ceiling of the auditorium, fold it, and tie it with a long string so that when the string was pulled, it would unfurl. On one side of the banner was printed, ""US out of UN"!" and on the other side was printed, ""UN out of US"!" This banner was to remain folded until after Stevenson began speaking.

Walker himself did not attend the planned disruption, nor did he take credit for the orchestration. The events in the auditorium proceeded exactly according to plan so that Stevenson felt he had to quit speaking before his presentation was finished and rushed out to his limousine. On his way there, he was spat upon by some protesters, and one protester struck him in the head with her placard. The spitter and the hitter were both arrested. Walker was not charged, although his role was well-known at the time. Stevenson warned President Kennedy not to go to Dallas following these events.

We described the full-page anti-Kennedy advertisement and handbill about Kennedy that was distributed on the day the president arrived and was assassinated. That was not the end of Walker's problematic behavior.

Angered by the negative publicity he was receiving for his conservative political views, Walker began to file libel lawsuits against various media outlets. At this point, Walker and his lawyers had won over $3 million in lawsuits. The Associated Press appealed the decision, as *Associated Press v. Walker*, all the way to the United States Supreme Court, and in 1967 the Supreme Court ruled *against* Walker. The Court, which had previously said that public *officials* could not recover damages unless they could prove actual malice, extended this to public *figures* as well.

Walker, from 1962 through 1967, displayed a full-size billboard on his front lawn with the slogan, *Impeach Earl Warren*. Supreme Court Justice Earl Warren was a key figure in the decision of *Brown v. Board of Education*, which mandated the racial integration of all US public schools. Warren was also the Supreme Court judge who heard 'Walker's case against the Associated Press. Walker and his lawyers walked away with nothing.

We shall wind up our discussion of Edwin Walker with what happened to him in later life. When he was 66 years old, he was arrested on June 23, 1976, for fondling and propositioning a male undercover police officer in a public restroom in a Dallas Park near his home and charged with public lewdness. He was arrested again for public lewdness on March 16, 1977. He pleaded no contest to one of the two misdemeanor charges and was convicted and sentenced to jail time, which the judge suspended. He was also fined $1,000.

Walker was a heavy smoker and died of lung cancer at his home on Halloween 1993, ten days before his 84th birthday. He never married and had no children.

Two years before his death, Walker wrote a letter to the Dallas Police Department, but he was very mixed up and confused about Lee Oswald and President Kennedy. He seemed to believe that President Kennedy had sent Lee Oswald to kill him on April 10, 1963. He seemed to think that Oswald was caught and released from jail the next day on orders from the President. Then, the president was killed himself by Oswald.

This letter is part of the collection entitled John F. Kennedy, Dallas Police Department Collection. Here is his letter to the Police Chief:

A common assassin with a dead President-Commander in Chief is an ugly experience since 1963.

The President went to Dallas knowing and protecting his November assassin Lee H. Oswald from prosecution for his April Crime "Attempted Assassination of the former General working at his desk in his Dallas home, 9:00 p.m. April 10."

The Kennedy protection included an early-morning, secret release of the prime suspect Lee H. Oswald, from Dallas Pollice Custody on Kennedy orders, April 11.

The president did not live to know that he knew his assassin but everyone else lived to know that he did and that his assassin could not be prosecuted for the November Crime because of his Kennedy protection from prosecution for his April Crime.

The law does not provide for protection and prosecution at the same time.

Only by the election of a new government could the protection be eliminated.

The common assassin was dead within forty-eight hours, Friday to Sunday.

SIGNATURE OF WALKER

NOV. 1991

EDWIN A. WALKER

DALLAS

Walker was said to have inspired the character of the Air Force General played by Burt Lancaster in *Seven Days in May*. He was also said to have inspired the character of General Jack D. Ripper, played by Sterling Hayden in the anti-war movie *Dr. Strangelove*.

Caroline Kennedy
After the Assassination

*"Children are the 'world's most valuable resource
and its best hope for the future."*

President John F. Kenned at UNICEF July 25, 1963

Caroline was born November 27, 1957, and was six years old when her father was assassinated. She and her brother John played in and outside of the White House in those early days. She was photographed riding her pony "Macaroni," a gift from Lyndon Johnson, around the White House grounds. That inspired Neil Diamond to write and sing his song "Sweet Caroline." He revealed that fact when he performed for her 50th birthday.

As a child, she received many gifts from dignitaries, such as a puppy from Soviet Premier Nikita Khrushchev. That came about, said Caroline, because Jacqueline ran out of things to say to Khrushchev at the state dinner in Vienna on June 4, 1961. So, she asked about the dog, Strelka, that the Russians had shot into space. She asked about Strelka's puppies. Three weeks later, a puppy arrived that President Kennedy was not expecting. It was Strelka's daughter, Pushinka, which means "fluffy." Pushinka mated with a White House dog and produced four puppies.

On June 21, 1961, President Kennedy wrote Chairman Nikita Khrushchev:

Mrs. Kennedy and I were particularly pleased to receive Pushinka. Her flight from the Soviet Union to the United States was not as dramatic as the flight of her mother, nevertheless, it was a long voyage and she stood it well. We both appreciate your remembering these matters in your busy life.

We send to you, your wife, and your family our very best wishes.

Sincerely yours,

John F. Kennedy

Little Caroline was delighted when Pushinka learned to climb a little ladder up to her playhouse. Then, it slid down a slide to return to the ground.

On November 22, 1963, the day of the assassination of their father, Caroline and John were taken by nanny Maud Shaw to the home of Jacqueline's mother, Janet Bouvier Auchincloss, who insisted that Shaw be the one to tell Carolyn about her father's assassination. That evening, they were brought back to the White House. While Caroline was in bed, Shaw told her about her father's death. Jacqueline soon arrived and was angry that she wasn't the one to tell the children.

In 1967, Caroline christened the US Navy aircraft carrier *USS John F. Kennedy* in a ceremony at Newport News, Virginia. Over that summer, Jacqueline took the children on a six-week tour of Ireland, where they visited the Kennedy ancestral home in Dunganstown. Too much attention was paid, and crowds were disruptive. Jackie notified Irish authorities to cease informing the public of their itinerary and whereabouts.

Robert Kennedy was a major presence in the lives of Caroline and John after their father's death. He accepted the role of running for president only after Jacqueline encouraged him to run. However, after his assassination in 1968, Jacqueline had said she didn't want her children to live in the United

States any longer where the Kennedy name was a target. She wanted to move to another country.[44]

Caroline endured the marriage of her mother to Aristotle Onassis. As part of her high school years, Kennedy attended Sotheby's Institute of Art in London, England from 1975-1976. She then returned to the United States and earned a BA in Fine Arts from Harvard University's Radcliffe College in 1980. She then studied law at Columbia University and graduated in 1988.

She worked at the Metropolitan Museum of Art, where she met her future husband, exhibit designer Edwin Schlossberg. She married Edwin Schlossberg, a quiet man who is 13 years older than Caroline. She has not changed her name to Schlossberg. She walked down the aisle with her uncle, Senator Edward Kennedy, and brother John was the best man. Caroline and Edwin have three children, Rose, Tatiana, and John, all with the last name Kennedy.[45]

Rose Kennedy Schlossberg was born June 25, 1988, named after her great-grandmother. She attended an all-girls private school in New York City and later attended Harvard University where she was awarded a degree in English, then earned a master's degree in interactive telecommunications. She has worked as a production associate on several TV series and married her girlfriend, restauranteur Rory McAuliffe, in May 2022.

Tatiana Celia Kennedy Schlossberg was born in 1990. She went through school at the Brearley and Trinity School, then went to Yale where she was editor-in-chief of the *Yale Herald.* She later received a master's degree in history from the University of Oxford in England. In 2014, she became a writer for *The New York Times* and wrote for various magazines such as

---

44 C. David Heymann, 2008. American Legacy: The Story of John and Caroline Kennedy, p. 152-54.

45 https://www.townandcountrymag.com/thescene/weddings/g10330712/caroline-kenne-dy-wedding

The Atlantic, Vanity Fair, etc. She married George Moran in 2017, and they have a son named Edwin, but some call him "Jack."

Caroline and Edwin had John Bouvier Kennedy "Jack" Schlossberg named after his grandfather, John F. Kennedy, and his maternal great-grandfather, John Vernou "Black Jack" Bouvier. He attended the Collegiate School in NYC and co-founded "ReLight New York, a non-profit organization that installed energy-efficient compact fluorescent lights in low-income housing developments. Jack graduated as high school valedictorian in 2011 and delivered the commencement speech. He also went to Yale, worked for the *Yale Herald,* and worked at a toxic waste removal company as an environmental technician in cleaning up hazardous wastes.[46]

In 2015, he moved to Japan, where his mother was serving as US ambassador and learned to speak Japanese. He graduated from Harvard in 2022, passed the New York State Bar in 2023, and enjoys paddleboarding along the Manhattan shoreline.

Caroline has been a spokesperson for her family's legacy, co-authored many books on civil liberties and her family, and served as co-chair for Barack Obama's Vice-Presidential Search Committee, which proposed Joe Biden as Obama's running mate. She spoke at the 2000 Democratic National Convention in Los Angeles. President Obama appointed Kennedy as the ambassador to Japan in 2013, where she served throughout his presidency. This was an important role because Japan had few leadership positions for women.

President Joe Biden appointed Kennedy as the ambassador to Australia, and she took office after her confirmation on June 10, 2022. She is based in Sydney, and one of her first duties was a trip to the Solomon Islands to commemorate the 80th Battle of Guadalcanal on August 7, 2022.

---

46 https://people.com/all-about-caroline-kennedy-kids-7965684

Since her father was a patrol boat captain in the Solomon Islands during WWII, it was a moving experience for her. The celebration included Caroline meeting the children of the two Solomon Island men who saved her father's life. They took the cocoanut with Kennedy's distress message to the Australian coast, and the PT 109 crew was rescued.

She and her husband went to Australia for their honeymoon in 1986, and she looks forward to continuing the values that her father set forth. She was happy to announce plans to reopen the embassy in Honiara that had closed some thirty years ago. This step was taken to increase US presence in the Pacific after a controversial security pact with China was signed.

Caroline Kennedy has tried to further the legacy of her family by creating the Profile in Courage Award, helping run the John F. Kennedy Presidential Library as its honorary president, and advising Harvard University's John F. Kennedy School of Government.

Caroline began writing books, and we will give brief descriptions of her books here. In 1987, she wrote with Phillip Knightley about the intermediary between the Soviets and the British government during the 13-day Cuban Missile Crisis in *How the English Establishment Framed Stephen Ward.*

In 1991, Caroline wrote with Beatrix Potter a colorfully illustrated garden book entitled *The Beatrix Potter Gardener's Year Book* with tips about planting and paintings from Potter's works. More closely related to her father's career was her 1991 *In Our Defense: The Bill of Rights in Action* with fellow law school graduate Ellen Alderman. It included true stories of original people who contributed to the Bill of Rights added to our Constitution. Continuing in this tradition about the Constitution, the two women wrote about trial decisions, anecdotes and important rights enjoyed by all Americans. They also co-wrote *The Right to Privacy* in 1995, which examined how a person's right to privacy has come under attack in the United States.

She returned to her mother's interests when she wrote *The Best Loved Poems of Jacqueline Kennedy Onassis* in 2001. These poems include photos of the Kennedy clan and poems by renowned authors.

She used her father's idea for *Profiles of Courage* about brave senators, for which he earned a Pulitzer Prize. She selected good authors who wrote about people who exemplified political bravery. She entitled her 2002 book *Profiles of Courage for Our Time.*

She began to focus on education when she wrote her 2003 *A Patriot's Handbook: Poems, Stories, and Speeches Celebrating the Land We Love* and made it readable by those 17 years old and up. Caroline Kennedy next wrote her 2005 *A Family of Poems: My Favorite Poetry.* This included 100 poems for young readers aged 10 to 14, grades 5-9. Her next book in 2007 was entitled *A Family Christmas* and described profound new information about the holiday of Christmas for readers 18 years old or more.

Caroline was on the committee that selected Joe Biden as President Obama's vice president in 2008.

She wrote two books in 2011. One was *Jacqueline Kennedy,* which contained seven interviews with Jacqueline Kennedy taped in 1964 describing her life with John Kennedy. The other was *She Walks in Beauty: A Woman's Journey in Life*, described in poetry.

In 2012, Caroline wrote the foreword and compiled two 75-minute CDs of her father speaking with others entitled *Listening In: The Secret White House.* In July 1962, John Kennedy had installed a hidden recording system in the Oval Office and the Cabinet Room. Day-to-day conversations and phone calls were recorded, and the president can be heard discussing the space race, Vietnam, the Cuban Missile Crisis, civil rights, etc. Reviewers had mixed reactions, from boredom to pleasure to excitement, depending on what was talked about.

In 2013, Caroline wrote two books. One was *Rose Kennedy's Family Album*, including 300 images and letters and photos collected by Rose Kennedy, John's mother, from 1878-1946. The other book was *Poems to Learn by Heart* for children from 10 to 14 years and all ages, with 100 poems interspersed with watercolor paintings.

Caroline's philosophy about raising children seemed to be that she measured success by the seeds she planted today and not by today's harvest. She used education as a tool to help children grow, think, plan, and strategize. Her efforts with her children are still coming to fruition.

Caroline's son, John Bouvier Kennedy Schlossberg, the only grandson of former President John Kennedy, spoke at the August 2020 Democratic National Convention with his mother, Caroline Kennedy. Their segment was called "We Lead from the Oval Office." The 27-year-old went to Collegiate School in Manhattan, Yale, and then Harvard, where he attained a JD and MBA. He has participated in the New Frontier Awards created by the John F. Kennedy Library Foundation and the Profiles in Courage Awards. He was a Senate page and an intern for Senator John Kerry.

Young John, frequently called Jack, delivered brief remarks at a ceremony on May 23, 2022, when he gave Liz Cheney a Profile in Courage award. He said, "In *Profiles in Courage,* my grandfather focused on the task of challenging your own party. Sometimes, it has to be done. Congresswoman Cheney found herself there in 2020." He described her as a life-long committed conservative Republican," who was ostracized from her party after publicly rebuking Donald Trump for his claims that the 2020 election was "rigged" because he lost. She was removed from the House Republicans leadership role last year after she voted to impeach Trump for his role in the deadly January 6th riot at the US Capitol building.[47]

---

47 http://people.com/politics/jfks-grandson-jack-schlossberg-awards-liz-cheney-profile-in-courage/

Jack Schlossberg criticized his cousin, Robert F. Kennedy Jr., who was running for president in 2023. He said that Robert was "trading in on Camelot, celebrity, conspiracy theories and conflict for personal gain and fame…. His candidacy is an embarrassment. Let's not be distracted, again, by somebody's vanity project."

Jack was clever to analyze how a man who lies to himself and listens to his own lies comes to a point where he cannot distinguish the truth within him or around him and so loses all respect for himself and for others.

He moved to Australia to join his parents after completing his education. He honored his grandfather, John Kennedy, in August 2023 by recreating his swim to safety when his PT-109 boat was sunk near the Solomon Islands. He said, "The swim was pretty difficult, so I have a lot of appreciation and admiration for what my grandfather did and the perseverance it must have taken to survive."

Caroline Kennedy continues to set goals for herself and spread the best part of her parent's ideology. In line with her father's wish to land a man on the moon, she has talked with Amazon chief Jeff Bezos about making another trip to the moon to transport the first woman there. She said, "If I keep hearing Jeff say it, then I am beginning to be able to imagine it."[48]

---

48 https://www.thelist.com/241227/the-untold-truth-of-caroline-kennedy/

John Kennedy, Jr.
After the Assassination

"Thus, the physical fitness of our citizens is a vital prerequisite to 'America's realization of its full potential as a nation, and to the opportunity of each individual citizen to make full and fruitful use of his capacities."

President John F. Kennedy in Sports Illustrated, December 26, 1960

John Fitzgerald Kennedy Jr. (November 25, 1960-July 16, 1999) was born two weeks after his father was elected president. His life began with a search for identification with an unknown father and moved further toward a search for purpose in his life until it was cut short.

He began with weak lungs that were allowed to develop more fully by staying in an incubator for his first six days of life. It was called Respiratory Distress Syndrome. Jacqueline delivered her baby through a C-section surgery and stayed at the hospital for two weeks. She used Dexedrine (an amphetamine) and other medications to endure three of the five inaugural balls dancing with the President.

John lived at the White House for his first three years. He had no distinct memories of his father or the White House as an adult. However, little John saluted his dead father at his mother's direction on his third birthday at the President's funeral service on November 24, 1963. Later in the day, his mother had arranged a birthday party where he opened presents.

Lyndon B. Johnson was very considerate of the Kennedys after the assassination. He wrote his first letter as president of the United States to John telling him that he "can always be proud" of his father. After the assassination, Jacqueline Kennedy moved with her children to a luxury apartment in New York City, where John Jr. grew up. In 1967, she took him with older sister Caroline for a six-week tour of Ireland. Both the children had dedicated nannies, but Jacqueline provided most of the tender loving care of a mother.

Books have been written about the impact of the assassination on John Kennedy, Jr. Author Edward Klein's St. Martin's Press, 2003, *The Kennedy Curse* described a conversation with Jacqueline Kennedy. She said that little John developed attention deficit hyperactivity disorder (ADHD), for which he took Ritalin (a form of amphetamine) throughout his life. He also had dyslexia, which he inherited from his father, who had it. John Kennedy is often listed as one of the presidents who had dyslexia and chronic back pain but went on to achieve great things.[49]

Russian writer Fyodor Dostoevsky, who had epilepsy and seizures, could have been describing Kennedy when he wrote, "Pain and suffering are always inevitable for a large intelligence and a deep heart. The really great men must, I think, have great sadness on earth."

President Kennedy had his IQ tested at Choate in his teens, and it was 119, or high average. His assassin's IQ was tested in his teens and was 118, also high average. The President's reckless hyperactivity and numerous spelling errors are clearly seen in Nigel Hamilton's *JFK Reckless Youth*, Random House 1991. John Jr. had no IQ tests that were available, but he had trouble passing grades in school and college. He also had trouble passing the bar to be an attorney, which he failed twice before success the third time.

Details of people with ADHD describe how it often starts at age three, sometimes due to major stress, but is certainly present by age seven. Such

49 9/27/23. https://www.history.com/news/robert-f-kennedy-death-funeral-train

patients are hyperactive, accident-prone, and disorganized, so they forget things, lose things, and often act before thinking of consequences. Perhaps an early example of his difficulties occurred on July 2, 1966, when five-year-old John fell into the coals of a dying cookout fire on a Hawaiian Island. He was flown to Honolulu, where he was treated for first and second-degree burns on his body.[50]

John's mother had him evaluated, and he was begun on Ritalin to control his hyperactivity. Despite that medication, he injured himself countless times, breaking bones and doing risky activities. His weekly doctor's appointments were well-known to his friends and family. He could not abide by William Shakespeare's warning: "Wisely and slow. They stumble that run fast."

After Aristotle Onassis' death, Jacqueline's brother-in-law, Edward "Ted" Kennedy, helped her obtain some $20 million from the tycoon's estate to tide her over in style and raise her children. The Secret Service continued to provide security for the two Kennedy children until they were aged sixteen but were no longer obliged to provide security for the dead president's wife.

John Kennedy, Jr. attended private schools in Manhattan, starting at Saint David's School, but had trouble in school and moved to Collegiate School in New York, which he attended from third through tenth grade. He completed his education at Phillips Academy in Andover, Massachusetts. After graduating, he accompanied his mother on a trip to Africa. He rescued his group while on a pioneering course, which had gotten lost for two days without food or water. For this, he won points for leadership.

On his 16th birthday, John Kennedy Jr.'s Secret Service protection ended, and he spent the summer of 1978 working as a wrangler in Wyoming. Kennedy attended Brown University, where he majored in American studies. By his junior year at Brown, he had moved off campus to live with several other students in a shared house.

---

50 https://www.nytimes.com/1999/07/19/us/john-f-kennedy-jr-heir-to-a-formidable-dynasty. html?pagewanted=all

In 1979, he made his first public speech at the dedication of the JFK Presidential Library and Museum in Boston. He cited British author Stephen Spender's 1928 poem "The Truly Great." This poet considered the passionate people who have made changes in our lives by putting aside things, including love, to focus on the highest goals, which are now a part of the air we breathe. Young John undoubtedly considered his father among the truly great.

The Truly Great by Stephen Spender

I think continually of those who were truly great. Who, from the womb, remembered the soul's history Through corridors of light, where the hours are suns, Endless and singing. Whose lovely ambition Was that their lips, still touched with fire, Should tell of the Spirit, clothed from head to foot in song. And who hoarded from the Spring branches The desires falling across their bodies like blossoms.

What is precious, is never to forget The essential delight of the blood drawn from ageless springs Breaking through rocks in worlds before our earth. Never to deny its pleasure in the morning simple light

Nor its grave evening demand for love. Never to allow gradually the traffic to smother With noise and fog, the flowering of the spirit.

Near the snow, near the sun, in the highest fields, See how these names are fêted by the waving grass And by the streamers of white cloud And whispers of wind in the listening sky. The names of those who in their lives fought for life, Who wore at their hearts the fire's centre.

Born of the sun, they travelled a short while toward the sun And left the vivid air signed with their honour.

While he treasured his father's role in the big things of life, John Jr. had trouble with the little things of life. For example, in January 1983, 'Kennedy's Massachusetts 'driver's license was suspended after he received more than three speeding summonses in a twelve-month period and failed to appear at a hearing. The 'family's lawyer explained he most likely was immersed in exams and just forgot the date of the hearing. But this behavior was, unfortunately, typical of his particular problems.

John Kennedy's Legacy Was *George*

The political magazine called *George* turned out to be 'Kennedy's legacy. John had also worked as a photojournalist for *The New York Times* in 1992. That led to the founding of a glossy monthly magazine called *George* beginning in 1995. His partner, Michael Berman, helped him develop the popular magazine until they began to scream and fight with each other. John gave it the tagline, "not politics as usual."

When asked about its mission, he once said that politics was the greatest show on earth, and he wanted a magazine that covered politics the way *Sports Illustrated* covered sports. *George* began with a bang due to Kennedy's name, and many people brought up issues. Gradually, the excitement dwindled, and it became harder to get ads when fewer people subscribed.

In 1997, Kennedy used the magazine as his forum to blast members of his own family as "poster children of bad behavior." That was extremely unusual in the Kennedy family where relatives went out of their way to cover up the wrongdoings of each other. In that issue, he exposed himself by posing seemingly nude on the cover. He admitted on a television program that he had on shorts and shoes, which cannot be seen on the magazine cover.

The magazine declined in sales and was nearly defunct shortly before his death. He had commented that he planned to have online chats with presidential candidates for the 2000 election to be placed in the magazine.

Around the time he founded *George*, he had tired of dating glamour women such as actresses Brooke Shields and Daryl Hannah. He fell in love with Carolyn Bessette who worked in the fashion industry as the publicity agent for Calvin Klein. She was a beautiful, excitingly attired, tall young lady, and she could be bossy. She had an edge as a strong-minded, determined woman like John's mother had been. He proposed marriage on July 4, 1995, at Martha's Vineyard. She held off her answer for some three weeks.

He was thrilled when she finally said she would marry him, but she wanted a private wedding without the intrusive paparazzi. John obliged her wish by arranging their wedding on the tiny island of Cumberland just off the shore of Georgia. It took extensive planning, but it turned into a beautiful candle-lit private wedding, which will be described in more detail shortly.

He graduated that same year with a 'bachelor's degree in American studies and then took a break, traveling to India and spending some time at the University of Delhi, where he did his post-graduate work and met Mother Teresa.

John was aged 25 and had no Secret Service protection after he was sixteen. He lived a rather reckless life of activities and did not go to great lengths to protect himself. Pleasure and action make the hours seem short and he became an obvious target. On May 14, 1985, police in Herndon, Virginia, received a call from "an intoxicated white male," stating that he and seven other individuals planned to kidnap John Kennedy that evening. Kennedy was informed and changed his evening plans. He was never one to change his lifestyle, however.[51]

While attending Brown, John acted in a few plays, always explaining that he was just dabbling and had no interest in an acting career. He acted in a play entitled *Winners* staged at the Irish Arts Center in Manhattan on August 4, 1985. It ran for six performances.

---

[51] "The Kennedy Tragedy: JFK Jr. Starring in Drowning Tragedy." Jack Holland, The Irish Echo. https://group.irishechol.com/2011/02/the-kennedy-tragedy-jrf-jr-starred-in-drowning-tragedy-2/

Kennedy played a serious young man in love with Mag. She was pregnant and wanted to go out on a rather risky boat trip so she could "dance on every island… stay out all night and sing and shout at the moon." Joe was reluctant due to the risks, but they did it. The couple and their boat did not arrive at their destination in the play. People were alerted. The search continued for three days. The bodies of Joe and Mag were found "floating face down" in the water. The similarities of this play are striking in comparing John's death and the actual trip with his wife some fourteen years later.

Not only are there similarities in the story, but they first announced a date for the play and had to delay it because Kennedy injured his foot in the gym. The year of his death, before John's airplane crash, he had broken his ankle parasailing and had the cast taken off the day of the crash. He was on crutches when he boarded and piloted the plane with his wife and her sister on July 16, 1999.

John also worked with some of the Kennedy special-interest projects, including the East Harlem School at Exodus House and Reaching Up. In 1989, John F. Kennedy, Jr. founded the non-profit Reaching Up to support higher education and career advancement of frontline workers in health, education, and social service occupations. In association with the City University of New York, the largest urban university system in the country, Reaching Up developed new college-level courses and specialized training programs for direct support workers.

After earning a bachelor's degree in American studies, John Jr. traveled to India. After meeting Mother Teresa, he was profoundly affected by her faith and life of service. That is how he chose to help with programs in East Harlem, such as one called Reaching Up and opportunities for people with disabilities.

He studied but did not pass the bar on his second try. That caused him great embarrassment. Finally, he passed it on his third try in July 1990. His dyslexia may have caused trouble reading as he tended to reverse letters in long words. Once he passed the bar, he went to work as a prosecutor in the Manhattan District Attorney's office for four years. He voiced his dissatisfaction with his work to his mother and friends.

The popular television show *Seinfeld* featured an episode about John Kennedy, Jr. This began with a mother catching her son George masturbating in her house while reading *Glamour* magazine. He vowed not to repeat that, but friends Elaine, Seinfeld and Kramer bet George that he would repeat it and yield to his instincts. In fact, they all four bet $100 to see who could go the longest with masturbating. Elaine must bet $150 since the fellows said it was harder for women but was part of a man's lifestyle. They bet using the honor system, where they simply admitted if they masturbated.

Kramer was almost immediately out and slammed down his $100 bill. Then Elaine visited her fitness club, which was supposedly patronized by John F. Kennedy, Jr. Viewers see only the elbow of Kennedy played by an actor. Elaine dreamt about Kennedy and heard that he wanted to meet her. Eventually, the pressure became too much for her, and she was the second person to be knocked out of the contest.

That show attracted so much attention that on the way to a trial where John Jr. was a prosecutor, people started honking at him and laughing. Entering the courtroom, the defendant said, "I saw you on *Seinfeld* last night." Then John heard someone say, "No wonder he failed the bar examination; he's an actor, too." So, some even imagined he was acting in addition to prosecuting.

A year before he died, Kennedy was a guest on the *Jay Leno Tonight Show* along with Jerry Seinfeld. He told about those details and added, "I've never seen that episode."[52]

---

52 https://www.cracked.com/article_38852_the-night-jerry-seinfeld-and-jfk-jr-discussed-the-contest-on-the-tonight-show.html

Kennedy made what was considered his debut into the world of politics at the 1988 Democratic National Convention in Atlanta, Georgia, where he introduced his uncle, Senator Ted Kennedy. His DNC speech was acclaimed — and reportedly was honored with "a two-minute standing ovation." He was extremely handsome and was pictured with voters for Ted and for his cousin Patrick J. Kennedy's campaign for the Rhode Island House of Representatives.

A third attempt on the life of John Kennedy, Jr. took place on July 13, 1995. It was well-known that John rode a bicycle alone all over Manhattan. He put his life in danger and made himself extremely vulnerable to criminals. The potential for kidnapping got the FBI's attention.

There was a woman named Griselda Blanco of mixed heritage, alias "Godmother of cocaine," who wanted her buddies to kidnap rich people for ransom. In an exceptional turn of events, one of the woman's former lovers named, Charles Cosby, blew the whistle on her plot to capture the wealthy biker. The FBI notified young Kennedy's security firm, and they appraised their client of those plans. This information about Kennedy's potential abduction was learned thanks to the Freedom of Information Act with a request for the FBI to yield all documents related to John Kennedy, Jr. Once alerted to danger, he tried to change things, but he seldom thought up his own solutions.

In a surprise finding by searching the Internet, we have found some unusual dim pictures of the unique marriage of John Kennedy, Jr.

John Kennedy, Jr. Marries

The couple selected about thirty of their closest friends and relatives. Those people were told that they would participate in a weekend occasion but would not be told where they were going. They gathered at the Teterboro Airport in New Jersey and boarded a special plane. They arrived and found themselves on a murky little island with unpaved roads and animals like spotted horses, boars, and other creatures.

They were driven about in large pick-up trucks, seated on the truck beds on Chippendale fine old chairs for a bumpy ride through water-filled ditches and rough terrain. They arrived at an inn where they spent the night. The next day involved preparations and training for the wedding. Excellent cuisine was prepared by a special chef.

The wedding the next day was to be in a small wooden chapel, the First African American Baptist Church, built for slaves in 1893. The choice of this location had connections to the work that President John Kennedy did with Rev. Martin Luther King.

The guests were taken there while Carolyn stayed at the Inn, where a special fashion designer arranged a dress which was to slide over her trim body. It was a bold fashion statement when she finally appeared so very late. The waiting guests mingled and talked in the pews and were entertained by a gospel singer whom John Kennedy, Jr. had selected because the man could sing "Amazing Grace." Some joined in with the hymns. There was no electricity, and it was darkening in the late afternoon.

While biding their time, ice-cold Heineken's beer arrived. Old candles were found and lit in the tiny confines of the church. Finally, the bride arrived, and the delay with a difficult dress fit was blamed. The service began and can be seen on the Internet. The tender scenes showed John fumbling with the ring he was to place on his wife's finger. She put her hand on his shoulder to comfort him, and he relaxed. In many ways, she had a calming influence on the hyperactive young man.

Following the service, all were trucked back to the Greyfield Inn for the reception and dinner where good wishes and short speeches took place. John danced with Carolyn in a very passionate embrace to the music of Prince and others.

Their day of marriage on September 21, 1996, was indeed a secret and special day.

The chef had chosen capons smothered in mushrooms, Irish potatoes, and other select treats. A capon is a castrated rooster that grows fatter in the absence of testosterone, having had a diet of porridge and milk. Dessert was vanilla buttercream-frosted cake.

At one point, reporters were swirling in helicopters above the group, but guides took the guests into a more private part of the jungle where they could not be seen. Reporters only learned for sure where the wedding was held after the group's return to Teterboro Airport. There, paparazzi descended upon the group as John took Carolyn off to fly to Turkey and the Greek islands for a two-week honeymoon. They were able to relax, enjoy drinking wine, and looking at the moon while thinking of all the civilizations the moon had seen passing by, but that ended.

Upon their return home, the paparazzi were ferocious in learning their schedules and following their activities, interrupting virtually everything they tried to do. John was more able to live with these prying media people during his lifetime. His wife was daunted and reluctant to share John's lifestyle. The paparazzi, which had also disoriented sister Caroline's life, craved news and often made up stories and negative descriptions of their subjects.

Steve Gillon, a friend of John Kennedy Jr., wrote a biography of young Kennedy. Gillon said that Jackie Kennedy told people she regretted naming John after his father. She realized it only added to his burden. The irony was that in her effort to honor her husband, she inadvertently made her son's life more challenging.[53]

Siblings John and Caroline had a dispute over how to dispose of their mother's possessions. Caroline took her husband's advice and had Sotheby's perform the auction, believing it might yield more money than a private

---

53 https://www.dailymail.co.uk/news/article-72058531/Jackie-o-regretted-naming-john-f-kennedy-jr-father.html

auction. John disagreed with letting someone who was not a Kennedy decide the issue, such as Caroline's husband. This caused the siblings some distress, but it was seemingly resolved when they promised to stay in closer contact with each other.

Carolyn Bessette-Kennedy was alarmed to read eleven months after their marriage that Princess Diana, on August 31, 1997, died with male friend Dodi Fayed as their driver raced to elude paparazzi in Paris. Carolyn's new marriage and lifestyle were not welcome, and John's wife came to hate the press. She could see that children would suffer in the same way that her husband, John Jr., had suffered as a child caught forever in the public eye night and day.

By this time, she not only knew that John's public lifestyle could not be changed, but he had problems that might be passed by inheritance, such as dyslexia and attention deficit hyperactivity disorder. She knew that he wanted children, but she did not. In fact, whenever he mentioned children, she refused to have sex with him, or so he told his male friends.

John had also shared with those close to him that his mother changed over the years after the assassination. She drank a lot more and was absent for long periods. Now, his wife was beginning to change. She kept to herself, and some thought she was using drugs of some sort. He thought she was depressed and urged her to take an anti-depressant.

John, with his ADHD, was a rather carefree fellow who was always late, lost items, couldn't remember things, and wanted to work out constantly in rather risky pastimes. He might say he didn't want to go somewhere or do something and preferred to just come home to have supper with his wife. Thus, she would expect him home, but he was very late or brought over an unexpected friend. She seemed afraid to go out due to the ever-constant paparazzi. She would pass up requests from friends for get-togethers. John seemed disorganized and unprepared to compromise his free ranging risky lifestyle for her more sedate preferences.

Although Carolyn-Bessette Kennedy chose not to go out as much, she tried to go on with her career with Calvin Klein and his products as John tried to find a new life in *George* magazine. An old friend and co-worker named Michael Bergin wrote a 2004 book entitled *The Other Man: A Love Story: John F. Kennedy Jr., Carolyn Bessette, & Me.* He wrote, describing himself as an old boyfriend of Carolyn, that she told him she was pregnant by John and miscarried a baby. There are several allusions to Carolyn cheating on her husband and perhaps taking a medicine prescribed for depression. His book did reveal that Senator Ted Kennedy asked Cardinal O'Connor to perform "emergency marital counseling" for the Kennedy couple.

Young John Kennedy tried to use the media attention to get ads for his magazine. The public didn't seem to know what to make of stories in *George* that involved movie stars talking about politics but lacked depth and understanding. Some of the articles were extremely interesting, but after a big splash due to his name, John Kennedy Jr. could not get the public to buy his magazine. It had life for nearly six years, having survived Kennedy's death by one year, but it was soon gone.

Jacqueline Kennedy Onassis had always feared he would die in an airplane crash and argued against him piloting until she died. She pled with her friend Maurice Templesman to stop young John's plans to become a pilot. She told Maurice that she had nightmares of John dying in a plane crash. How surprisingly correct she was in her prognostication.

But young John was a pleasant enough young man and close friends realized that the two most important meetings in John's life were a weekly therapy appointment (ADHD and Ritalin management) and weekly massage appointments. Friends thought he was a good listener when they had problems and seemed to understand people at a deeper level.[54] This may have

---

54 Inside the Heartbreakingly Tragic Final Days of John Kennedy Jr.: Family Strife, Financial Woes, and Talk of Divorce. Sarah Grossbart January 4, 2019. http:www.eonline.com/news/1001130/inside-the-heartbreakingly-tragic-final-days-of-john-f-kennedy-jr-family-strife-financial-woes-and-talk-of-divorce

come from psychological counseling, which would have accompanied his therapeutic management. Maurice knew of this counseling, and there was little else he could do to prevent John's urge to fly.

We do not know of conversations about flying between the young, frisky president's son and the elderly friend and investment counselor for his mother. John and Maurice did not pal around much with each other, but there were occasions when they would meet important people together, such as Nelson Mandela, the first president of South Africa, when he visited the US in 1993. In a picture of the three men, John Kennedy Jr. has facial hair with a moustache and something of a goatee beard.

After Jacqueline Kennedy's death, John had taken up learning to fly. He purchased a plane and went through many hours of training, where his flying was observed and improved by in-flight instructors. He had done day and night piloting and was working on flying by instrument only but had not earned a certificate yet in 1999. He kept the secret of his flight training from his wife at first. But finally, he wanted to take her up on a plane. However, she consented only when a certified instructor accompanied them.

The couple finally decided to live apart after 2½ years of marriage. It seemed to her that she and John were not on the same side. She saw John as a disorganized risk-taker who enjoyed running, rollerblading, biking, and piloting. He had several injuries from these sports, such as a broken ankle in a 1985 gym workout and a 1997 wrist injury for which he wore a small cast on his arm. Later, he fell while parasailing and broke his left ankle on early June 2, 1999.[55] After orthopedic surgery, a cast was applied to his left foot and ankle. He went flying with his flight instructor but could not use the rudder pedals well.

By March 1999, they were working with a marriage counselor. Additionally, in the summer of 1999, they even talked with Cardinal John O'Connor.

---

55 "JFK Jr. Puts His Best Foot Forward," Kirsten Davis. 6/6/99 New York Post.
https://nypost.com/1999/06/jfk-jr-puts-his-best-foot-forward/

Before he had completed his ankle recovery, John and Carolyn were invited to the wedding of Rory Kennedy on July 17, 1999. Carolyn's sister, worried about their separation, thought that might be just the thing to get the couple back together again. She invited them to lunch with her and proposed the following trip. The three would fly to Martha's Vineyard, where she would leave the Kennedys to see some friends. The two would then fly on to Hyannis Port on July 19, 1999, where the wedding was to take place. She talked them into getting along for the weekend. They agreed. The three were to meet at the airport.

Carolyn went to Saks Fifth Avenue and purchased a $1600 dress for the occasion. She told her saleslady that she was not looking forward to an upcoming flight but would go anyway. John had his cast removed on the day of the flight, July 17, 1999, and hobbled around on crutches with a cane. He called the airport to have his plane ready for take-off Friday afternoon and told his flight instructor that he did not have to go with him since his cast was off. He also visited his sick uncle, who was dying of cancer.

The three were late in getting to the airport on that Friday evening. Even though it was getting dark, an airport observer saw John using crutches to move their luggage onto the airplane. They settled into the plane and strapped themselves in. As they began their flight, they may have talked about Rory Kennedy, whose wedding they would attend.

Rory was the youngest child of Robert Kennedy, who was born after he was assassinated. That remarkable circumstance of Rory's birth to a mother who had been widowed brought an unusual decision. Her mother assigned her older brother Michael as a godparent when she was born after the death of her father. Michael and Rory were extremely close and talked almost every day during their lives. When she was 29, they were skiing together, and he had a terrible accident. She tried to use mouth-to-mouth resuscitation, but it was not successful due to all the blood in his mouth. She had lost another brother, 28-year-old David, to a drug overdose when she was 15. It was a family filled with tragedies but here was going to be this bright moment for their youngest.

The family had erected a huge tent for the wedding in Hyannis Port. People were coming in from all over. Suddenly, there was a call from Martha's Vineyard airport that John Kennedy, Jr.'s plane had not arrived when expected. The tent for the wedding became the gathering place for prayers and mourners during the search for the Kennedy plane. It wrecked the wedding event, and Rory and Mark Bailey changed their wedding date from July 17 to August 2, 1999.

It took five days to find the actual bodies of the passengers who were still strapped in their seats, having died from the impact of the nosedive hitting the ocean at a speed of over fifty miles per hour.

The National Transportation Safety Board determined that pilot error was the cause, stating: "Kennedy's failure to maintain control of the airplane during a descent over water at night was a result of spatial disorientation." Some writers have commented that a more experienced pilot would have avoided the heavy fog by heading for land and better visual clarity until the fog lifted.

The Washington Post reported that radar data showed 'Kennedy's Piper Saratoga dropping from 2,200 feet to 1,100 feet in a span of 14 seconds, well beyond the safe descent rate for the aircraft. The last known radar capture of the plane was taken at 9:40 and 34 seconds, at which point the aircraft was at about 1,100 feet (about twice the height of the Washington Monument) and plummeting at about 53 miles per hour toward the ocean. Investigators claimed that the speed of the descent, combined with Kennedy not making a distress call, indicated the drop was rapid. Experts also doubted potential mechanical failures, as the plane passed its annual inspection less than one month before the crash.

The three bodies were autopsied to see if there was any use of drugs or alcohol, and no trace of either was found. Young John Kennedy Jr. was careless for the last time as his riskiness cost three lives.

At the funeral service, Senator Ted Kennedy gave the eulogy in a private service at St. Thomas More Church in Manhattan, where Jacqueline Kennedy once worshipped. He said, "We are to think in that other Irish phrase that this John Kennedy would love to comb gray hair with his beloved Carolyn by his side. But, like his father, he had every gift but length of years."

John Kennedy Jr. and the two Bessette sisters were also given shipboard rites with cremation and burial at sea. In an ancient naval ritual honoring John Kennedy's service as a naval hero, an officer in dress whites carried three brass urns of ashes down a ladder to the water, where they were swept into waves. Four Navy chaplains and Father O'Bryne, all

Roman Catholics, presided over the 35-minute service. A brass quintet from the Newport Naval Base played Christian hymns in place of the military "Taps." There were no sung words, but one participant said the words so well known to the two families: "Abide with me, fast falls the eventide, the darkness deepens, Lord with me abide. When other helpers fail and comfort flee, help of the helpless, o abide with me."

While cremation and burial at sea was once thought to deny Catholic belief in the resurrection of the body on Judgment Day, that ban was lifted in 1963. The church does expect cremated remains to be treated much like a whole body, so scattering of the ashes is usually not included.[56]

Some 17 relatives, including Senator Edward Kennedy, Caroline Kennedy Schlossberg, and Bessette mourners, attended. President John Kennedy's

---

56 https://www.washingtonpost.com/wpsrv/national/longterm/jfkjr/stories/ kennedy072399.html

booming voice was heard on tape-recorded as he declared a toast to the America's Cup racing crews on September 14, 1962. He said:

> It is an interesting biological fact that all of us have in our veins the exact same percentage of salt in our blood that exists in the ocean, and therefore, we have salt in our blood, in our sweat, in our tears. We are tied to the ocean. And when we go back to the sea—whether it is to sail or to watch it—we are going back from whence we came."

This special celebration was described in "Kennedy, Bessettes Given Shipboard Rites" by Barton Gellman and Pamela Ferdinand, *Washington Post* staff writers, on July 23, 1999.

What would have happened had John F. Kennedy Jr. lived? The chances are that he would probably have gotten into politics in one place or another. Edward Klein wrote *The Kennedy Curse: Why Tragedy Has Haunted America's First Family for 150 Years.* He wrote that John told a friend just a few days before the crash that it was hard to talk to his wife, and they were headed for divorce. So marital harmony eluded him in his short life.

Another excellent book about the president's son was by his friend Steve Gillon, who wrote *America's Reluctant Prince* in 2019. He had known John for 18 years and wrote that John was thinking of running for governor of New York. "Isn't it pretty to think so?" as Ernest Hemingway concluded at the end of *The Sun Also Rises.*

In a surprise at the Dallas site of the assassination of President John Kennedy, a group of people arrived on November 2, 2021. Hundreds gathered to await the return of the slain president's son, JFK Jr., whom they believed to be in hiding for the last 22 years. For these QAnon devotees, Donald J. Trump, reinstated as president, would name JFK Jr. as his unelected vice president. The younger Kennedy would ultimately succeed Trump, who would then become "one of seven new kings—most likely the King of Kings."

However, JFK Jr. did not appear on November 2, 2021. Some expected he might show up later for a Rolling Stones concert in Dallas. Consider that these possibilities may exist in the minds of some people: The QAnon goal has Trump oversee the arrests, trials and death sentence of Satanic instigators, the resurrection of Kennedy Jr. to American life and leadership, the elevation of Trump from presidency to "king of kings," and the acquisition of Christian theology for their own socio-political agendas. John F. Kennedy Jr. would certainly have had that story in his *George* magazine.

Since John Kennedy Jr. left a legacy that included his magazine, *George,* we will end with a commemoration about that magazine done on its tenth anniversary. The Kennedy School of Government paid tribute to JFK Jr. and *George* on October 13, 2005. Journalist Tom Brokaw moderated a panel featuring *Fox News* Chairman Roger Ailes, political analyst Paul Begala, Rock the Vote President Jehmu Greene, former President Bill Clinton, former California Governor Arnold Schwarzenegger, with a conclusion by Senator Edward Kennedy, and an introduction by Caroline Kennedy.

Caroline began, "John was one of those revolutionary spirits, and *George* was his way to reach people on the issues of the day." Brokaw said, "John wanted to force this country to look at politics in fresh and interesting ways… and he did it with passion." Clinton said, "I think he saw that people don't divide their lives between politics and culture." Senator Kennedy ended his comments by saying, "He brought popular culture and politics together in a new and creative way. He was far ahead of his time![57]

John Kennedy Jr. was honored in 2000 when Reaching Up, the organization he founded in 1989, joined with The City University of New York to establish the John F. Kennedy Jr. Institute. In 2003, the ARCO Forum at Harvard was renamed the John F. Kennedy Jr. Forum of Public Affairs. Kennedy had been

---

57 https://news.harvard.edu/gazette/story/2005/10/not-just-politics-as-usual/

an active member of the Senior Advisory Committee of Harvard's Institute of Politics for 15 years. His uncle, Ted Kennedy, said the renaming linked Kennedy with his father, while his sister, Caroline, stated that the renaming represented his love of discussing politics.

In a psychobiography where Kennedy's words, letters, and speeches from 1995 to 1999 were analyzed and counted, these themes were noted: lack of privacy, seeking to know about his father and family members, efforts to understand, encouragement to engage in public life, how people use their influence, using humor to engage or deflect, and comparisons between current situations and previous ones. Words that increased over the five years of his life are about analytical thinking, anxiety, sadness, and death.[58]

58 The Qualitative Report 2020 Vol. 25, No. 10, Art. 7, 3583-3601 Exploring the Final Years of the Life of JFKJr: A Mixed Methods Psychobiographical Case Study. Caitlin R. Ferrer and Joseph G. Ponterotto.

Ted Kennedy
After the Assassination

"Mothers all want their sons to grow up to be president, but
they don't want them to become politicians in the process."
Senator John F. Kennedy at the University of Illinois, January 27, 1957

Edward (1932-2009) was the youngest of the nine Kennedy children born to Joseph and Rose, Irish Catholics of Boston, Massachusetts, and was lucky to live until he was 77 years old. John was 15 years old when Ted was born. He asked to be Ted's godfather and wanted to name him George Washington Kennedy, but his parents did not approve of that name. Ted served as a U.S. senator for almost 47 years, from November 7, 1962, to August 25, 2009. In 1963, John, Robert, and Ted Kennedy all served in elected offices at the same time. John was president, Robert was attorney general, and Ted was a senator.

Ted wrote eight books, and his last was a memoir, *True Compass*, finished just days before his death from brain cancer. Some of this information is from that memoir.[59]

He was a poor student throughout his life but was very good at sports and received a recruiting feeler from the Green Bay Packers. At Harvard, he had a classmate take his place on a Spanish exam, and he copied answers from another student for a final exam in a science class. In his schooling, teacher

59 Edward M. Kennedy (2011) True Compass: A Memoir. London, England: Hachette.

and student did not get along. He was expelled for cheating but could re-apply in a year or two if he demonstrated good behavior.

He signed up for the U.S. Army in June 1951 and trained in the Military Police Corps. He was on the honor guard at SHAPE headquarters in Paris, France, and his father made sure he was not sent to Korea. After 21 months, he was discharged in March 1953 as private first class. He re-entered Harvard, where his behavior in the military was judged well. He graduated at age 24 with a degree in history and government. However, his grades were so low that he was not accepted by Harvard Law School.

He entered the University of Virginia School of Law in 1956, where Bobby Kennedy had gone, and it took a full faculty vote to admit him after his Harvard behavior. He was a middling student but brought speakers to the campus using his family connections. While attending law school, he was charged with reckless driving and driving without a license. However, he was good at meeting people and managed John's 1958 Senate re-election campaign. He graduated from law school in 1959.

He met Joan Bennett during law school, and they married in a service by Cardinal Francis Spellman in 1958 at Bronxville, New York. He was admitted to the bar in 1959. Ted and Joan had Kara (1960-2011), Ted Jr. (b. 1961), and Patrick (b. 1967). Their marriage was stormy because of Ted's infidelities and Joan's growing use of alcohol. Though he claimed religion, Ted did not do unto others as you would have them do unto you.

Ted managed brother John's campaign for the presidency in the Western states. When John resigned his U.S. Senate seat from Massachusetts, Ted was not eligible until age 30 in 1962, but John asked the governor to name Kennedy friend Ben Smith as interim senator for John's unexpired seat to keep it open for Ted.

Meanwhile, Ted worked as an assistant district attorney for Suffolk County, Massachusetts. He went on Latin American trips in 1961, and the FBI reported that he often met with former Soviet spies such as Lauchlin Currie. They also reported that he rented a brothel and used bordellos. Kennedy soon changed his actions in 1962 when the state Attorney General, Edward J. McCormack, Jr., mounted a campaign against him. However, Kennedy won the election and was sworn into the Senate on November 7, 1962. Meanwhile, Vice President Johnson liked Ted.

On November 22, 1963, Kennedy was presiding over the Senate when an aide told him President Kennedy had been shot. Ted and sister Eunice Kennedy Shriver flew to the family home in Hyannis Port, Massachusetts, to give the news to their invalid father, who had been afflicted by a stroke two years earlier. They could tell that old Joseph Kennedy understood.

When Ted Kennedy returned to work, he was in a plane crash some eight months after John's assassination. His pilot and aide were killed, and he was badly injured. He spent months in a hospital recovering from a severe back injury, broken ribs, punctured lung, and chronic back pain. This hospital experience caused him to pay much attention to health care, and his work played a large part in Obama's health care planning and insurance. Despite his illnesses and medical care, John Kennedy never did for health care what younger Ted accomplished.

Walking with a cane, Ted resumed work on the Voting Rights Act of 1965 and banned poll tax at the state and local level. He pushed through an immigration plan that ended the quota system based on national origin. He was upset by the lack of U.S. programs in the Vietnam war and made a trip there in 1968. He advised brother Robert not to challenge President Johnson in the 1968 presidential election.

When Robert was assassinated, Ted gave this eulogy:

My brother need not be idealized, or enlarged in death beyond what he was in life; to be remembered simply as a good and decent man, who saw wrong and tried to right it, saw suffering and tried to heal it, saw war and tried to stop it. Those of us who loved him and who take him to rest today, pray that what he was to us and what he wished others will some day come to pass for all the world. As he said many times to those he touched and who sought to touch him: "Some men see things as they are and say why. I dream things that never were and say why not."

After the deaths of his brothers, Ted Kennedy took on the role of a surrogate father for his 13 nephews and nieces. He was involved in examining the 1968 marital contract between Jacqueline Kennedy and Aristotle Onassis after she decided that Robert's assassination meant the Kennedys were targets. Ted Kennedy wore the crown as the oldest of the clan still alive. However, "uneasy lies the head that wears the crown," as William Shakespeare cited.

On July 18, 1969, Ted Kennedy was at Chappaquiddick Island at Martha's Vineyard, hosting a party for six women who had worked on Robert's 1968 presidential campaign. It was a party of emotions as the workers were mourning the loss of Robert Kennedy.

Ted left the party at about 11:15 p.m. with 28-year-old Mary Jo Kopechne. She did not tell anyone she was leaving for the evening and left behind her car keys and hotel room keys as if she intended to return to the party later.

About 15 minutes later, Ted took a wrong turn and was speeding when he suddenly realized there was a lake ahead. His car skidded and went over the embankment, plunging upside down into the water. Ted escaped through a window he opened on the driver's side of the car, but Mary Jo drowned.

As he realized what had happened, Ted dove into the water to try to get her out but was unable to do so. Worn out and weary, he stumbled back to the site of the party. He told only two friends, who returned with him to the wrecked car and tried to get Mary Jo out. After their failed attempt, he asked them to say nothing.

He went into a tiny office cabin where a telephone was located and made 17 telephone calls, according to the records on his credit card. He had no phone numbers on him, so he called around to get phone numbers. Among the people he called was his mistress, Austrian Helga Wagner, whom he asked for Stephen Smith's phone number. Stephen had married Ted's sister, Jean, and was a financial analyst and political strategist in the 1960 United States presidential campaign of his brother-in-law John F. Kennedy.

When interviewed in 2009, Helga Wagner said Kennedy called and seemed to be trying to keep things together and had not wanted to hurt the young woman. He called Ted Sorenson several times that night, as well as lawyer Burke Marshall.

In 1968, Sorensen, a former speechwriter for President John Kennedy, was an important adviser to Senator Robert Kennedy when he ran for president in the fiercely contested Democratic primaries against vice-president Hubert Humphrey and Senator Eugene McCarthy. Ted called several times to ask Sorenson what to do. Someone suggested that Kennedy see a physician for memory loss.

Other information was learned from James Schlesinger, friend of the Kennedys, who wrote about this in his journal. Ted had three drinks before the accident that night. In addition, his driver's license had expired five months earlier, and he was driving without a license. Schlesinger wrote that Ted asked all his friends and family to say nothing about all this.

When Ted saw some others that morning, he made no mention of the crash. People soon after came running up and told of the crash and police getting a body out of the car. His car was identified, and he went with the police to try to explain what happened. The EMS firefighter who got Mary Jo's body out of the car described how she had scrunched up to a little area where she may have had some breath for quite a few minutes before she suffocated or drowned.

That afternoon, Ted went to see Robert D. Watt, M.D., and the doctor put out word that Kennedy had a concussion with minor memory loss. He wore a neck brace to the funeral of Miss Kopechne, whose parents he had called to inform them of her death. His collapse was growing more and more glorious until it had become almost a halo around his head.[60]

An inquest into the death was held in 1970 in Edgartown, Massachusetts. A week after the incident, Kennedy pleaded guilty to leaving the scene of the accident and was given a suspended sentence of two months in jail. That night, he gave a national broadcast in which he said, "I regard as indefensible the fact that I did not report the accident to the police immediately."

Senator Kennedy's driver's license had expired on February 22, 1969, and although driving with an expired license was only a misdemeanor, it provided evidence of negligence needed to prove a manslaughter charge in the death of Mary Jo Kopechne. But as a Kennedy, he was given the extreme benefit of a doubt. He seemed bereft of morals, as if conduct had nothing to do with good and evil.

He even had to struggle to convince his father, who was belabored by a stroke, that he did not kill a woman. He said that she had died in a car accident where he was driving.

---

60 https://www.theguardian.com/world/2010/nov/01/theodore-sorensen-obituary

Ted wanted to get away, hoping that this news would die down. He went overseas for a short time but, upon return, was astonished at how seriously everyone seemed to feel about his actions. He knew that his chance of being president was now near zero. However, he had always said he might be killed if he became president. He simply exhibited a disregard for his actions that did not look like tact, consideration, or politeness. It looked like pure indifference or callousness.

Apparently, he began to dedicate himself to creating beneficial legislation so that he could atone for this tragedy. By the end of 1968, he had joined the Committee for National Health Insurance. This fit in with President Richard Nixon's proposed health insurance reform. Hearings on national health insurance were held in 1971. He finally sponsored the Limited Health Maintenance Organization Act of 1973 and played an important part in the passage of the National Cancer Act of 1971.

Other presidents had paid little attention to the troubles in Northern Ireland, but he advocated the withdrawal of British troops from the northern countries. He traveled to India and wrote of the plight of ten million Bengali refugees. He was asked to be George McGovern's vice president in 1972, but he declined, so McGovern chose Kennedy's brother-in-law, Sargent Shriver.

In 1973, Ted Kennedy's 12-year-old son was diagnosed with bone cancer. His leg was amputated, and he underwent an experimental two-year drug treatment. Their son Patrick was suffering from severe asthma attacks. Pressures pushed his wife, Joan, to seek treatment for alcoholism and emotional strain after she was arrested for a drunk driving traffic accident. Their separation would grow into a divorce by 1981.

As health issues grew within his own family, Kennedy and others introduced a bill for near-universal national health insurance in 1974. But Nixon's resignation shook up support for that plan. After the Watergate scandal, Kennedy helped pass the Federal Election Campaign Act limiting contributions for presidential elections. In that year, he also travelled to meet Soviet leader Leonid Brezhnev and advocated a full nuclear test ban.

Although Kennedy first opposed integration by busing school children, he came to support it as an important part of civil rights efforts. He appeared at a September 1974 anti-busing rally but was insulted and pummeled with tomatoes and eggs.

He visited China and gained permission for several Chinese nationals to leave the country. He continued arguments for nuclear disarmament and spoke on this at Hiroshima University. He tried to work with President Jimmy Carter on national health insurance. He had been the most important Democrat in Washington since Robert Kennedy's death, but now Carter had that role.

As Ronald Reagan became more popular, Kennedy criticized his confrontation policy toward Russia. He tried to offer Moscow other ways to work with the United States, but Yuri Andropov was not impressed.

On August 12, 1980, Kennedy delivered his most famous speech at the 1980 Democratic National Convention when he realized that Carter would win the nomination. It included these words:

> For me, a few hours ago, this campaign came to an end. For all those whose cares have been our concern, the work goes on, the cause endures, the hope still lives, and the dream shall never die.

Carter found it difficult to convince Kennedy supporters to rally around him, so he was defeated by Ronald Reagan in the 1980 election.

Kennedy traveled to South Africa in January 1985, undertaking a dangerous mission to defy the apartheid government by visiting Bishop Desmond Tutu and Winnie Mandela, wife of imprisoned black leader Nelson Mandela. Kennedy worked with Reagan to approve travel to the Soviet Union in 1986 to negotiate arms control with Mikhail Gorbachev.

Despite excellent work in politics, Kennedy's habits of overdrinking, harassing women, and behaving rudely were well-known and widely discussed. He continued to use his skills to pass the COBRA Act, which allowed employees to continue receiving health benefits for a while after leaving a job.

He co-sponsored the Fair Housing Act of 1968, which prohibited discrimination. He directed the passage of the Americans with Disabilities Act of 1990. That was of interest due to his sister Rosemary's condition and his son's amputated leg. He struggled against other senators to provide funding to combat the AIDS epidemic and provide care for low-income people affected.

Kennedy and other relatives went to Palm Beach, Florida, for the Easter holidays in 1991. His son Patrick and nephew accompanied him. They met women and had sex on the beach. One woman called it rape when local police arrived. Jokes about their activities emerged, and *Newsweek* called Kennedy "the living symbol of the family flaws."

In September 1991, Clarence Thomas was nominated to the Supreme Court, and hearings began. Kennedy pressed Thomas about his dismissal of *Roe v. Wade,* but soon Anita Hill brought the sexual harassment charges against Thomas. Kennedy's malicious reputation kept him from commenting. One biographer, Adam Clymer, believed the Thomas hearings and Kennedy's silence were the worst offenses in his Senate career. Kennedy voted against the nomination, but Thomas was confirmed by a narrow 52-48 vote.

Kennedy married Victoria Reggie in 1992. She was said to have helped him be more productive in the Senate. He supported President Bill Clinton on the North American Free Trade Agreements (NAFTA) and the Clinton health care plan first run by Hillary Clinton. In 1994, he became the first senator with a computer home page, which showed that he was not as old and out of touch as some thought.

In 1994, he faced Mitt Romney. They had a televised debate, and Kennedy narrowly won re-election to the Senate. His career as the "Liberal lion in the Senate" was used to secure an increase in the minimum wage in 1996. He worked with others to pass the Health Insurance Portability and Accountability Act in 1996 and the Mental Health Parity Act, forcing insurance companies to treat mental health payments the same way medical practitioners do. In 1997, he pushed the use of tobacco taxes to expand health insurance coverage for children. He helped President Clinton during the 1998 Lewinsky scandal, cheering up the president and bucking the impeachment of the president.

On July 16, 1999, his nephew John F. Kennedy Jr. plus his wife and sister-in-law were killed in an airplane crash near Martha's Vineyard. He consoled the family as their patriarch.

Kennedy was in his Senate office meeting with First Lady Laura Bush when the September 11, 2001, attacks took place. Two of the airplanes involved had taken off from Boston. In the next few weeks, Kennedy telephoned each of the 177 Massachusetts families who had lost members in the attacks to express sympathy and maintained a bond with them in subsequent years.

In retaliation to the attacks, he supported the 2001 overthrow of the Taliban government in Afghanistan. He strongly opposed the Iraq War, however. He sought immigration reform with Republican Senator John McCain and produced the Comprehensive Immigration Reform Act of 2007.

In 2006, he wrote a children's book about politics from the view of his dog Splash entitled *My Senator and Me: A Dog's-Eye View of Washington, D.C.* The same year, he wrote another book called *America Back on Track*.

Kennedy supported Barack Obama for president in 2008 after Obama promised to make universal health care a top priority. "Obamacare" or the Affordable Care Act resulted and is still the law of the land. Those who qualify for financial help are able to ensure continued health care through good times and bad.

On May 17, 2008, Kennedy suffered two seizures. Doctors announced that he had a cancerous brain tumor called malignant glioma. He underwent surgery to remove as much of the tumor as possible. He then underwent chemotherapy and radiation, which helped him continue to work for some bit until his death.

Impaired vision caused him to be unable to read teleprompters or speeches, so he memorized them in short lines. He spoke briefly at the 2008 Democratic National Convention on August 25, 2009. He promised to see Obama inaugurated. He did see it on January 20, 2009, but had a seizure at the luncheon afterwards. He was taken by wheelchair and ambulance to the hospital. He was released the following day.

He continued work and attended meetings when he could. In March 2009, he was granted an honorary knighthood by Queen Elizabeth II for his work in the Northern Ireland peace process.

As time passed, awards and favorable documentaries were being shown. He was awarded the Presidential Medal of Freedom but could not attend the ceremony. He could not attend the funeral of his sister, Eunice Kennedy Shriver, who died at age 88 in August of 2009.

Ted Kennedy died on August 25, 2009, at age 77, in his home at Hyannis Port, Massachusetts. The family thanked everyone who gave him care and support over the last year and everyone who stood with him in his public service career. Upon his death, his sister Jean was the only one of the nine Kennedy siblings alive.

At his funeral were presidents Obama, Carter, Clinton, Bush, and Biden, along with Bob Woodward, Tom Brokaw, Tony Bennett, Placido Domingo, Yo-Yo Ma, Jack Nicholson, Lauren Bacall, Boston Celtics player Bill Russell, and many others. He was laid to rest at Arlington National Cemetery near the graves of his assassinated brothers.

Kennedy's widow, Vicki, attended the signing of the Patient Protection and Affordable Care Act, at which both she and President Obama wore blue "Tedstrong" bracelets. A 65-year period in which a Kennedy held Federal elective office ended but resumed in 2013 when Ted's great-nephew, Joseph P. Kennedy III, became a member of the House.

In 1957, John Kennedy said:

Just as I went into politics because Joe died, if anything happened to me tomorrow, my brother Bobby would run for my seat in the Senate. And if Bobby died, Teddy would take over for him.

Kennedy's obituary in the *New York Times* described him thusly:

He was a Rabelaisian figure in the Senate and in life, instantly recognizable by his shock of white hair, his florid oversized face, his booming Boston brogue, his powerful but pained stride. He was a celebrity, sometimes a self-parody, a hearty friend, an implacable foe, a man of large faith and large flaws, a melancholy character who persevered, drank deeply and sang loudly. He was a Kennedy.

OTHER POST-ASSASSINATION INFORMATION

A. The Peace Corps

"For every young American who participates in the Peace Corps—who works in a foreign land—will know that he or she is sharing in the great common task of bringing to man that decent way of life which is the foundation of freedom and a condition of peace."

President John F. Kennedy Statement on March 1, 1961

On March 1, 1961, President John F. Kennedy established the Peace Corps as a new agency within the Department of State. The same day, he sent a message to Congress asking for permanent funding for the agency, which would send trained American men and women to foreign nations to assist in development efforts. The Peace Corps captured the imagination of the U.S. public, and during the week after its creation, thousands of letters poured into Washington from young Americans hoping to volunteer.

The immediate precursor of the Peace Corps, the Point Four Youth Corps, was proposed by Representative Henry Reuss of Wisconsin in the late 1950s. Senator John Kennedy learned of the Reuss proposal during his 1960 presidential campaign and sensed growing public enthusiasm for the idea. He decided to add it to his platform as it matched his inauguration challenge: "Ask not what your country can do for you but what you can do for your country."

This is perhaps the longest-surviving accomplishment of President Kennedy, who would surely be happy to know that his idea is still working around the world more than sixty years after it began.

On October 14, 1960, he first publicly spoke of the Peace Corps idea at an early morning speech at the University of Michigan in Ann Arbor. The night before, he had engaged Vice President Richard Nixon in the third presidential debate and was surprised to find an estimated 10,000 students waiting up to hear him speak when he arrived at the university at 2 a.m. This was proof that his administration was of great interest to young people. The assembled students heard the future president issue a challenge: How many of them, he asked, would be willing to serve their country and the cause of freedom by living and working in the developing world for years at a time?

The Peace Corps proposal gained momentum in the final days of Kennedy's campaign, and on November 8, he was narrowly elected the 35th president of the United States. On January 20, 1961, in his famous inaugural address, he promised aid to the poor of the world. "To those peoples in the huts and villages of half the globe struggling to break the bonds of mass misery," he said, "we pledge our best efforts to help them help themselves, for whatever period is required—not because the communists may be doing it, not because we seek their votes, but because it is right." He had created a method for people to answer "what you can do for your country."

After March 1, thousands of young Americans answered this call to duty by volunteering for the Peace Corps. The agency was headed by Kennedy's brother-in-law, Sargent Shriver, who eventually chose some 750 volunteers to serve in 13 nations in 1961. By August, Kennedy hosted a White House ceremony to honor some of the first Peace Corps volunteers. The 51 Americans who later landed in Accra, Ghana, for two years of service immediately made a favorable impression on their hosts when they gathered on the airport tarmac to sing the Ghanaian national anthem in Twi, the local language.

President Kennedy had followed Shriver's development and career and learned Sargent had experienced the very sort of program that he would direct for the United States. Robert Sargent Shriver (1915-2011) married Eunice Kennedy, John Kennedy's sister, on May 23, 1953.[61] He graduated from Canterbury School in Connecticut and won a scholarship to spend the summer in Germany as part of the Experiment in International Living. He returned in 1934 to begin college at Yale University. There, he was the senior editor for the *Yale Daily News.*

The following summer, he was invited to participate in the Experiment for International Living as leader of a group of students graduating from Yale in 1938. While in law school, he led a third group of students to France in the summer of 1939, when WWII was just beginning.

He reported to duty in the Navy in 1941 and was assigned to the *USS South Dakota* battleship, where he served as a gunner during the 1942 Battle of Santa Cruz and Battle of Guadalcanal. He next trained as a submariner and was a gunner and torpedo officer on the *USS Sandlance.*

He returned to New York and worked for the Joseph P. Kennedy Enterprises, where he met Eunice Kennedy. He became the assistant general manager of the Merchandise Mart for Joseph Kennedy. He then moved to Washington, D.C., in 1947 to help Eunice with the National Conference on Prevention and Control of Juvenile Delinquency.

The Shrivers' had five children, and in 1955, Sargent began directing Chicago schools for the desegregation of schools. In 1960, he coordinated two state primaries for John Kennedy's presidential campaign. When Kennedy was elected, Shriver was first appointed to direct a Talent Hunt committee to find candidates for top administrative and ambassadorial positions.

Shriver's most important accomplishment soon came with the creation of the Peace Corps. He prepared a report on the feasibility of a volunteer

---

61 https://www.jfklibrary.org/learn/about-jfk/the-kennedy-family/r-sargent-shriver

corps that would work on projects in other countries. Shriver served as the Director of the Peace Corps from 1961 to 1966. He made overseas trips to Latin America, Africa, the Middle East, and Germany to review Peace Corps work being done and to make new connections for future programs.

After President Kennedy's death, Shriver continued directing the Peace Corps and helped launch President Johnson's War on Poverty. In 1964, Johnson signed the Office of Economic Opportunity (OEO) Act, and Shriver became its first director. It led to other programs such as VISTA (Volunteers in Service to America), Head Start, and Job Corps.

In 1968, Shriver was appointed the U.S. Ambassador to France. Relations with French President Charles de Gaulle had become very strained as France aligned with China withdrew from NATO, and denounced the American war in Vietnam in 1967. France was unhappy that the U.S. refused to aid France in its plan to become a nuclear power. Shriver arrived amidst strikes and student unrest. Shriver helped de Gaulle by setting up President Richard Nixon's visit to Paris in 1969 and President Pompidou's visit to Washington, D.C. in 1970.

Eunice Kennedy Shriver's first international Special Olympics Games in 1968 for the retarded was a victory of sorts. Its aftermath has been a spectacular promotion of help and attention to retarded citizens across this country. Unfortunately, Its inception was shortly followed by the assassination of her brother, Robert Kennedy.

This dreadful tragedy led to decisions for politics within the Kennedy family. Shriver ran for vice president on the George McGovern ticket in 1972. They lost to Richard Nixon and Spiro Agnew. After the election, Shriver joined a law firm. In 1976, he ran a short campaign for the presidency but soon returned to his private life. He died on January 18, 2011, at age 95.

The Peace Corps continues to operate and has about 7,300 Peace Corps volunteers service in 61 countries. Some 45% of volunteers serve in African countries, 19% in Central and South America, 13% in Eastern Europe and Central Asia, 12% in Asia, and some in Fiji and countries like Morocco.

In each country, Peace Corps volunteers help society meet their need for trained women and men. They promote a better understanding of Americans among locals, as well as gain a better understanding of the local culture and people. This is why the Peace Corps is crucial to maintaining positive relations between America and countries around the globe.

Volunteers must be at least 18 years of age, an American citizen, and have 27 months available for 3 months of training in the USA and a two-year assignment elsewhere. Volunteers can pick the locations they desire, understanding that they must live like the natives live and make ends meet with little money provided beyond basic needs. Volunteers work in one of six Peace Corps sectors – Education, Health, Youth in Development, Agriculture, Community Economic Development, and Environment. This work may involve things people have done before, or it may involve learning new skills that may be valuable in a later career search.[62]

The current Peace Corps Director is Carol Spahn. Here is contact information:

Peace Corps
1275 First Street NE
Washington, DC 20526
(865) 855-1961

---

62 http://www.peacecorps.gov/contact/

B. Secret Service Study: "Fame Through Assassination"

"There is always inequality in life. Some men are killed in a war and some men are wounded and some men never leave the country. Life is unfair."

President John J. Kennedy

The Secret Service did a study of 83 people who tried to gain fame through assassinations, including Lee Harvey Oswald, John Hinckley, Sirhan Sirhan, and many others.

People have wondered for more than sixty years why Lee Harvey Oswald wanted to kill President John Kennedy and why, six months earlier, he wanted to kill Major General Edwin Walker. The Secret Service has compiled a study about assassins who kill political figures and celebrities. They described people who kill for *Fame Through Assassination*. Let us look at some of their information.[63] They published their results in *The Journal of Forensic Sciences,* hoping that those in charge of protecting important individuals would know of their findings.

There was such an attack against Gabrielle Giffords. She was a member of the U.S. House of Representatives, representing Arizona's 8th congressional

---

63 https:www.npr.org/2011/01/14/132909487/fame-through-assassination-a-secret-service-study

district from January 2007 until January 2012. She resigned because of a severe brain injury resulting from an assassination attempt while campaigning at an Arizona Safeway store on January 8, 2011. She was shot in the head by Jared Lee Loughner. He hit 19 people, killing six, including a 9-year-old little girl. She is married to Mark Kelly, a U.S. senator from Arizona who is a retired Space Shuttle Commander. He and medical professionals have helped Gabrielle regain the ability to walk, speak, read, and write, and she is now a strong gun control advocate.

Agent Robert Fein, who worked in the mid-1980s with the Secret Service as a psychologist, was shocked by four situations within 18 months of people with weapons intending to kill public representatives. All four cases were prosecuted with two convictions and two being sent to psychiatric facilities. Secret Service psychologist Fein and Secret Service agent Bryan Vossekuil began the most extensive study of assassins and would-be assassins ever done. They identified 83 people who had completed or made attempts to assassinate people between 1949 and 1996. They not only studied records but went to visit many of these assassins in jail.[64]

They explained to these offenders that they were trying to protect people and wanted to learn about assassins and their lives and viewpoints. They asked prisoners how they chose targets, how they prepared, what were their motives, etc.[65]

Among those studied was Sirhan Sirhan, who killed Senator Bobby Kennedy; Mark Chapman, who killed John Lennon; Lee Oswald, who tried to

---

64 "Fame Through Assassination: A Secret Service Study" by Alix Spiegel, January 14, 2011. NPR https://www.npr.org/2011/01/14/132909487/fame-through-assassination-a-secret-service-study

65 "Assassination in the United States: An Operational Study of Recent Assassins, Attackers, and Near-Lethal Approachers." Robert A. Fein, Ph.D. and Bryan Vossekuil. Executive Director of the National Threat Assessment Center, U.S. Secret Service, Washington, D.C. 20223 published in The Journal of Forensic Sciences, Vol. 44, No. 2, March 1999.

kill Major General Edwin Walker and did kill President John Kennedy; Arthur Jackson, who tried to kill actress Theresa Saldana, who was in *Raging Bull,* Members of the Order who tried to kill radio talk show host Alan Berg, and John Hinckley who tried to kill President Ronald Reagan to impress actress Jodie Foster. Hinckley killed one man, caused permanent brain damage and paralysis in press secretary James Brady, and wounded another man and the president. He was recently set free after years of treatment by psychiatrists in a confined facility.

This Secret Service study described incorrect assumptions about assassins. For example, many people believe they are insane and divorced from reality. But despite some mental health issues, most of them were quite organized as they attacked a public official.

Many writers have asserted or assumed that American assassins have been mentally ill. Some people assume that the assassination of the President or others is an irrational act. Trials of assassins often feature testimony by mental health professionals. However, the belief that almost all assailants are mentally ill is incorrect and misleading. None of the attackers was a model of emotional well-being, but they were sufficiently organized to mount an attack on a prominent person of public status.

Assassins whose primary targets are celebrities are more likely to be mentally ill than subjects whose targets were public officials. But, reliance on ideas that mental illness causes assassination can lead to errors. Sometimes, after a life crisis, attackers begin to see the idea of assassination as acceptable and a way to become famous or notorious. Some write their ideas in a journal or diary, and others tell friends, family, or colleagues about their thoughts. Attackers often consider more than one target, ultimately choosing an unexpected opportunity for an attack. Some assassins plan an escape, and others expect to be killed and make no plans.

The Secret Service authors concluded by saying, "Understanding these patterns of ideation and action may permit those 'with protective responsibilities' to prevent future attacks." Readers may wish to obtain the article on the Internet to see discussions about various cases in more detail.

Most of the assassins felt like failures and nobodies. They wanted to be 'somebody.' They chose political targets because they would become famous instantly if they succeeded in their plan. In some cases, they picked a target to associate themselves with a purpose that would make their crime seem not so bad. For example, Oswald tried to kill Major General Edwin Walker, who was becoming an autocratic leader and, in the assassin's mind, needed to be removed. But he only had fame in mind when he killed President Kennedy.

The research led to several surprising conclusions. For example, it was very, very rare for the primary motive to be political, even though there were several assassins who seemed to cover their motives with some political rhetoric. It seemed to make it okay for them to kill a certain politician. But when a problem arose, such as another politician who came into town before their chosen target, they might seize the opportunity near at hand. That illustrated less interest in a point of view and more interest in getting publicity by killing an important person.

John Hinckley clearly stated that he murdered someone famous to impress young actress Jodie Foster. Was it a question of whether Oswald wanted to murder President Kennedy to impress his wife or people in general? He certainly had not shot at Major General Walker to impress his wife, as we know from the way he hid his actions and left written instructions on how to manage if he was arrested.

The night before Oswald left his wife for the Texas Schoolbook Depository, he asked her three times to get back together. He offered to purchase laundry facilities for diapers, but she was not amenable. Nor did she want to cuddle or have sex with him that night.

He appeared resolved by the time he left for work the next morning, so he left her almost all his money and his wedding ring. He had broken apart his rifle and wrapped it in paper he brought from his work site, calling it curtain rods to his co-worker who drove him to work. His goal seemed to be "fame through assassination" since he could not have the woman he wanted.

His plan to enjoy his fame was destroyed on November 24, 1963, when he was killed. He could no longer toy with the police and the press after Jack Ruby shot him at the police station. Later in the day, on November 24, 1963, Marina, the two baby girls, and Lee's mother, Marguerite, were taken to see Oswald's body at Parkland Hospital. Marina noted that he had cried because his eye was wet. The doctor addressed Oswald's wife and mother, saying, "You were satisfied it was your son?" His mother had taken leave of her senses when Marguerite Oswald said, "I think some day you will hang your heads in shame."

Oswald's mother was delusional and was convinced that her son was being supported by the government for some mission when he went to Russia. She had gone to Washington, D.C., to speak to President Kennedy just after his election to tell him that if they were supporting him, they must send her some financial support as well. Of course, the President's spokesmen tried to explain that they had nothing to do with Oswald's decision to go to Russia. After Lee's assassination by Ruby, his mother told a hospital chaplain that she wanted her son buried at Arlington Cemetery, where she had heard President Kennedy was to be buried.

Oswald was buried on Monday, as were the President and Officer Tippit. The Oswald burial, through a mix-up, had no minister. The funeral home director conducted the service. Reporters and officers who were guarding the site carried the casket. Fame did not elude Oswald because his name has been widely known ever since the Kennedy assassination.

Here is a summary of the findings of Fein and Vossekuil's study of assassins. The Secret Service Exceptional Case Study Project (ECSP) is the latest effort to study all persons in the United States known to have attacked or approached to attack a prominent public official or figure since 1949.

Handguns were the most common weapons used. Various motives were found, such as wishes for notoriety, revenge, idiosyncratic thinking about the target, hopes to be killed, interest in bringing about political change, and desires for money. In more than 40%, there was a wish to save the world, a desire to bring attention to a perceived wrong, or a longing to achieve a special relationship with the target.

Characteristics of the 83 attackers studied were 86% male, 77% white, average age of 35, 51% single and never married, 61% had children, 25% had some college, 52% were unemployed, 56% had one or more adult arrests for a non-violent offense, 66% had never been incarcerated, 75% were not delusional at the time of the incident, 61% had been treated or evaluated by a mental health professional, 44% had a history of serious depression or despair, 39% had a history of substance abuse, 67% had a grievance, 44% had a history of interest in assassinations, and 77% had a history of verbal or written communication about the target.

About one-third wished or expected to die or be killed in their attack. A few family members are known to have been told directly about plans for the attack on a public official. Lee Oswald made his wife take his picture while he held a rifle, dressed in combat clothes, shortly before he attempted to kill General Edwin Walker in April 1963. Oswald also communicated to her his disappointment that he had missed Walker with his bullet.

C. Why Are There So Many Conspiracy Theories?

"We are opposed around the world by a monolithic and ruthless conspiracy that relies primarily on covert means for expanding its sphere of influence--on infiltration instead of invasion, on subversion instead of elections, on intimidation instead of free choice, on guerrillas by night instead of armies by day."

President John F. Kennedy to American Newspaper Publishers Association, April 27, 1961

Why have conspiracy theories played such a prominent role in the minds of many who think about the assassination of people like President John Kennedy, Senator Robert Kennedy, Jack Ruby's assassination of Lee Harvey Oswald, and the Warren Commission?

There have been many studies of people in several countries who have determined what kind of people believe in conspiracy theories. Here are the results from some recent studies.

The *European Journal of Social Psychology* published an article in December 2019, 48(7), entitled "Belief in Conspiracy Theories: Basic Principles of an Emerging Research Domain" by Jan-Willem van Prooijen and Karen M. Douglas. They concluded that conspiracy theories are *consequential* (they have a real impact on people), *universal* (they are widespread across time and cultures), *emotional* (they give negative emotions rather than rational deliberations), and *social* (they involve intergroup conflict).

The scientists described how conspiracy theories reflect beliefs about a group that colludes in secret to reach malevolent goals. They might be propagated by someone important like President Donald Trump, who said that Barack Obama was not born in the U.S., climate change is a hoax, and vaccines cause autism. There might be people who say things such as Princess Diana was murdered or the U.S. caused the 9/11 catastrophes.

National Geographic reporter Jillian Kramer wrote an article on January 8, 2021, entitled "Why People Latch on to Conspiracy Theories, According to Science." She described how on January 6, 2021, insurgents swarmed the U.S. Capitol to create chaos and defy legislators who followed ex-President Donald Trump's claim, "They rigged an election." That assertion implied that powerful people are dishonestly manipulating society and must be stopped. The assertion was misinformation that offered a simple answer for a random event, and the answer seemed to restore control for many people.

The article described how people who feel insecure in their relationships and lives tend to catastrophize life's problems and are more prone to believing in conspiracy theories. "The brain mistakes familiarity for truth," said one researcher. This has been called "collective narcissism," or a group's belief in their own significance, such as the rioters on January 6, 2021. For some people, conspiracy beliefs are the best way to deal with their own possible failures.

When Trump told supporters: "The media is the biggest problem we have," some supporters smashed media crew equipment, tied a camera cord into a noose, and scrawled "murder the media" on the door of the Capitol building. They singled out an adversary who had qualities that represented their own view of evil so they could gain control over what was happening to them. They play the old game of "Follow the leader," who seems like a savior who will help them protect their in-group from conspiring enemies.

Lukasz Stasielowicz wrote "Who Believes in Conspiracy Theories?" which was published in June 2022 in the *Journal of Research in Personality.* He wrote that conspiracy theories are ubiquitous and can have negative consequences like prejudice and even harm. Those who are more likely to believe in such theories are people who believe in pseudoscience, suffer from paranoia, have low cognitive ability, and may be narcissistic (thinking they know everything) and sometimes religious (believing a higher force condones the theories). For example, ex-Major General Edwin Walker rallied people to stop the integration of black veteran James Meredith at the University of Mississippi, which was established by what he called "the anti-Christ Supreme Court."

Jonathan Jarry wrote an article for the *Office for Science and Society* entitled "Who Is Likely to Believe in Conspiracy Theories?" published on July 28, 2023. He wrote, "The more likely you are to believe in one conspiracy theory, the more likely you are to believe in others." He offered ideas for those who know a conspiracy theory advocate. To deal with that person, use empathy, avoid confrontations, and keep the dialogue going if you can. He wrote: "Studies looking at who has a tendency to believe in conspiracy theories reveals the best portrait we have so far: people who see danger in the world around them, who use their intuition a lot, who have odd beliefs and experiences, and who tend to be antagonistic and feel superior to others."

We will probably always have conspiracy theories about one thing and another. As regards the JFK assassination, perhaps *CBS News* anchor Walter Cronkite said it well on the evening that the Warren Commission Report came out in September 1964.[66]

Two further impressions are inescapable from even a casual reading of the commission report. First, Oswald was a liar. During the few

---

66 https://www.britannica.com/video/166075/Walter-Cronkit-murder-part-Warren-Commission-Lee-September-1965

hours between his arrest and his death, he was repeatedly interrogated. The commission report reveals that he had lied on important matters of substance. He lied about his rifle, his revolver, his movements, the documents found on his person. Second, no investigation could have been more painstaking than that carried out by this commission. Every resource of criminology was called into play; ballistics tests, analysis of the guns themselves, handwriting analysis, the blanket in which the rifle was wrapped, the photographs and documents linking Oswald to the crime. And Earl Warren was a judge of men and was not too dignified to race down the stairs at the Depository Building watch-matching his time against Oswald's.

In the end, we find confronting each other the liar, the misfit, the defector on the one hand and seven distinguished Americans on the other. And yet, exactly here we must be careful that we do not say too much. Oswald was never tried for any crime, and perhaps, therefore, there will forever be questions of substance and detail raised by amateur detectives, professional skeptics, and serious students as well. For the Warren Commission could not give Lee Harvey Oswald his day in court and the protection of our laws.

Suspects are not tried by seven distinguished Americans; their cases are heard under law by twelve ordinary citizens. If it had not been for Jack Ruby's revolver in the basement of the Dallas police station, twelve such citizens would have heard the evidence, would have heard Oswald—if he had chosen to speak. That jury would have represented our judgments, our conscience, and, in the end, would have spoken for us. Now we must depend upon our own judgments and look into our own consciences. The Warren Commission cannot do that for us. We are the jury, all of us, in America and throughout the world.

D. How Did the Assassination Change America?

"And so, my fellow Americans: ask not what your country can do for you—ask what you can do for your country."
President John F. Kennedy Inaugural Address
January 20, 1961

Various people have offered opinions about the impact of President Kennedy's assassination. Each of us has our own opinions, but let us note some major changes that have attracted attention.

Secret Service Agent Clint Hill's Comment

Clint Hill, who jumped aboard Kennedy's limousine and covered the president and his wife as they sped to the hospital, in his new book *Five Days in November* had this to say:

> It was the end of the age of innocence. People no longer trust the government. The conspiracies continue to thrive, get worse and worse, and have ever since. The biggest change is that people don't really have trust in institutions or others, or the government like they used to have. And it's a shame because it really damages our way of life.

The 25th Amendment Was Added

Scott Bomboy is the editor-in-chief of the National Constitution Center and wrote "How JFK's assassination led to a constitutional amendment" in the *Constitution Daily Blog* on November 22, 2022. Technically, the Constitution never spelled out how a Vice President would become President if a President died, resigned, or was unable to perform the office's duty.

Presidential successions happened after the deaths of six presidents. Furthermore, there was no constitutional way to replace a Vice President who had vacated office or to handle a situation where a President became incapacitated while in office.

Within three months, the House and the Senate agreed on the wording of what would become the 25th Amendment. Section 1 of the 25th Amendment made it clear that the Vice President became President when the presidency became vacant under three circumstances: death, resignation, and removal from office. Section 2 gave the President the power to name a new Vice President, with the permission of Congress, if that office became vacant. The amendment's other two sections detail the process for the Vice President to serve as Acting President if the President is unable to perform his or her official duties and how to resolve disputes about the President's ability to discharge official powers.

The 25th Amendment would receive its first test in October 1973, when Vice President Spiro Agnew resigned. Gerald Ford became the new Vice President in December 1973 after President Richard Nixon nominated Ford for congressional approval. Ford himself invoked the 25th Amendment nine months later when he nominated Nelson Rockefeller as Vice President after Nixon's resignation.

News Came from Television Instead of Written Word

News journalist Bob Schieffer recalled a chaotic weekend, from the jubilation in Fort Worth when the president arrived late Friday night at Carswell Air Force Base to massive crowds greeting him at the Texas Hotel to the time he drove the suspect's mother to police headquarters in Dallas. A riveted nation followed the dramatic events unfolding, even viewing the press in a new light, Schieffer said. "We came to have a new understanding of the media," he said. "Up until that weekend, for most people all they knew about news was the news product – a story written and edited in a newspaper. They saw a story edited on television. That weekend, they saw the news process, and people discovered it's not always orderly. It doesn't always make sense."

It also changed how news is consumed, he said. "Most people in America depended on the printed word for their news. From that weekend on, with the country — for the first time in its history — all focused on one news story at the same time… television would be the place most people would get their news."[67]

ABC News did a program on November 22, 2013, about five more ways the JFK assassination made changes. The Secret Service has been part of American history since its creation in 1865, but it wasn't until after President John F. Kennedy's assassination that the organization began to expand and evolve into the high-tech, massive, secret operation that it is today. Here are the changes that have occurred.

1. No More Riding in Open Cars. On Nov. 22, 1963, President John F. Kennedy waved to spectators from the back of a midnight blue 1961 Lincoln four-door convertible in Dallas. After Kennedy's assassination, presidential ground transportation greatly evolved. The president's limo is equipped with 8-inch-thick plates of armor that are capable of stopping an IED, 5-inch

---

67 https://magazine.tcu.edu/fall-2013/schieffer-jfk-assassination-changed-america/

multi-layer windows that make the vehicle's door's weight equal to the weight of a door on a 757 airplane, a night vision system, on-board systems for fresh oxygen and even a blood bank, located in the trunk, stocked with the president's blood type.

2. The End of the Presidential 'Stroll.' Before JFK's assassination, presidents had much more freedom to travel around the capital without extreme protective detail. President Coolidge and Truman were known for frequent walks around the capital with limited protective detail. But Northeastern University Political Science Professor Robert Gilbert notes that after Kennedy's assassination, unaccompanied, unplanned strolls were no longer an option for presidents. The distance between the public and its leader has grown significantly."

3. Lifetime Coverage: As a direct result of Kennedy's assassination, Congress passed legislation in 1963 to continue to protect Jackie Kennedy and her children for two additional years. This extended protection was new for former first families. Before Kennedy's assassination, families of the president were not afforded this protection after they left the White House. In 1965, Congress again expanded the protection for former presidents and first ladies, creating a law that authorized the protection of former presidents and their spouses during their entire lifetime and their minor children until age 16, unless they declined protection.

These laws were changed by Congress in 1997 when a law was created that afforded presidents and their families serving after 1997 only 10 years of Secret Service protection. But, in 2012, President Obama signed the Former Presidents Protection Act of 2012, which reversed the previous law that limited Secret Service protection. Under the law that Obama signed, former President George W. Bush and future former presidents will receive Secret Service protection for the rest of their lives. Children of former presidents up to the age of 16 are assured protection under the new law.

4. President Kennedy decided during his campaign that the people were his asset and wanted no Secret Service men on the back of the car. He was often seen standing in an open car, waving to crowds, and shaking many hands of spectators. Now, there are long road closures, more police and Secret Service presence, and extended perimeters of protection.

5. From July 1, 1962, to June 30, 1963, the Secret Service had an average strength of 513, of whom 351 were special agents. Today, the Secret Service employs more than 3,200 special agents, 1,300 Uniformed Division officers, and more than 2,000 other technical, professional, and administrative support personnel.

Michael Barone of the *Washington Examiner* wrote about the impact of the JFK assassination on American politics on November 1, 2013. Kennedy's death occurred when *Time* and *Newsweek* were influential national voices. Suddenly, television and cable news networks took over. In the recent past, the Internet has destroyed newspapers and weekly news. Many of these have a point of view or a bias rather than strictly neutral news stories. This left a distrustful audience in something of a quandary as a result of the JFK assassination.[68]

The former Ambassador to Great Britain whom the author knew in London was John "Jock" Hay Whitney, who served in that role from February 11, 1957, to January 14, 1961. He left that role because he had purchased the *New York Herald Tribune* and opened a subsidiary to that newspaper in Paris, France. On the day of the assassination, he was pressed into service as a copyreader. Three days later, he gave a talk about that day to a group of professional journalists at Harvard. Here are a few of his remarks:

---

68 https://www.aei.org/articles/how-jfks-assassination-changed-american-politics/

In this period of national involvement, the nation has turned to its news media—and especially to its press. Throughout the country, millions watched the funeral, the burial—even the moment a man was killed—on television, and then they turned to their newspapers. For together, the papers have served to crystallize the moment. Men will not remember these days as a long period of a continuing event... Their personal history will be a succession of images—a President shot in an open car; a careening drive to the hospital with a wife holding her husband's head; a hurried swearing-in; a face of grief behind a dark veil; the roll of muffled drums; a flag-draped caisson; a eulogy perhaps; a little boy saluting; white-gloved hands slowly, precisely folding the last flag...

Most of the country's editors were conscious that they were preparing a record for the future. When the television pictures had gone, the people in my city went out to buy the papers they would put away and save as recollection for some future time.[69]

---

69 The Life and Times of John Hay Whitney, E. J. Kahn, Jr. Doubleday & Co., New York, 1981.

E. Lee Harvey Oswald
Before the Assassination

Lee Harvey Oswald (1939-1963) lived an extraordinary life full of excitement. He had a poor early history, which will be described later, but apparently hoped to do something important. He disliked his early childhood in the United States and his time in the Marine Corps. So, he went to Russia but soon became disillusioned and decided to return home. Thinking he might still be important by describing details of Russian life, he wrote a book about that country. He described himself at the beginning of that book thusly with his own spelling errors unchanged:

Lee Harvey Oswald was born in Oct 1939, in New Orleans La. The son of a Insuren [insurance] Salesmen whose early death left a far mean streak of indepence [independence] brought on by negleck [neglect], entering the US Marine corp at 17 this streak of independence was strengthened by exotic journeys to Japan, the Philipines and the score's of odd Islands in the Pacific, immianly [immediately] after serving out his 3 years in the USMC he abonded [abandoned] his American life to seek a new life in the USSR. Full of optimism and hope he stood in red square in the fall of 1959 vowing to see his chosen course through After, however, two years and a lot of growing up I decided to return to the USA. This book is not a story about himself. He is only the narrator. He dose think, however that not too many people, at least Americans, had had the oppitunity to look into a often incredible and sometimes terrifying world, but a world whose outward appearance is very like our own.

As a youth, Oswald had no father in the household, and his mother was constantly at work as a caretaker or clerk. His two older brothers were military examples, but he had little contact with them. He was so unruly that his mother moved with him from Louisiana to New York so that her oldest son could bring some order to their life. Lee skipped school in New York City and was brought in for evaluation to understand why he defied the authorities. His psychiatrist, Renatus Hartogs, wrote this report:

> This 13-year-old well-built boy has superior mental resources and functions only slightly below his capacity level in spite of chronic truancy from school which brought him into Youth House. No finding of neurological impairment or psychotic mental changes could be made. Lee has to be diagnosed as "personality pattern disturbance with schizoid features and passive-aggressive tendencies." Lee has to be seen as an emotionally, quite disturbed youngster who suffers under the impact of really existing emotional isolation and depression, lack of affection, absence of family life, and rejection by a self-involved and conflicted mother.

Upon discharge, Dr. Hartogs wrote that Lee should be on probation, should have therapy with a male psychiatrist, and his mother should have counseling. If these things were not done, Lee was to be removed from his home and placed elsewhere. Lee's mother did not tell the court that she would not comply. She simply moved the two of them to New Orleans, where Lee attended school to some extent until he was old enough to join the Marine Corps.

In 1965, Renatus Hartogs and Lucy Freeman wrote *Two Assassins* about Lee Oswald and Jack Ruby. They believe that both assassins were loners who killed for themselves and not for some conspirators or other people.

Before Lee left home for military service, he had become interested in the American Socialist Party and wrote for information about membership. This came about, according to the story he told a reporter in Russia because he was given pamphlets to support Mr. and Mrs. Julius Rosenberg, communists who were accused of giving A-bomb secrets to Russians.

The execution of Mrs. Rosenberg was urged by counselor Roy Cohn, who had many clients, such as Senator Joseph McCarthy, Donald Trump, and Aristotle Onassis. Unfortunately, after three jolts, the executioners unstrapped Mrs. Rosenberg and found her heart was still beating. Thus, they had to re-attach her and send charges a fourth time. Their children were adopted by Abel Meeropol and his wife. Meeropol created the lyrics for *Strange Fruit,* a song that made Billie Holliday famous for singing about lynchings of blacks that swung from trees. Some of this news created Oswald's interest in communism.

Lee entered the Marine Corps on October 26, 1956. He disliked being told what to do, so he violated rules. He bought his own gun, which was discovered when he accidentally shot himself in the elbow. He liked his service in Japan so much that he asked for an extra tour of duty there. When his sergeant declined, he argued with him in a bar, spilling a drink on him and inviting him outside for a fistfight. He received two court-martials, a demotion from E-3 to E-2, and served a month in the brig.

On October 4, 1957, the Russian satellite Sputnik was launched. The world was shocked to see that the USSR was superior in technology. Oswald began to read about Russia, study the Russian language, and took a USMC language test in February 1959 to gauge his learning. He scored poorly but continued with a growing plan to go to Russia.

He went home briefly after discharge and left after two days. He pretended that he wanted to attend a college in Turku, Finland, but he was seeking a passport to get into Russia. He finally obtained one at the Soviet Embassy in Helsinki, Finland. It was a five-day student tourist visa to Russia.

Thanks to Soviet Premier Boris Yeltsin, who gave President William Clinton several documents in August 1999, here is the letter Oswald wrote on October 16, 1959, requesting citizenship in the Soviet Union:

I, Lee Harvey Oswald, request that I be granted citizenship in the Soviet Union. My visa began on Oct. 15, and will expire on Oct. 21. I must be granted asylum before this date, while I wait for the citizenship decision.

At present, I am a citizen of the United States of America. I want citizenship because I am a communist and a worker, I have lived in a decadent capitalist society where the workers are slaves. I am twenty years old; I have completed three years in the United States Marine Corps. I served with the occupation forces in Japan. I have seen American military imperialism in all its forms.

I do not want to return to any country outside of the Soviet Union.

I am willing to give up my American citizen ship and assume the responsibilities of a Soviet citizen.

I had saved my money which I earned as a private in the American military for two years, in order to come to Russia for the express purpose of seeking citizenship here. I do not have enough money left to live indefinitely here, or to return to any other country. I have no desire to return to any other country. I ask that my request be given quick consideration.

Sincerely,

Lee H. Oswald.

Lee was so obsessed with his goal that his guide, Rimma, was not able to show him around as she was assigned to. He was keeping a diary and wrote this on October 21, 1959.

Received word from police official. I must leave country tonight at 8:00 p.m. as visa expires. I am shocked! My dreams! I have $100 left. I have waited for 2 years to be accepted. My fondest dreams are shattered because of a petty official; because of bad planning. 7:00 p.m. I decide to end it. Soak wrist in cold water to numb the pain. Then slash my left wrist. Then plunge wrist into bathtub of hot water. I think "when Rimma comes at 8 to find me dead, it will be a great shock." Somewhere a violin plays as I watch my life whirl away. I think to myself "How easy to die" and "a sweet death" (to violins). About 8:00, Rimma finds me unconscious (bathtub water a rich red color). She screams (I remember that) and runs for help. Ambulance comes. Am taken to hospital where five stitches are put in my wrist. Poor Rimma stays by my side as interpreter (My Russian is still very bad) far into the night.

When Oswald was discharged from the hospital, he was taken to the Metropole Hotel. During his five-day visa, he had visited the U.S. Embassy to renounce his American citizenship, and they had told journalists of this. Thus, two journalists visited him at the hotel, but he refused to talk to them at first. He finally did, and news arrived in American newspapers about his request for Soviet citizenship.

He finally received word that he was allowed to stay for one year. His request for citizenship would be reconsidered at that time, provided he was still interested.

Richard Snyder at the American Embassy in Moscow sent this telegram to the U.S. State Department on October 31, 1959.

Lee Harvey Oswald. Unmarried age 20, passport 1733242 issued September 10, 1959. Appeared at Embassy today to renounce American citizenship. Stated applied in Moscow for Soviet citizenship following entry to USSR from Helsinki Oct. 15. Mother's address and his last address U.S. 4936 Collinwood St. Ft. Worth, Texas. Says action contemplated last two years. Main reason "I am a Marxist." Attitude arrogant, aggressive. Recently discharged Marine Corps. Say has offered Soviets any information he has acquired as enlisted radar operator. In view of Petrulli case [another American defector to Russia]; we proposed delaying executing renunciation until Soviet action known or department advises. Dispatch follows. Press informed.

Oswald had two interviews with American female journalists about his reasons for leaving the U.S. and coming to Russia. He wrote his brothers and his mother to finalize contacts with them.

He continued his diary, and here is a note from January 4, 1960:

I am called to passport office and finally given a Soviet document. Not the Soviet citizenship as I so wanted. Only a residence document, not even for foreigners, but a paper called "for those without citizenship." Still, I am happy. The official says they are sending me to the city of Minsk. I ask "Is that Siberia?" He only laughs. He also tells me that they have arranged for me to receive some money through the Red Cross to pay my hotel bills and expenses. I thank the gentleman and leave. Later in the afternoon, I see Rimma. She asks, "Are you happy?" Yes. [He filled out papers for an occupation called "assembler Minsk radio plant" and a residence card to expire on January 4, 1961.]

Other papers turned over to President Clinton by Premier Yeltzin explained why he had been denied citizenship.

"In reviewing an application for Soviet citizenship, the competent authorities of the Soviet Union consider first of all the extent to which the applicant can fulfill the obligations of a citizen of the USSR and enjoy the right granted to him. Oswald's motives for submitting the application were unclear. Thus, his application for Soviet citizenship was rejected."

He was to be given a furnished apartment in Minsk, and the Red Cross would provide an allowance of 700 rubles monthly for one year. He was sent to Hotel Minsk, where he met the city mayor and was welcomed by some co-workers.

He gradually learned more Russian, found some buddies at work, and met some girls, a few of whom he dated. He was quite the center of attention in the beginning. But after a couple of months, he was just another worker, rather lazy and doing shoddy work, according to his supervisor's reports.

On May 1, 1960, he wrote this in his diary.

Zeger [older co-worker] advises me to go back to U.S.A. It's the first voice of opposition I have heard. I respect Zeger. He has seen the world. He says many things and relates many things I do not know about the USSR. I begin to feel uneasy inside. It's true!!

He wrote this in his diary during August-September 1960.

As my Russian improves, I become increasingly conscious of just what sort of a society I live in. Mass gymnastics, compulsory after work meetings, usually political information meetings, compulsory attendance at lectures and the sending of the entire shop collective (except me) to pick potatoes on a Sunday at a state collective farm—a "patriotic day" to bring in the harvest. The opinions of the workers (unvoiced) are that it's a great pain in the neck. They don't seem to be especially enthusiastic about any of the "collective" duties—a natural feeling. I am increasingly aware of the presence in all things of Lebezen, shop party secretary, fat, fortyish, and jovial on the outside. He is a no-nonsense 'Party' regular.

On September 26, 1960, John Kennedy and Richard Nixon had the first of four televised Presidential debates. One of the principal subjects was communism. In the second debate on October 7th, Kennedy said that President Eisenhower should have apologized to Premier Khrushchev for the U-2 spy plane incident (where pilot Gary Power was in a plane shot down) because it prevented an important summit meeting. Kennedy also blamed the Eisenhower administration for losing Cuba to Fidel Castro. These debates received coverage in the Soviet press.

Oswald's diary note of January 2, 1961, described his marriage proposal to a girl he was dating. She turned him down. He wrote:

I realize she was never serious with me but only exploited my being an American in order to get the envy of the other girls who consider me different from the Russian boys. I am miserable.

He had timed his marriage proposal to coincide with the January 4 renewal of his request to become a Soviet citizen. So, he wrote this in his diary on January 4, 1961.

One year after I received the residence document, I am called in to the passport office and asked if I want citizenship (Russian). I say no, simply extend my residential passport to agree, and my document is extended until January 4, 1962.

I am starting to reconsider my desire about staying. The work is drab. The money I get has nowhere to be spent. No nightclubs or bowling alleys. No places of recreation except the trade union dances. I have had enough.

About January 26, 1961, unbeknownst to Lee, his mother had scraped up enough money to visit the White House to see President John Kennedy, who had been inaugurated six days earlier. She said she had lost contact with Lee after he moved to Minsk, even though he had written that he wanted no more contact with family.

White House officials met with her as a stand-in for President Kennedy. She told them that she thought Lee must be an American agent sent to spy on the Soviets, an idea which probably helped her accept his defection and rejection of her and America. Here is the Department of State document recording the visit of Marguerite Oswald with Messrs. Hickey, Stanfield, and Boster.

Mrs. Oswald came in to discuss the situation regarding her son, Lee Oswald, who had gone to the Soviet Union and attempted to renounce his citizenship in a visit to the Embassy on October 31, 1959. Mrs. Oswald said she had come to Washington to see what further could be done to help her son, indicating that she did not feel the Department had done as much as it should in his case. She also told she thought there was some possibility that her son had in fact gone to the Soviet Union as a U.S. secret agent, and if this were true, she wished the appropriate authorities to know that she was destitute and should receive some compensation.

Mrs. Oswald was assured that there was no evidence to suggest that her son had gone to the Soviet Union as an "agent," and that she should dismiss any such ideas. With respect to her son's citizenship status, Mr. Hickey explained that he [Lee] had not yet taken the necessary steps in order legally to renounce his citizenship. At the same time, we did not know whether he had taken any action which would deprive him of his American citizenship under our laws. Mrs. Oswald conceded that there was a good possibility that her son was acting in full knowledge of what he was doing and preferred the Soviet way of life. If this were the case, she would respect his right to do so.

It was agreed that the Department would send a new instruction to the Embassy in Moscow asking that the Soviet Foreign Ministry be informed that Mrs. Oswald had not heard from her son in several months and was very anxious to have word from him.

Mrs. Oswald said that her address at the present time was Box 30, Boyd, Texas.

On February 1, 1961, Oswald sent a letter to the American Embassy in Moscow with a request to return to the United States. He received a letter from Richard E. Snyder of the American Embassy stating he could come in for an interview any time he wanted. He wrote back that he could not leave the city of Minsk without permission. He did not wish to jeopardize his position, so he wondered if much of the work could be done through correspondence.

In April 1961, the publication *Overseas Weekly* ran an article about Major General Edwin Walker. He had called Harry Truman, Eleanor Roosevelt, and Dean Acheson "definitely pink." Walker was indoctrinating Army troops with John Birch Society literature, urging them to vote for a radical right platform. For this, he was officially admonished. Following this humiliation, he resigned from the Army and became a spokesman for the John Birch Society in Dallas, Texas. He was publicly critical of Secretary of State Dean Rusk and President Kennedy's foreign policy. This information is included because Oswald would try to kill Walker when he returned to the U.S.

Oswald's diary showed him falling in love with a new lady friend who would become his wife and the mother of his two daughters.

March 17, 1961: I and Erich went to trade union dance. Boring, but at the last hour I am introduced to a girl with a French hair-do and red dress with white slippers. I dance with her. Then ask to show her home. I do along with 5 other admirers. Her name is Marina....

April 30, 1961: We are married. At her aunt' home, we have a dinner reception for about 20 friends and neighbors who wish us happiness.

Lee wrote his brother on May 5, 1961, telling of his marriage and his plan to return to the United States. Now, his new plan to bring his wife complicated the paperwork required for a move. It took many letters, documents, and procedures to leave Russia. His wife became pregnant, and their first child was born just before they could leave. It all took so long that he wrote Senator John Tower of Texas on December 6, 1961, hoping that a politician could expedite matters.

Oswald did not have enough money to pay for the transportation from Russia to the U.S., so the government loaned him some money, and he would pay it back quickly once he got a job in the U.S. His brother loaned him the rest of the money to get to Texas from New York.

Earlier, when it became public news that Oswald intended to renounce American citizenship, the USMC had changed his discharge to dishonorable. Now that he was to return and seek work, he wanted that to be reversed. He wrote to John Connally, who used to be Secretary of the Navy, but he had resigned to run for governor of Texas. Thus, that letter was forwarded to Fred Korth, who replaced Connally. In 1963, Connally was injured when Oswald killed the president in the Dallas motorcade.

Meanwhile, Marina delivered their baby on February 15, 1962. Papers needed to be set up for his Russian wife and his baby before their trip to the

U.S. could take place. The Oswalds both needed to resign from their jobs, and that was difficult because of very critical comments from friends, co-workers, neighbors, and authority figures.

There was constant tension and bickering between the newly married couple. Norman Mailer wrote a 1995 book called *Oswald's Tale: An American Mystery* and learned that the KGB recorded conversations in Oswald's apartment. He recorded some of it in his book. Here is an example from July 21, 1961:

Lee: Well, why are you crying? I told you it won't do any good.

Marina: You know, I never said that I was a very good person. Why did I get married? You tricked me.

Lee: You shouldn't cry. I understand. You don't understand yourself why.

Marina: My friends don't recognize me.

Lee: Well, I've also lost weight, right?

Marina: Why did I get married?

Lee: Well, what am I supposed to do? Is it my fault that you have a lot of work? I mean you don't ever cook, but other women cook. And I don't say anything about it. I don't yell. You never do anything, and you don't want to do the wash. What do you do? The only thing you ever talk about is how tired you are at work.

Marina: I didn't get any rest.

Lee: Well, what can I do?

Marina: Everything was so good, but lately everything has gotten bad. Nothing's right. You can't please a man like you.

When documents were finally ready, the three Oswalds sailed on the *Holland America* line to the United States. Lee spent much time writing questions he might be asked and possible good answers he could give reporters. To his surprise, there were no reporters. Perhaps he forgot that he wrote asking his brother to contact no reporters. The answers he prepared were found in his possession when he was arrested after the assassination of the president, along with many other papers.

The Oswalds arrived in New York on June 13, 1962, and Lee's brother, Robert, paid their fare to Dallas, Texas. The family all talked for a few days in Texas, and Lee then wrote to the Marine Corps to try to undo his dishonorable discharge. He had little money but used ten dollars to hire a stenographer to type his fifty pages for the book he wrote on Russia. After she had typed ten pages of his barely legible writing, he had no more money to pay her.

Lee helped Marina and the baby get registered under the Immigration and Naturalization Service. He went to the Texas Employment Office to apply for jobs and gave his brother's address.

On July 6, 1962, FBI agents interviewed a sullen Oswald about his course of action in Russia and his return. He began his payments to the State Department for his transportation loan. He also wrote the Socialist Workers Party on August 12, 1962, for membership information. The FBI interviewed him again on August 16, 1962. He promised to let them know if any Soviets attempted to contact him. He did not answer why he went to Russia, saying, "I went, and I came back. It was something that I did." And he certainly didn't tell them that he was staying in contact with communist and socialist organizations.

On August 17, 1962, he wrote the Russian Embassy a letter reflecting his rapidly developing discontent in America. He ended his letter by saying, "I would like for the Embassy to send us any periodicals or bulletins which you may put out for the benefit of your citizens living, for a time, in the USA."

Lee set up a library membership and began to check out James Bond books and would eventually read Kennedy's 1957 *Profiles in Courage* about eight courageous senators. He probably did not know that Kennedy had help in research and writing but added punchy dialogue. Thus, Kennedy was a bit more like the editor of the book.

In Dallas, the Oswalds were put in touch with Russians, including George de Mohrenschildt, who became a particular friend of Lee and Marina. He was born in Minsk, had royal connections, and moved to Long Island, New York, in 1938. He had been a friend of Jacqueline Kennedy's mother, socialite Janet Lee Bouvier Auchincloss, and bounced little Jacqueline on his knee when she was about nine or ten.[70]

George met his fourth wife, Jeanne LeGon, in 1955, and they married in 1959. She worked with Abraham Zapruder, who filmed the JFK assassination. Abraham was born in the Ukraine and immigrated to the United States in 1920. In 1941, he moved to Dallas to work for Nardis Sportswear, and he worked with Jeanne LeGon from 1953 to 1954. His office was in the Dal-Tex Building across the street from the Texas School Book Depository, to be discussed later.

George and Jeanne de Mohrenschildt helped Lee and took Marina to get some needed low-cost dental work. There were many Russian friends who helped Marina and baby June while Oswald roomed at the Dallas YMCA looking for work through the Texas Employment Commission. There were some fifty or more Russians who kept in contact with each other in the Dallas area.

On October 1, 1962, everyone reading the *Dallas Morning News* and watching TV in Dallas learned of the riot at the University of Mississippi. Dallas resident Major General Edwin Walker was charged with insurrection and was evaluated at Parkland Hospital as was described earlier.

Lee took a job at the Leslie Welding Company but had worked there only a few weeks when he did not show up for work on October 9, 1962. He

---

70 https://www.nytimes.com/1964/11/24/archives/friend-of-oswalds-knew-mrs-kennedy.html

did not give notice and just began work on October 12, 1962, at the Jaggers-Chiles-Stovall company, where he was a photography trainee.

On October 21, 1962, the nation heard President John Kennedy announce that the Soviets had constructed missile sites in Cuba. On October 25th, U.N. Ambassador Adlai Stevenson exhibited aerial photographs of the Cuban missile bases at the U.N. for the world to see. Premier Nikita Khrushchev agreed on October 28 to dismantle the bases and return missiles to Russia.

That was perhaps the finest hour of John Kennedy's presidency. He had to make a choice about how to deal with Russia, going against some of his people and agreeing with others. He saved the world from the brink of disaster, averting World War III by preventing Russia from installing nuclear missiles ninety miles from the United States.

He was not always so noble. A closer look at John Kennedy presents some surprising behavior by someone like the president of the United States, a nation held in high esteem by so many other nations. Oswald did not know about the ignoble side of the president. He focused only on how important the president was that a puny little ex-Marine sharpshooter could kill him.

Lee craved attention as he had craved love, but he never received either during his short life. Lee's assassin became famous for having avenged the president, but Jack Ruby deprived the world of knowing more about Oswald to settle questions of his guilt. Ruby's act of vengeance satisfied his need to be a hero but left conspiracy theorists with many tidbits to weave into malevolent assumptions.

Chronological Record of Lee Harvey Oswald

- 10/18/39 Lee was born in New Orleans, Louisiana, after his father died
- 12/26/42 Lee was placed in an orphanage with his two older brothers
- 1/29/44 His mother removed Lee from the orphanage to live with her
- 4/18/45 Lee had a mastoidectomy and tonsillectomy
- 1949-52 Lee lived with his mother in Ft. Worth, Texas, and became unruly
- 4/15-5/7/53 In NYC with mother, on probation for truancy, had psychiatric evaluation
- 1/26/54 Lee moved to New Orleans with mother
- 10/10/55 Lee dropped out of tenth grade to enlist in the Marine Corps
- 10/19/55 Lee was rejected by Marines for being underage

- 7/1/56 Lee moved with his mother to Ft. Worth, Texas
- 10/3/56 Lee applied for membership in the Socialist Party of America
- 10/24/56 Lee enlisted in the Marine Corps
- 1/20/57 Stationed in Camp Pendleton, San Diego, California
- 3/18/57 Stationed at NATTC, Jacksonville, Florida
- 5/4/57 Stationed at Kessler AFB, Mississippi
- 7/9/57 Stationed at MCAS, El Toro, California
- 9/57 Stationed in Fleet Marines in the Pacific
- 10/4/57 USSR launched Sputnik 1, the first man-made satellite
- 1/31/58 U.S. launched their first man-made satellite— Explorer 1
- 3/58 Khrushchev became the Premier of the Soviet Union
- 4/11/58 Lee had a Court Martial: Guilty of owning unregistered weapon

- 6/17/58 A second Court Martial: Used provoking words to staff NCO. Demoted
- 12/22/58 Stationed at MCAS, El Toro, California
- 2/25/59 Requested Russian test after using Berlitz book—poor score
- 3/4/59 Applied to Albert Schweitzer College, Switzerland
- 5/6/59 Scored 212, sharpshooter. Fired riot gun, M-1, and 45-caliber pistol
- 8/59 Mother was hurt, so got hardship discharge from USMC to help her
- 9/4/59 Completed passport application in Santa Ana, California
- 9/10/59 Passport issued from Los Angeles, California
- 9/11/59 Early honorable discharge from active duty to serve in reserves
- 9/14/59 Arrived at mother's home in Ft. Worth, Texas
- 9/16/59 Completed Passenger Immigration form in New Orleans, LA.
- 9/21/59 Sailed from New Orleans to Le Havre on *SS Marion Lykes*
- 10/16/59 Lee arrived in Moscow and requested Soviet citizenship
- 10/21/59 After citizenship denial, Lee attempted suicide-hospitalized
- 10/28/59 Hospital discharge, renewed request to stay in USSR. Severed family contact
- 10/31/59 Asked the American Embassy to dissolve American citizenship
- 11/3/59 Lee filed a complaint that the Embassy delayed his request
- 11/15/59 Interviewed by UPI Aline Mosby
- 11/19/59 Interviewed by NANA correspondent Priscilla Johnson
- 1/4/60 Issued residence permit for those without citizenship
- 1/7/60 Sent to Minsk radio factory to work as "assembler"
- 9/13/60 Lee received an undesirable discharge for defection to USSR

- 2/1/61 After 13 months, asked US Embassy for return to U.S.
- 3/17/61 Met Marina at trade union dance in Minsk
- 4/30/61 Lee married Marina
- 6/61 Lee told Marina he wanted to return to the U.S.
- 7/8/61 Visited Moscow to get passport and papers for U.S.
- 10/4/61 Lee wrote U.S. Ambassador to expedite exit visas
- 12/25/61 Lee learned Soviet exit visas were granted
- 1/2/62 Lee wrote to his mother to request transportation money to return to U.S.
- 1/30/61 Lee wrote John Connally, Navy Sec. to reverse undesirable discharge
- 2/15/62 Marina gave birth to June
- 3/22/62 Lee wrote USMC to review undesirable discharge
- 5/16/62 Lee wrote Radio Factory resignation letter
- 5/30/62 Oswalds left Moscow for the U.S. with travel fund loan

- 6/7-13/62 Oswalds sailed from Holland to New York
- 6/14/62 Oswalds arrived in Ft. Worth to stay with brother Robert
- 6/18/62 Lee submitted papers to reverse USMC discharge
- 6/18/62 Lee took his book about the USSR to Steno to be typed
- 6/26/62 Lee was interviewed by the FBI
- 7/17/62 Lee was hired by Leslie Welding Co. in Ft. Worth
- 8/4/62 Lee subscribed to *The Worker*, U.S. Communist Paper
- 8/12/62 Lee wrote for membership in Socialist Workers Party
- 8/14/62 Lee was interviewed again by the FBI
- 8/18/62 Lee sent payment to the State Dept. for transportation loan
- 9/30/62 Jas. Meredith enrollment in U of Miss. blocked by Walker
- 10/9/62 Separated from wife, Lee got Dallas P.O. box

- 10/12/62 Hired by Jaggers in Dallas as photo trainee
- 11/3/62 Lee moved into an apartment with family in Dallas
- 1/1/63 Lee ordered communist info on "Coming American Revolution"
- 1/25/63 Lee paid off State Dept. transportation loan
- 1/27/63 Lee ordered a pistol under alias A. J. Hidell
- 1/28/63 Lee began evening typing class
- 2/22/63 Oswalds met Ruth Paine at party-she wanted to learn Russian
- 3/9-11/63 Lee photographed Walker's house and yard
- 3/12/63 Lee ordered rifle & sight from Kleins using Hidell alias
- 4/6/63 Lee was fired from the photo job
- 4/8/63 Lee dropped the typing class. Sought unemployment compensation
- 4/10/63 Shot at Gen. Walker left instructions for Marina if arrested

- 4/12/63 Marina visited Ruth Paine, Lee sought unemployment comp.
- 4/63 Lee wrote Fair Play for Cuba for literature, wrote *The Worker* for a job as a photographer
- 4/24/63 Lee left Marina with Paine and sought work in New Orleans
- 4/26/63 Lee filed for unemployment compensation in Louisiana
- 5/4/63 Marina sent a photo of Lee with a rifle & pistol to Mohrenschildt's Wrote on the back, "Hunter of fascists-ha-ha!"
- 5/9/63 Hired as a maintenance man with Wm. Reily Co. in New Orleans
- 5/10/63 Ruth Paine drove Marina to join Lee in New Orleans
- 5/26/63 Lee wrote Fair Play for Cuba Committee to open a branch

- 5/29/63 Lee ordered FPCC flyers using the alias Lee Osborne
- 6/3/63 Lee opened a P.O. box in New Orleans for him and Hidell alias
- 6/63 Lee wrote FPCC to change rules for his branch
- 6/8/63 Lee made a fake vaccination form using the alias Dr. A. J. Hidell for passport
- 6/24/63 Lee completed a passport application for renewal
- 7/1/63 Lee requested USSR visas for Marina and self to be processed separately
- 7/19/63 Lee was fired from Wm. Reily maintenance job
- 7/21/63 Lee filed again for unemployment compensation
- 7/27/63 Lee spoke to seminary students of cousin about Soviet life
- 8/1/63 Lee wrote the FPCC that he put on a demonstration for them
- 8/5/63 Lee tried to infiltrate Cuban exile group pretending to be anti-Castro
- 8/9/63 Lee was arrested and fined for fighting with Cuban exiles, covered by media
- 8/10/63 Lee was interviewed by the FBI in jail and omitted USSR residence
- 8/12/63 Lee wrote FPCC bragging about press coverage of his arrest
- 8/13/63 Lee sent *The Worker* press clippings of his arrest
- 8/16/63 Lee hired two men to hand out pro-Castro flyers and called media to cover
- 8/17/63 Lee was on the radio as 'secretary' of FPCC New Orleans branch
- 8/17/63 Lee wrote the FPPC about his demonstration and radio interview
- 8/21/63 Lee was humiliated on a radio debate about his lies and communist ties
- 8/28/63 Lee wrote Communist Party of the USA and asked for advice on where to live
- 8/31/63 Lee wrote *The Worker* for a photo job, saying moving to NY soon

- 9/1/63 Lee wrote for Communist Party USA to say he was moving to D.C.
- 9/17/63 Lee applied for a tourist card to Mexico using alias H.O. Lee
- 9/23/63 Lee left Marina with Ruth Paine, intending to go to Cuba via Mexico
- 9/26/63 Lee went to Mexico City but could not get a visa to Cuba
- 9/27/63 Lee completed a visa for Cuba but was told of 4-month delays
- 10/3/63 Lee returned to the U.S., buying a bus ticket as H. O. Lee
- 10/7/63 Lee rented a room from Mary Bledsoe in Dallas and began looking for work
- 10/14/63 Lee was evicted by Bledsoe for speaking a foreign language on the phone
- 10/15/63 Lee was hired by Texas School Book Depository with Ruth Paine's help
- 10/20/63 Marina gave birth to second daughter, Rachel
- 10/23/63 Lee attended U.S. Day Rally led by General Walker
- 10/25/63 Lee attended an ACLU meeting at the invitation of Ruth & Michael Paine
- 11/1/63 Lee opened the P.O. Box for self, FPCC, and ACLU. Wrote *The Worker,* asking whether to infiltrate the ACLU on behalf of communism.
- 11/4/63 Lee applied for membership in ACLU
- 11/9/63 Lee wrote the Soviet Embassy in D.C. for visas to return to the USSR
- 11/12-15/63 Lee left a warning note for FBI agent Hosty to stop bothering Marina
- 11/16/63 Lee completed an application for a Texas Drivers' License
- 11/18/63 Marina was mad that Lee rented a room under an alias of H. O. Lee
- 11/21/63 Lee visited Marina a day early and tried in vain to make up with her. He went into the garage where he kept

his rifle and carried special
wrapping paper from work to
break it down and cover it up to
carry to work the next morning.

- 11//22/63 Lee left his wedding
ring and $170 in cash for Marina
on her dresser before leaving
for work. Lee was arrested for
killing Patrolman J. D. Tippit,
who tried to question him after
President Kennedy was shot.
- 11/24/63 Lee Oswald was killed
by Jack Ruby.

F. John Kennedy's Health Problems

There was a very good chance that John Fitzgerald Kennedy (1917-1963) would die an early death from life-threatening medical problems. He lived his life as if to cram everything possible into each moment. His marriage to Jacqueline had lasted only ten years, but the way he lived influenced his wife, his children, his siblings, and many others. We will examine his life, which produced memories and gossip that many people carry on, whether they knew him or not.

John was born to politician and businessman Joseph P. Kennedy Sr. and wife Rose. Joseph Patrick Kennedy wanted to be president himself. He is the reason that his son was elected president, and his life will be described briefly at the end of this book.

John's paternal grandfather had served as a Massachusetts state legislator, and his maternal grandfather was a U.S. Congressman and Mayor of Boston. His family was of Irish heritage, and he had eight siblings.

John's health problems ruled his life. At age two, he contracted scarlet fever on the day his mother gave birth to his sister, Kathleen. Fearing he might transmit the fever to his sibling, he was rushed to Boston City Hospital. He became so sick that a priest was called in to deliver his last rites. But he pulled through and received treatment for six weeks, then spent six weeks in isolation until he could return home.[71]

---

71 https://www.cbc.ca/radio/undertheinfluence/john-f-kennedy-was-given-last-rites-5-different-times-1.6362855

John became a sickly youth with a weakened immune system that made him slow to recover from childhood and other illnesses. Unlike his brothers, who were taught by their father to compete physically and mentally, he was seen as less able to do so. He was a challenge for his parents, teachers, and doctors. His life was so precarious from early childhood and required so many treatments of various kinds that he became a "devil-may-care" reckless youth. He tended to burn his candle at both ends of the stick and live it up while he could.

John's favorite poem was by Alan Seegar, a New York man who graduated from Harvard in 1910 and went to Paris to live. When war broke out between France and Germany, he joined the French Foreign Legion and was shot to death on the 4th of July in 1916. He had written many poems, but John's favorite was *I Have a Rendevous with Death:*

I Have a Rendezvous with Death

I have a rendezvous with Death
At some disputed barricade,
When Spring comes back with rustling shade
And apple-blossoms fill the air—
I have a rendezvous with Death
When Spring brings back blue days and fair.

It may be he shall take my hand
And lead me into his dark land
And close my eyes and quench my breath—
It may be I shall pass him still.
I have a rendezvous with Death
On some scarred slope of battered hill,
When Spring comes round again this year
And the first meadow-flowers appear.

God knows 'twere better to be deep
Pillowed in silk and scented down,
Where Love throbs out in blissful sleep,
Where hushed awakenings are dear...
But I've a rendezvous with death
At midnight in some flaming town,
When Spring trips north again this year,
And I to my pledged word am true,
I shall not fail that rendezvous.

It was clear to Joseph Kennedy's sons that their father had not only a very close relationship with his secretary but also a very close relationship with the actress Gloria Swanson. He began their friendship by offering help to her to avoid bankruptcy, but it became a long and emotional love affair. He became involved with Hollywood, and much of his early income came from his ownership of movie and booking studios. See his book *The Story of Films*, published in 1927 by A. W. Shaw Company. The boys followed in their father's footsteps in many ways.

At age 14, John attended Choate School, a prestigious boarding school in Connecticut. His IQ was 119 when he was tested before entrance, according to biographer Robert Dallek's *An Unfinished Life: John F. Kennedy, 1917-1963*, published in 2004. Assassin Lee Harvey Oswald was tested at age 13 in a psychiatric institution and found to have an IQ of 118; thus, both John and Lee had a bright average intelligence. Both John Kennedy and Lee Oswald suffered from dyslexia, and John would transmit that problem through genes to his son, John Kennedy Jr.

At Choate, he and school chum Lem Billings pulled tricks and were nearly expelled. The Kennedy sons knew that their father had many affairs outside of marriage to well-known women who sometimes visited their house. Those affairs also included actress Marlene Dietrich. Thus, his sons followed him in such pursuits, and young John began having sexual adventures quite early.

Nigel Hamilton's excellent 1992 book *JFK Reckless Youth* described John's early letters to his friend Lem Billings. On page 149, 18-year-old John is writing Billings about his health on January 27, 1936:

They have not found out anything as yet except that I have leukemia, + agranulocytosis. Took a peak [sic] at my chart yesterday and could see that they were mentally measuring me for a coffin. Eat, drink and make Olive [a girl he met], as tomorrow or next week we attend my funeral.

This was young John's effort to make fun of early death and find momentary satisfaction in sex whenever possible. John probably thought that despite a short life, he might find some meaningful adventures. Perhaps he downplayed illness and death as insignificant.

At age 19, his father sent John and his older brother Joe to the Jay Six dude ranch in Benson, Arizona, for a summer to toughen up frail John. By this time, he was often called Jack. The boys built an office for the boss and tended horses while there.

Jack slipped across the nearby border several times with a male friend to have unprotected sex with Mexican prostitutes. He required treatment for gonorrhea then and later in his life. He described that in letters to chum Lem Billings, which can be found in Nigel Hamilton's book. There is a letter he wrote Lem in May 1936 entitled "Travels in a Mexican Whore-house with Your Roomie," and he signed himself "your gonnereick roomie."

Some young men who get sick after doing something wrong believe that God has visited their bodies with rot and decay. But John apparently did little soul-searching after each treatment for venereal disease and was hale and hearty again. The body triumphs and has plans other than those of the soul.

In 1937, young John, at the age of twenty, decided to travel around Europe with Lem Billings. He kept a diary of his travels and called it *My Trip Abroad.* This was over twenty years ahead of Lee Harvey Oswald, who went to Russia and kept a diary he called *Historic Diary,* which he began on October 16, 1959, two days before he turned twenty. Both young men reveled in their opportunities to see the world and wanted to record their discoveries.

When Jack was twenty-one, his father took the family on vacation at Hotel du Cap near Cannes, France, in August 1938. Joseph had served six months as Ambassador in England. He had a habit of inviting his paramours to his home, and his wife did nothing about that except go on trips and spending sprees. So, John Kennedy saw his father going into Marlene Dietrich's cabana. Her husband was aware that she was bisexual and didn't worry too much about her disappearance from time to time.

When John became president, he invited Marlene to the White House when she was doing her one-woman show nearby. They had a quickie, and she was ready to go back to the theater when he asked if she had sex with his father. She merely said, "He tried." Obviously, the Kennedy boys followed their father's example when it came to women.[72]

John graduated from Harvard University in 1940. He wrote a college thesis called *Why England Slept.* His father differed from Roosevelt about war against Hitler. Joseph was rather narrow-minded, didn't care for Jews, and wasn't that offended by Hitler's antisemitism. He disagreed with his son's ideas but wanted fame for the lad, so he had his friends help John do a foreword, corrections, and rewrite it so that it could be published in 1940. His father also bought numerous quantities of those books so that they seemed to be a best-seller.

---

72 https://www.vanityfair.com/news/2009/03/dietrich-kennedy200803

John joined the U.S. Naval Reserve the following year, having concealed his medical problems by lies. While serving as an ensign, he met Danish journalist Inga Arvad, who was living with his sister Kathleen, called Kick, in Washington, D.C.

Arvad was a beautiful young lady who had married a man in 1931. After their divorce, she married a Hungarian film director in 1936 and starred in three movies. She turned journalist and was invited by Adolf Hitler to the Summer Olympics in 1936, where she interviewed him. She left her husband and was thought to be a potential spy by the FBI when she came to America as a journalist.[73]

When Kathleen introduced them, Jack and Inga were immediately attracted to each other and began dating. Perhaps all men are wistful until they meet the right woman, which, in John's case, was Arvad. By then, the FBI was checking Inga, wondering if she was a Nazi spy. They spoke with John's superior officer since he was working in the Naval Reserves intelligence office, looking over documents. They decided to transfer him to Charleston, South Carolina, just in case she was spying.

FBI agents tapping her phone learned that she was making trips to Charleston so she could be with Kennedy. The two lovers stayed at a particular hotel, and agents put listening devices under their bed at J. Edgar Hoover's insistence. While no important intelligence information was passed, some comments were made. Kennedy's superior officer was advised, and John was transferred to a seagoing unit since they wanted to remove contact in case Arvad was a spy.[74]

Inga and John exchanged letters, which can be seen at: https://www. jfklibrary.org/asset-viewer/archives/JFKPP/004/JFKPP-004-052.

---

73 "Kennedy Affair with Spy Suspect Reported" Los Angeles Times January 19, 1976., p. B8
74 Jack Kennedy by Chris Matthews, 2011, p. 44 and https://warfare historynetwork.com/article/wwii-secrets-the-mysterious-inga-arvad/

Those letters show that she was very much aware of his bad back and frequent pain, which may have interfered with his bodily positions during intercourse. Kennedy's Catholic father told him to stop the affair because she was a divorcee, which would reflect badly on his Catholicism. Jack told her about that just before his transfer to the Pacific Theater. They were heartsick at parting.

During WWII, he commanded a PT boat in the Pacific theater, survived its sinking, and, although wounded, rescued fellow sailors, earning Navy and Marine Corps medals. When Kennedy returned to the United States, Arvad helped make him a hero by her story of January 13, 1944, in *The Pittsburgh Press.* Here is the beginning of that article:

"Lt. Kennedy Saves His Men as Japs Cut PT Boat in Half. All but two returned after destroyer rams them" by Inga Arvad.

This is a story of the 13 American men on PT boat 109 who got closer than any others to a Japanese destroyer and of the 11 who lived to tell about it. It is about the skipper hero, 26-year-old Lt. John F. Kennedy, son of Joseph Kennedy, former U.S. ambassador to Great Britain, now home on leave, who thought he saved three lives, and swam for long hours in shark-infested waters to rescue his men, today says: 'None of that hero stuff about me. The real heroes are not the men who return, but those who stay out there like plenty of them do, two of my men included.[75]

There was no doubt that his courage in battle saved lives. He was wounded, but he served his men well. How did he do it? Despite unbearable conditions, he ignored what he could not control. Just as he had ignored warnings by doctors about his health, he ignored warnings and thoughts of difficulties.

---

75 http://news.google.com/newspaper?Id=3XUbAAAAIBAJ&sjid-kowEAAAAIBAJ&p-g=3103,31675&dq=arvad&hl=en

There was freedom in that mindset. In health emergencies, others had taken over or put him to sleep. This time, he was the captain of his own fate. His attitude now was, "Oh, so what!"

Surely, through his sicknesses, he felt like a God struggling with the devil to go further and further. He used that inner power to mask the fear of death. Damn the torpedoes. Full speed ahead. He learned to "play king" by daring the worst conditions with bravado. He would run the show and carry out strategies to help rescuers find his men. He carved an SOS on a coconut and asked natives behind the lines to take it to the American base. He kept that coconut on his desk in the Oval Office. It said: "NAURO ISL... COMMANDER... NATIVE KNOWS POS'IT... HE CAN PILOT... 11 ALIVE... NEED SMALL BOAT... KENNEDY."

Jack and Arvad continued to correspond lovingly as she signed her name Binga, so Kennedy referred to her as Inga Binga. Arvad went on with her life and understood Kennedy's need to conform to his religion for his future in politics. She thought he was an exceptional young man and expected to hear great things about him in the future.

She was hired by movie producer David O. Selznick to promote 1945 *Duel in the Sun* by traveling across the country at various movie openings. She worked for MGM and met wealthy cowboy actor Tim McCoy, whom she married in 1946 until her death in 1973 near Nogales, Arizona. Author Seymour Hersh wrote about her affair with Kennedy in his 1997 book, *The Dark Side of Camelot*.

John's older brother, Joseph Jr., was about through with his combat mission in Europe, where he and his pilot were to fly an airplane wrapped in bombing materials. The plan was for the two men to parachute out, and the plane would go as one of the very first unmanned drones to its target and explode. The operation was called Anvil, but the combat drone exploded, and they both died a sudden death on August 12, 1944. Similar to brother John, Joe Jr. had fallen in love with a woman who had been married and had children, and he was reluctant to part with her. Details of his life and unusual final mission can be found on *Wikipedia.*

John Kennedy put together a small book with memories by friends and family called *As We Remember Joe* in 1945, with a first run of 390 copies and a second run of 250 copies. They are now available at special bookstores for over $10,000 each.

Following the death of John's brother, old Joe wanted John to prepare for the presidency. Did John want to be president? He had always followed his father's wishes as all his siblings and wife did. So, he began to imagine himself in the role of president. To be in politics is to want the most power to do the most good. John had been led to believe that humans can't live together peacefully and harmoniously without government.

Many young men experience the thrill of brushing up against powers that could destroy them. His father's position as Ambassador had given him a taste for such thrills. How would John capture and keep office in the business of politics? His sense of humor had always made others enjoy being around him. He was quick-witted and could demean himself much as Ronald Reagan did to good effect. How could he practice and build that capacity?

Being quite sick after his PT boat service, John's father sent him to Castle Hot Springs, Arizona, for rest and recuperation beginning in January 1945. This had been like a tubercular sanitarium in the early days, with frivolity provided as patients and doctors laughed at death and made jokes about it. This might be good for him, so he agreed to go.

He was treated with the curative waters at that site, proper food with meat sent by his father, and medicines, and he gradually strengthened. He saw some old people who seemed to enjoy illness because it made them the center of attention. He just bantered and joked with them briefly but focused on a self-made investment millionaire, Patrick J. Lannan, who became an excellent soulmate during this time. They spent their time together and finally went searching for some better female company at high-class hotels in the Phoenix area.

John disliked how illness made him overemphasize the physical side of his life. His father called him every day at 5 p.m. for months. He did not want to be a wimp, and there was constant reassurance that he was becoming healthier, tougher, and more ready for public service. A family aims to sustain the life of its members, and the Kennedys had certainly been doing that with their brood.

The Castle Hot Springs Resort is now a high-class dude ranch near Lake Pleasant in the Phoenix area, attracting a well-heeled clientele who want to see the place where John Kennedy recuperated and have their own adventures. In earlier times, Cecil B. DeMille filmed *The Squaw Man* in 1931, and the cast stayed at the resort. They included Warner Baxter, Charles Bickford, Lupe Velez, Roland Young, Raymond Hatton, and Dickie Moore. Other guests were Presidents Calvin Coolidge, Herbert Hoover, Theodore Roosevelt, Franklin Roosevelt, and Woodrow Wilson.

In April 1945, John left treatment and was given an assignment by William Randolph Hearst, thanks to Joseph Kennedy's intervention. Hearst asked John to write on topics such as the founding of the United Nations. Kennedy's dyslexia produced writing that needed spelling and grammatical corrections, but it gave him exposure. Others, like aide Ted Sorenson, wrote his speeches and papers with great aplomb at a later point.

Gene Tierney met the handsome young Kennedy when he was visiting the movie set of *Dragonwyck* in 1946. They began a romance that ended the following year after Kennedy told her he could never marry her because of his political ambitions. He and his father felt he needed to be seen as a proper Catholic who did not marry a divorcee. She was broken-hearted for quite some time but sent Kennedy a note of congratulations on his 1960 victory in the presidential election.

In September 1947, a spell of indolence was upon Jack. He became ill in London and was diagnosed at a London Clinic with Addison's disease, a rare endocrine disorder. His physician estimated that Kennedy would die of this within a year. His family insisted John be sent home, and his condition deteriorated while crossing the Atlantic Ocean. A priest was summoned to perform last rites. He held on until he arrived home, where doctors saved his life. He was living in his head and steeled his body to defy every obstacle.

Former Vice President Dick Cheney and his long-time cardiologist, Dr. Jonathan Reiner, wrote the 2013 book *Heart: An American Medical Odyssey* about Cheney's thirty-five-year battle with heart disease. That book covered the incredible medical breakthroughs that have changed cardiac care over the last four decades. Kennedy and his doctors could have written a book about how the treatment of Addison's disease with cortisone in John Kennedy kept changing throughout the patient's lifetime. He was always just a step away from death but survived thanks to his physicians and new medical discoveries.

In 1951, John was on a trip to Asia with brother Robert when he suffered a recurrence of his Addison's disease in Tokyo. His temperature surged to 105.8 degrees. He became delirious and then comatose. Those around him did not think we would survive, so a priest was called in to deliver the last rites. Robert Kennedy found a way to transport John to a military hospital in Okinawa. They saved John's life, and the 34-year-old slowly convalesced until he was well enough to travel back home.[76]

---

76 https://www.cbc.ca/radio/undertheinfluence/john-f-kennedy-was-given-last-rites-5-diferent-times-1.6362855

In 1954, two years after being elected to the U.S. Senate, Kennedy underwent surgery to fuse his spinal disks. It was a risky operation, but Jack was told that if he didn't have surgery, he might be confined to a wheelchair for life. After the operation, he developed a urinary tract infection that became profoundly serious due to his Addison's disease. His temperature again spiked so high that he fell into a coma and was not expected to live through the night. A priest was again called to administer the last rites. Fortunately, he managed to pull through and spent five months recovering.[77]

If this medical history sounds repetitive, think about how this felt to John. He became so used to these close calls that he gave his doctors permission to try anything to remove his pain and suffering. It would always only last for so long until another bout of illness hit him again, over and over.

John Kennedy met Jacqueline Bouvier when she interviewed him as a reporter for the *Washington Times-Herald*. Perhaps he recalled his relationship with reporter Inga Arvad. John and Jackie announced their engagement on June 24, 1953. Earlier, she had dropped an engagement to stockbroker John Husted Jr. when she learned he only made $17,000 per year. She and John married on September 12, 1953, and honeymooned in Acapulco and Santa Barbara, California. But John was his father's son, and on August 23, 1956, Jackie delivered a stillborn daughter while her husband yachted in the Mediterraneum with a mistress.[78]

John Kennedy had to recover from illness in 1956 and used that year to do most of the writing of *Profiles of Courage*. He had the help of future speech writer Ted Sorenson and one of Jacqueline's professors so that he could describe courageous senators. The finished product received the Pulitzer

---

77 https://www.cbc.ca/radio/undertheinfluence/john-f-kennedy-was-given-last-rites-5-diferent-times-1.6362855
78 "JFK and Jackie Kennedy's Relationship Timeline" by Nicole Briese for People Magazine, July 12, 2023.

Award for Biography in 1957, thanks to his father's contacts with columnist Arthur Krock and others. It brought Senator Kennedy some accolades.

His book contained the heroic acts of eight senators: John Quincy Adams, Daniel Webster, Thomas Hart Benton, Sam Houston, Edmund G. Ross, Lucius Lamar, George Norris, and Robert A. Taft.

In 1958, Jacqueline Kennedy's friend, Adele Astaire Douglass (sister of dancer and movie star Fred Astaire), introduced Jackie to Bunny Mellon. The wealthy woman was 19 years older than Jackie, but they became long-time friends, and Bunny helped her create her life after the assassination of her husband. Bunny Mellon, of the Mellon banking magnate, was the style icon who designed the White House Rose Garden for the Kennedys.[79]

While John Kennedy was Senator, one of his actions was recently alluded to in the movie *Oppenheimer,* released in 2023. In 1959, Lewis Strauss went before lawmakers to be confirmed as the new secretary of commerce. However, his appointment was blocked by a swing vote cast by Kennedy.

Jumping ahead with a *USA Today* article of 7/22/2023, in mid-1963, President Kennedy was urged by advisors to bestow the Enrico Fermi Award on Dr. Robert J. Oppenheimer to restore his reputation. Kennedy died just before that event, so that President Lyndon Johnson awarded it on December 2, 1963. Johnson told the crowd: "I know every person in this room grieves with me and Dr. and Mrs. Oppenheimer that the late president, who gave his all for his country, could not present this award as he anticipated."

Let us return to the Kennedy-Nixon debates, which determined who would be elected president. Miss Theodate Johnson, publisher of *Musical America*, wrote to the two candidates requesting their views on music in relation to the federal government and domestic world affairs. Senator Kennedy's answer was dated September 13, 1960, and was published in the October issue of their magazine. He said:

---

79 https://www.townandcountrymag.com/society/money-and-power/a41916235/jackie-kenne-dy-bunny-mellon-friendship-true-story/

There is a connection, hard to explain logically but easy to feel, between achievement in public life and progress in the arts. The age of Pericles was also the age of Phidias. The age of Lorenzo de Medici was also the age of Leonardo da Vinci. The age of Elizabeth also the age of Shakespeare. And the New Frontier for which I campaign in public life, can also be a New Frontier for American art.

On September 26, 1960, John Kennedy was running for the presidency and was to debate Richard Nixon, but he was feeling under par. Their traveling campaign left him exhausted. A week earlier, Kennedy's Harvard classmate investment banker Charles "Chuck" Spalding described having injections by Dr. Max Jacobson when he sought relief from exhaustion. Spalding told Kennedy about his treatment, "I went over the top of the building. I felt wonderful, full of energy, capable of doing just about anything. I didn't know exactly what he was giving me, but it was a magic potion." Kennedy had also heard from his *Life Magazine* photographer Mark Shaw, who covered Kennedy's campaign, that he was greatly energized after seeing Jacobson and having some shots.[80]

Kennedy asked Spalding to set up an appointment. John did not tell his own physicians about this and eluded his security detail to see Jacobson one afternoon shortly before the first debate in September 1960. His arrival was expected by Jacobson, and he was served with courtesy and dispatch. He told Jacobson that the grind of campaigning left him tired and weak, but he must be alert and keen to debate Richard Nixon. Kennedy allowed Jacobson to give him a shot, and his muscle weakness immediately disappeared. In addition, Jacobson gave Kennedy a bottle of vitamin drops to be taken orally, and he departed.[81]

---

80 https://www.historynet.com/jack-kennedy-dr-feelgood/
81 https://www.historynet.com/jack-kennedy-dr-feelgood/

Kennedy met secretly with Jacobson a few minutes before taking the stage for the Nixon debate. The senator was complaining of his lethargic voice, and Jacobson injected his throat, pumping methamphetamine into the larynx, his voice box. That allowed Kennedy to debate without muscle pain and tension. Nixon, who decided to wear no makeup for television, began to sweat profusely and looked very tense.

These debates made all the difference about who was elected president in this very tight election; thus, Kennedy valued Max Jacobson highly.

John must always have wondered, "Who can deliver me from this body of pain?" Was this man a kind of savior for John? Was his impairment of the body brought on by sin, as Biblical writers proposed? Was disease the consequence of bad actions such as sex? Was pain the price to be paid for indulgences? Whatever the pain relief concoction was, Kennedy's best friend said, "Don't ask anyone. Just do it."

John Kennedy wanted Dr. Max to move to Washington and give up his New York practice. The doctor declined, so Kennedy's photographer, Mark Shaw, piloted his own Cessna and flew Jacobson to the Kennedys whenever needed. Jacobson carried his medical supplies in a briefcase for such trips.[82]

Kennedy and Jacobson set up a secret code. Whenever the president wanted to see Jacobson, he or his staff were to call Jacobson's office and say, "There is a call from Mrs. Dunn." Then, Jacobson made himself available when and where a treatment was needed. As the Secret Service became aware of Dr. Jacobson's treatments and often knew when the president was being whisked away to see Jacobson, they nicknamed him "Dr. Feelgood."

As we think of the various difficult tasks of the presidency, these were years with greater problems than many presidents have faced. Kennedy inherited a plot dreamed up by the previous Eisenhower administration. He

---

82 "President Kennedy's Nutrition Physician, Dr. Max Jacobson" by David A. Jeand'Heur and Andrew W Saul published by Orthomolecular Medicine.

did not have the right questions to ask his people, nor did he know how to check on such things as a raid of Cuba.

The fiasco of the Bay of Pigs invasion plunged Kennedy into deep humiliation. Advisors to President Kennedy had counted on support for invading exiles to create an overthrow of Castro. By April 19, 1961, the Cuban government had captured or killed the invading exiles. Kennedy was forced to negotiate for the release of the 1,189 survivors. The stress and humiliation were so deep that Press secretary Pierre Salinger found him weeping in his room on that day.[83]

The ailing president learned that he could not confide in his father and expect sympathy or understanding. Despite a lifetime of physical pain and suffering, here was a new and deep emotional suffering over his own mistakes with little time to make corrections. He undoubtedly took advantage of one of the quickest ways to distract oneself—sexual intercourse in some exciting rendezvous.

One day in May 1961, Dr. Jacobson was asked to fly to Palm Beach, where the first family was vacationing. Upon arrival, John told the doctor that Jackie was suffering from depression after giving birth to their son, John Jr., in November. That made the president wonder if she could accompany him on his upcoming trip to Europe, where she was to converse in French with General Charles De Gaulle and his wife. John was quite aware that he would be operating on foreign soil and wanted all the help he could get. The president wanted the doctor to pep her up and called her condition "post-partum depression."

However, Jacqueline may have been more depressed over the many affairs her husband was having. It was only four months since taking office, and he began an affair during his first month at the White House with 19-year-old

---

83 Dallek, Robert. An Unfinished Life: John F. Kennedy 1917-1963, Boston: Little, Brown, 2003, p. 366.

intern Mimi Alford, according to her memoir *Once Upon a Secret: My Affair with John F. Kennedy and its Aftermath.*

In addition, John had urged Jacqueline Kennedy to hire Pamela Turnure as her press secretary since she had been his secretary when he was a senator. She became another lover, and Jacqueline may have known of their two-year affair. That was described in *The Kennedy Half-Century* by Larry J. Sabato.

Books have been written about Jacqueline's decision to divorce John Kennedy due to his love affairs and especially his relationship with Marilyn Monroe. Such books describe an offer by Joseph Kennedy to Jacqueline to stay with his son for one million dollars and her counteroffer that if he brought home venereal disease, she would demand 20 million dollars. We have no idea whether the statements of these various authors are valid. There are enough facts about his many affairs without adding more sketchy rumors to this history.

Mrs. Kennedy probably did not describe John's affairs to Dr. Jacobson. After he gave her a shot, her mood changed completely. Ten days later, he was summoned to treat her again. After receiving an injection, she told the doctor that her husband wanted to see him as well. John had injured his back during a tree-planting ceremony in Canada and needed an injection to stand up straight and move about normally.

The president's doctor, Janet Travell, had been injecting the anesthetic procaine into his back several times a day. That was in addition to corticosteroids for his Addison's disease. Combining medicines and doctors without their knowledge of what each was doing risked life and limb. So, Travell did not know details about Jacobson's injections, and we do not know how much Jacobson knew about Travell's treatments.

Facial and bodily changes had begun to appear on John Kennedy's body. His steroid treatment caused a flushed countenance and a full rounded face, and fat deposits between the shoulders ("buffalo hump") caused by fluid retention in the tissues. Other side effects of steroids include euphoria, agitation, nightmares, hallucinations, and even paranoia. By 1961, photographers noticed the pudginess of Kennedy's face, which doctors had already noted on television clips of the president. The president had a year-round tan, often commented upon by the press, but it came from extra pigmentation of the skin stemming from his Addison's disease. His full head of hair of brown color also came from Addison's disease and the medication and steroids he was taking.[84]

Jack was hobbling about on crutches and, in a week, would fly to Europe to meet Khrushchev after meeting De Gaulle. He did not want to appear weak or inadequate after his humiliation over the defeat at the Bay of Pigs six weeks earlier when Fidel Castro crushed the CIA-backed invasion of Cuba. He was extremely delighted when Jacobson gave him an injection, and he was immediately able to walk across the room without crutches. He asked Jacobson to accompany him to the summit in Europe.

A week later, Kennedy had Dr. Jacobson give him an injection aboard Air Force One. He then had the doctor fly on Air France with nobody else on the plane chartered by the White House. That was surely an outrageous use of taxpayers' money, but he wanted to shield his injections from public attention and criticism.

In France, Jacobson injected the president and his wife for conversations with Charles De Gaulle. On June 1, 1961, Jackie was the star of the evening at a state dinner in Versailles, where she spoke fluent French with De Gaulle and his wife.

That night, John soaked his back in a giant gold-plated bathtub in the "King's Chamber" of a nineteenth-century palace on the Quai d'Orsay. He

---

84 Ailing, Aging, Addicted. Bert E. Park, M.D. The University Press of Kentucky, 1993.

received another injection from Jacobson that evening. Mr. and Mrs. Kennedy both received injections when they prepared to meet Queen Elizabeth II during that same trip.[85]

Now comes the reckoning. Perhaps Nikita Khrushchev had spies who told him of Kennedy's use of stimulants. Shortly before this trip, Dr. Jacobson's office had been ransacked by what some authorities thought was the KGB. So, Kennedy's addiction to methamphetamines may have been known. This may explain why Khrushchev arrived to meet Kennedy much later than the original time set for their meeting in Vienna on June 3-4, 1961.[86] Jacobson's injection was wearing off, and the president suddenly felt out of sorts with heavy eyelids and a feverish disposition. He murmured a word or more with his blurry tongue.

Kennedy's debilitating weakness and his drug addiction gave Khrushchev a decided advantage in negotiations. Thus, Nikita's delay left Kennedy in no condition for the important things they were to discuss. Mr. Khrushchev insulted the president, and Kennedy could say little to defend himself or his actions.

Kennedy got into futile debates about communism. The overpowering fatigue of travel and amphetamines gradually became so obvious that they ended their tete-tete but on a very bad note. Khrushchev declared that he was going to sign an agreement to divide Berlin and deny access to part of the city. He promised to respond with force if the United States challenged the USSR on that issue. Kennedy reacted by saying, "Then, Mr. Chairman, there will be war. It will be a cold winter."

John Kennedy was not smart enough to change his behavior and give up these chemicals. The consequences of his bad experience with Khrushchev

85 https://www.atlanticcouncil.org/content-series/thinking-global/berlin-1961-kennedy-s-dr-feel-good/

86 nypost.com/2013/04/21/the-kennedy-meth/

did not rouse him to action. Nothing of that sort took place. He was powerless to tear himself away from addictive methamphetamine. If we are under the advice of those who have no understanding of how life should be lived (like Dr. Jacobson), we destroy our health. Will life be worth living if that higher part of man, his ability to think clearly, would be destroyed?

Peggy Noonan, who worked for President Ronald Reagan, wrote a 2001 book entitled *When Character Was King.* On page 244, she wrote of Truman, who took charge when Roosevelt died and did many admirable things. Eisenhower came in and built highways across the country and settled things down some. John Kennedy came in with commitments to education and getting a man on the moon, but he didn't accomplish that much during his time in office. Was it a lack of character?

During his last year of life, the movie about his military duty, *PT-109,* was made. He had three requirements: it should be accurate, profits should be distributed to his crew, and he had a choice of the actor who was to portray him. He met Cliff Robertson and chose him after a heart-to-heart discussion. He approved of the picture once made.

John Kennedy was very reckless in his responsibilities as a president. He was also very reckless in his love affairs, which included Judith Campbell Exner, whom he knew was also seeing mob boss Sam Giancana. That man had worked with Al Capone on his way up the ladder to run illegal gambling operations in Chicago. Exner was invited to Las Vegas by Frank Sinatra as part of the rat-pack Hollywood crowd. On February 7, 1960, she was introduced to presidential candidate John Kennedy in Dean Martin's hotel suite. Her affair with Kennedy began in March 1960 in New York.

In her autobiography, Exner denied being a go-between but admitted passing messages to Giancana from entertainers like Jerry Lewis and Eddie Fisher. She became a patient of Dr. Max Jacobson. Since she was under close observation by the FBI, at J. Edgar Hoover's request, Kennedy finally dropped her.[87]

Kennedy's White House physician, Janet Travell, was aware of John's search for painkillers but not specifics. She may have shared this information with another of John Kennedy's physicians. In November 1961, Dr. Cohen, Kennedy's endocrinologist for the last five years, wrote this note to the president:

> You cannot be permitted to receive therapy from irresponsible doctors like M.J. who by forms of stimulating injections offer some temporary help to neurotic or mentally ill individuals… this therapy conditions one's needs almost like a narcotic and is not for responsible individuals who at any split second may have to decide the fate of the universe.[88]

Now that important doctors and men were telling Kennedy that he and/or the police ought to condemn his drugs, he resisted their advice and continued his pain relief injections for two more years up until his death.

White House physician Janet Travell had tried to help Kennedy. She found that he had one leg shorter than the other and had a lift made to insert in his left shoe so he could walk more evenly. She recommended a rocking chair, which helped relieve his discomfort and relax him. Other doctors criticized her overuse of procaine for his back pain and overuse of penicillin. That antibiotic can induce a fatal allergic reaction or could become ineffective with overuse.

Although Kennedy had many infections that responded to penicillin, his main use was to prevent venereal disease. He was like so many men who walked in the door of their doctor's office and announced, "I need a shot

---

87 https://www.nytimes.com/1977/06/13/archives/frank-jack-sam-judy.html
88 http://hnn.us/articles/1124.html

of penicillin." They did not even have to say why. Chlamydia, gonorrhea, and syphilis are caused by bacteria that usually respond to penicillin or other strong antibiotics with a single injection.

In June 1962, Kennedy's brother Bobby, the U.S. attorney general, grew so suspicious of Jacobson that he sent a sample of his formula to the FBI to learn what was in it. When he found out it contained amphetamines, he urged his brother not to use it. JFK told him flat out, "I don't care if it's horse piss. It makes me feel good. It works."

Although it is damning to say so, John Kennedy's corruption lay in his choice of gratifications. Ordinary citizens who do as Kennedy did find themselves in jail or in psychiatric treatment. However, the presidents' wants were supplied. By May 1962, Jacobson had visited the White House 34 times to give the president injection boosts for his maladies and struggles.[89]

John Kennedy owned an apartment at the Carlyle Hotel in New York City's Upper East Side for ten years. It was known as "the New York White House" during his administration.

Dr. Jacobson was sometimes sent there, and on July 15, 1962, the injection of amphetamines was apparently too high a dose. After Kennedy's injection, he went into the living room where the staff were waiting. He started stripping off his clothes and danced around the room naked.

First, his staff men were amused. He was completely naked and on the verge of paranoia, thinking his people were against him by trying to restrain him. But he was feeling so free of pain that he almost wanted to perform gymnastic acts as he ran out the door into the hallway. He began running from door to door, looking for Mimi Alford, the young aide who had been his earliest and most regular mistress since his election to the presidency. She was waiting in a room at the end of the hall where they were to have a fling.

---

89 https://telemachusunedited.wordpress.com/tag/max-jacobson/

His staff grabbed him and dragged him back into his room as he screamed. They pondered whether they should put the president in a straitjacket if they could secure one. They called prominent New York psychiatrist Lawrence Hatterer, who came quickly and recognized the psychotic symptoms. He gave the president an anti-psychotic medicine, and within minutes, he returned to more normal behavior.[90]

Dr. Hans Kraus, who treated the president's back pain, had also heard of Kennedy's treatment by Dr. Jacobson and had said in December 1962: "If I ever heard he took another shot, I'd make sure it was known. No President with his finger on the red button has any business taking stuff like that." All the Kennedy staff went out of their way to be sure Dr. Kraus did not hear of his continued shots.

President Kennedy tried to go along with Jacqueline's efforts to bring in arts and spoke about the arts in America. These comments were reported in *Look Magazine* in the December 18, 1962, issue:

> To further the appreciation of culture among all the people, to increase respect for the creative individual, to widen participation by all the processes and fulfillments of art—this is one of the fascinating challenges of these days... The life of the artist is, in relation to his work, stern and lonely... He has turned aside from quick success in order to strip his visit of everything secondary or cheapening. His working life is marked by intense application and intense discipline.

Jacqueline tried to ignore what she knew was going on. She busied herself with bringing the arts into the White House. With Jacqueline's initiative, pianist Van Cliburn was invited to perform for Presidents Kennedy and Dwight D.

---

90 "Amphetamines Used by a Physician to Life Moods of Famous Patients" by Boyce Rensberger, Dec. 7, 1972, The New York Times, and https://www.nytimes.com/1972/12/04/archives/amphetamines-used-by-a-physician-to-lift-moods-of-famous-patients.html

Eisenhower during the American Pageant of the Arts on November 29, 1962. The purpose of the event was to raise funds for the National Cultural Center, which began under the Eisenhower administration and was encouraged under the Kennedys. Two months after President Kennedy's assassination, Congress passed and President Johnson signed into law legislation renaming the National Cultural Center as a "living memorial" to John F. Kennedy.

The 23-year-old Van Cliburn, a tall 6'4" Texan, had been nicknamed the "American Sputnik" when he won the first Tchaikovsky competition in Moscow in 1958. It was an important win at a time when Russia seemed to have moved ahead of the U.S. with its Sputnik launch. The only ticker tape parade for a musician in New York City took place when he returned to the United States. Mr. Cliburn was also invited by President Kennedy to perform at the White House on May 2, 1963, for a Congressional Club Breakfast.

When asked one day on a radio show what was the President's favorite song, he said, "Hail to the Chief has a nice ring to it." That song was performed at his funeral a few months later, on November 24, 1963.

Returning to the President's health, he was being given steroids that enhanced his sex drive. England's Prime Minister Harold Macmillan saw some of Kennedy's lovers hiding nearby on their visits, and Kennedy confided that if he did not have sex often, he got a headache.[91]

On February 22, 1963, Mrs. Kennedy called her Secret Service agent, Clint Hill, with an unusual request. The president announced that he would put his White House staff to a 50-mile walking test, expecting to kick-start a national fitness campaign. Mrs. Kennedy told Clint that her brother-in-law, Stash Radziwill, and Chuck Spalding were going to begin the hike that night. She wanted Clint to be there to ensure that things were okay. She, about three months pregnant, and the president were going to check on the hike from time to time, and Dr. Max Jacobson was to be there for medical help.

---

91 https://nypost.com/2013/11/10/all-the-presidents-women-3/

Clint reluctantly agreed because he had no time to get other shoes than his dress shoes. Big blisters resulted after several hours. Some walkers took oxygen administered by Jacobson. Photographer Mark Shaw took pictures of the participants, the Kennedys, and the doctor. He published them before he died of amphetamine poisoning caused by the shots from Dr. Jacobson. Clint Hill subsequently wrote of this in *Mrs. Kennedy and Me,* published in 2012 by Simon and Schuster.[92]

On August 7, 1963, Jacqueline Kennedy gave birth to little Patrick, who died the next day. The Kennedys mourned together. Jacqueline could not attend Patrick's funeral because she was recovering from a C-section. So, John attended and took his St. Christopher medal from his wallet and placed it in the casket. He then asked White House physician Janet Travell to go with Jackie to Palm Beach to help her recover.[93]

When Jackie learned that John had buried his medal with Patrick, she had a new one made for him. At the president's funeral three months later, Jacqueline was standing by Bobby Kennedy next to the president's casket. She put some items and scribbles from little John and Caroline in the casket. Robert saw that and pulled his own St. Christopher's medal out of his wallet to drop into the casket as well. It had been a gift from his wife, Ethel.[94]

On September 20, 1963, President Kennedy made his speech before the United Nations. His speech ended with this phrase: "Let us take our stand here in this assembly of nations… and move this world to a just and lasting peace." John Kennedy had laryngitis the night before and had Jacobson inject him at the Carlisle Hotel. The talk went well, and the president thanked him at a reception following the speech.

---

92 https://clinthillsecretservice.com/2017/02/23/jackie-jfk-50-mile-hike/

93 Oral History Interview with Janet G. Travell on January 20, 1966, in Washington, D.C. by Theodore C. Sorenson for the John F. Kennedy Library.

94 https://historical.ha.com/itm/political/presidential-relics/john-f-kennedy-his-well-used-leather-wallet-and-1959-61-massachusetts-driver-s-license/a/6142-48013

So many people close to the president saw what he was doing and tried to stop him, but he was living the good life. He was the most important man in the United States and in the world, according to many. At the end of John Kennedy's life, he was having a glorious moment riding in a limousine as Texas Governor John Connally's wife Nellie said, "Mr. President, you can't say Dallas doesn't love you." Those were the last words John Kennedy ever heard.

Kennedy's Guilt

It seemed that most of Kennedy's physicians wanted what was best for him and for the country, but they were hampered by a patient who sought treatment from doctors on his own and failed to inform them of treatments by others. He did not reveal his medical history to the Navy or to the public when his health was questioned during the presidential campaign. He did not care that Max Jacobson had no hospital privileges and wrote no prescriptions. Dr. Feelgood made his own medicines in his filthy laboratory with his dirty fingernails touching syringes and used his own drugs, which clouded his mind. See such details about this at historynet.com/jack-kennedy-dr-feelgood/

There is no doubt that Kennedy's actions often resulted from his background of suffering. However, his desires for sex and pain relief were like someone saying, "I want what I want when I want it." He gave little thought to serving his country with a clouded mind that might plunge the world into war. He eluded the bagman carrying the satchel of vital communications when he desired a sexual tryst. He cared little about hurting the feelings of those in his life, like his wife, his brother, other relatives, and mistresses.

President Kennedy, his wife, his friends, and some of his doctors lacked integrity. President Thomas Jefferson said, "God grant that men of principle shall be our principal men." We must hope that future presidents will be more honest and care more for the country they serve. Many believe that the successful whitewash of Kennedy's medical history and health should push the United States to explore how this might be prevented in the future.

Jerrold M. Post (1934-2020) was an American psychiatrist and author. He was an analyst for the Central Intelligence Agency and the founder of the Center for the Analysis of Personality and Political Behavior. He also helped found the International Society of Political Psychologists in 1978, of which this author is a member. Post created several "psychobiographies" of notable individuals during his tenure at the CIA and wrote *Dangerous Charisma* about Donald Trump, correctly predicting that he would not accept election results if he lost.

Post wrote *When Illness Strikes the Leader* in 1995 and discussed John Kennedy and others. He also wrote an article entitled "Substance Abuse" for *The Washington Post* published on January 28, 1990.[95]

Here is an excerpt of that article:

It appears that amphetamine abuse, which had spread to the general population in the 1960s, began in elite groups in the 1940s and '50s. "Celebrity doctors" may have played an important role in first establishing this pattern.

Dr. Max Jacobson had fled Hitler's Germany in 1936 and soon took up medical practice in New York City. Although he had no staff privileges at any hospital after 1946, he acquired a reputation as a doctor for celebrities, among whom he was known as "Doctor Feel-good."

Among the initial effects of amphetamines which make it attractive to a leader in a crisis are an increase of alertness, lessened fatigue, feelings of well-being and lessened need for sleep. In a crisis, an

---

95 https://www.washingtonpost.com/archive/opinions/1990/01/28/substance-abuse/e2c9a3da-12a5-4893-908a-3f2b92f19925/

individual "high" on stimulants may be insufficiently cautious or unduly optimistic. Under sustained stress, some will utilize serially stimulant amphetamines and hypnotic drugs, producing a "high-low" sequence.

Decisions are made without judicious consideration, in impulsive haste. Continued amphetamine use can lead to confusion about time and place, distractibility, vagueness, rambling speech, delusions of persecution, hallucinations and psychological behavior resembling paranoid schizophrenia.

World leaders operate under unusual stress and often feel entitled to special treatment. Substance abuse by major political leaders is not a private illness. For the leader under the influence of drugs or alcohol... every aspect of his functioning is affected--his perceptions, judgment, decision-making and the balance between his own needs and those of his followers. Especially during crises, when the mighty are high, the lowly should tremble.

When John Kennedy became president, he hoped that his health problems would not prevent him from handling the job. By hiding his medical problems, he kept voters from deciding whether they wanted to take a chance on him or not. If the public had known more about him and his medications, would he have even been nominated or elected?

G. Joseph Patrick Kennedy
1888-1969

Joseph Patrick Kennedy is the reason that John Kennedy became president. He was an Irish American businessman, investor, and politician. He was the son of politician Joseph Kennedy and his wife, Mary August Kennedy. He attended Boston Latin School and was elected class president before graduating in 1908. He attended Harvard and gained admittance to the prestigious Hasty Pudding Club, graduating in 1912 with a bachelor's degree in economics.

He married Rose Fitzgerald in 1914, daughter of Boston Mayor John "Honey Fitz" Fitzgerald and Josephine Hannon. Joseph and Rose had Joseph Jr., John, Rosemary, Kathleen, Eunice, Patricia, Robert, Jean, and Edward. His father was in the whiskey importation business, and he made a fortune as a commodity and stock investor who reinvested proceeds into film studios, real estate, and shipping lines.

He liked to brag that he was the youngest bank president in America at age 25. When people asked him why he wanted to be a banker, he would say, "If you want to make money, go where the money is."

He oversaw the production of transport and warships and met Franklin Roosevelt, who was then the Asst. Secretary of the Navy. He moved to Hollywood in 1926 to run three film studios, one of which became the Radio-Keith-Orpheum (RKO) as they developed into talkies.

He had relationships with Gloria Swanson, "the reigning movie queen of Hollywood," and later German actress Marlene Dietrich. While supposedly helping Swanson straighten out her business affairs, she discovered that he was charging her for some of his expenses. She wrote an autobiography at age 81 telling all about her six husbands and Kennedy, her lover.

Rose Kennedy believed that sexual intercourse was only for the purpose of having children. After their fourth child, she told Joseph that she wanted to stop having children. She left him and returned to her parents. Her father told her in no uncertain terms that she could not stay and must return to her husband. She did so, and they continued to have children until the last one. Thus, some may argue that Joseph had affairs because there was no passion for his wife, and she was an unwilling partner.

Kennedy was rather open about his relationships with Swanson and Dietrich, and his boys also knew about Kennedy's secretary, who became a long-time lover. He mingled with many famous people, and some of them have memories of the Kennedys from their early days.

A good example is Katherine 'Kay' Murphy Halle (1903-1997), who was an American journalist, broadcaster, and socialite. She worked with the OSS during WWII and was good friends with people like George Gershwin, Averell Harriman, Robert Sherwood, Franklin Roosevelt, Walter Lippman, Buckminster Fuller, Randolph and his father Winston Churchill, and Joseph and his son John Kennedy. She wrote *Irrepressible Churchill, A Treasury of Winston Churchill's Wit.*

She met John Kennedy when he was hospitalized at age twelve for an appendectomy. She learned that young John had counseling with Columbia University psychologist Dr. Prescott Lecky. He helped John understand that he had withdrawn from competition with his older brother, Joseph Kennedy, Jr., by allowing himself to become thoughtless, sloppy, and inefficient. With therapy and a willingness to change, he discarded those symptoms and became a much better student.

This therapy also helped him learn to stand up against his father, who had strongly influenced each of his nine children to do his bidding. Although he listened to his father's wishes, he reserved the right to be his own man and make decisions, which sometimes opposed old Joseph.

Joseph had a hot and cold relationship with President Franklin Roosevelt. He had raised well over one hundred thousand dollars for Roosevelt and wrote the book *I'm For Roosevelt* in 1936. He was less interested in being an ambassador to Great Britain than being involved with money. He was especially interested in being the head of the Securities Exchange Commission (SEC), and Roosevelt finally appointed him to that position. The president was reluctant to do so because he knew that Joseph Kennedy had pulled some illegitimate money deals. But he told insiders he appointed Kennedy because "It takes a crook to catch a crook."

Joseph Kennedy had a falling out with Roosevelt over Germany and Hitler. He thought Hitler's plans to remove, sterilize, and eliminate Jews were good moves. He spoke with both sons about letting things be instead of going to war with Hitler. Joseph Jr. wrote favorably about Hitler, but John wrote his early book *Why England Slept,* which demonstrated why Hitler was to be feared.

In December 1937, Joseph Kennedy, father of the future President John F. Kennedy, was appointed U.S. Ambassador to Great Britain. It was among the most prestigious of all the diplomatic posts—one he had lobbied for over many months. When he and his large family arrived in London in March 1938, English society welcomed them with open arms.

In the spring of 1938, the couple enjoyed English hospitality, hobnobbing with aristocrats and royalty at the many balls, dinners, regattas, and derbies of the season. On one April weekend, they were guests at Windsor Castle, the home of King George VI and his wife, Queen Elizabeth. Rose Kennedy chronicled those unforgettable days in her diary. That can be found at: archives.gov/exhibits/eyewitness/html.php?section=20

In June 1938, Future British Prime Minister Winston Churchill published a book entitled *Arms and the Covenant,* which was published in the United States in September 1938 as *While England Slept; A Survey of World Affairs, 1932-1938.* That book may have been why Churchill was elected Prime Minister.

In 1940, John Kennedy was in his senior year at Harvard University. He had traveled in Europe for quite some time and feared the Nazis. Thus, he used almost the same title for his book, published in 1940. While his father saw things differently, he promoted the book for his son, and other writers helped John so that the book became quite a success. Joseph also bought hundreds of copies to help it become a best-seller.

Here are some quotations from that book:

No discussion on Britain's psychology would be complete unless some mention were made of the natural feeling of confidence, even of superiority, that every Englishman feels and to which many Americans object. This feeling, while it is an invaluable asset in bearing up under disaster, has had a great effect on the need Britain felt for rearming. The idea that Britain loses every battle except the last has proved correct so many times in the past that the average Englishman is unwilling to make great personal sacrifices until the danger is overwhelmingly apparent. This notion that God will make a special effort to look after England, and that she will muddle through, took a great toll of the British rearmament efforts of the 'thirties...

We can't escape the fact that democracy in America, like democracy in England, has been asleep at the switch. If we had not been surrounded by oceans three and five thousand miles wide, we ourselves might be caving in at some Munich of the Western World.

To say that democracy has been awakened by the events of the last few weeks is not enough. Any person will awaken when the house is burning down. What we need is an armed guard that will wake up when the fire first starts, or, better yet, one that will not permit a fire to start at all.

We should profit by the lesson of England and make our democracy work. We must make it work right now. Any system of government will work when everything is going well. It's the system that functions in the pinches that survives.

Although his father disapproved of his anti-war feelings at that time, after John was elected president, Joseph was pleased with his progress and position. They allowed him to vicariously enjoy being president of the country, a role which he longed to play himself. He was shattered when John was killed, and he lived another six years despite being very limited in speech by his strokes. However, he seemed to know and understand much of what was happening.

When Joseph Kennedy was 81 years old, he went into a coma and died on November 11, 1969. His son, Ted Kennedy, gave the eulogy and said that his main interest had been his children. His legacy was that all his children had tried to make this country a better place to live. His torch had been passed to his children, and they had passed it on to their children.

Sad to say, John Kennedy could have been an even better president if he had used more self-discipline. His father could have shown more self-discipline in his female relationships, and he could have kept his infidelities a secret and never allowed them to enter his life. All of Joseph's sons became unfaithful to their wives and filled their lives with lies and bad faith.

Even so, John and Jacqueline Kennedy made some interesting changes in the White House and the presidency. Kennedy was better able to use brilliant wording that made his statements quotable for many generations, thanks to his knowledge of history and his choice of words suggested by speechwriter Ted Sorenson.

He did some formidable things with his White House. For example, there had never been a meeting of such notable people as on April 29, 1962, when the White House held a dinner honoring all living Nobel Prize Winners of the Western Hemisphere. He said:

> I think this is the most extraordinary collection of talent, of human knowledge, that has ever been gathered together at the White House, with the possible exception of when Thomas Jefferson dined alone.

The president's opening remarks at that dinner meeting were these:

> I am proud to welcome to the White House winners of the Nobel Prize in the western hemisphere.... With brisk disregard for his fellow countrymen Alfred Nobel even took care to specify in his will, "I declare it to be my express desire that in the awarding of prizes, no consideration whatever be paid to the nationality of these candidates."
>
> I hope you will forgive me too if I express satisfaction over the fact that more Nobel peace prizes have been awarded to citizens of the United States than of any other nation. The record of thirteen American winners of the peace Prize suggests, I think, how deep-rooted the quest for peace is in the American tradition and the American ethos.

Prior to the dinner, the President and Mrs. Kennedy received in their private quarters the 1961 Nobel Prize winners: Dr. Melvin Calvin, cited for work in photosynthesis; Dr. Robert Hofstadter, cited for work in atomic physics; and Dr. George von Bekesy for discoveries on the mechanisms of the inner ear. Following the dinner, actor Fredric March gave a reading of excerpts from Sinclair Lewis' *Main Street* (Nobel Prize for Literature, 1930), George C. Marshall's *The Address* (Nobel Prize for Peace, 1953), and one of Ernest Hemingway's books, (Nobel Prize for Literature, 1954).

Some guests were chosen as good conversationalists, and here are some of the most familiar names of attendees: Leonard Trilling, Arthur Schlesinger, Mrs. Norman Cousins, Dr. Linus Pauling, Robert Frost, Mr. and Mrs. George C. Marshall, Mrs. Ernest Hemingway, Clark Kerr, James Baldwin, Pierre Salinger, Mr. and Mrs. William Faulkner, John Dos Passos, Katherine Ann Porter, and Dr. Harold Urey.

In addition to the Peace Corps, the other most important contribution of President John Kennedy was the emphasis on the space program. President Kennedy described it to Congress on May 25, 1961, including these words:

We go into space because whatever mankind must undertake, free men must fully share…I believe that this nation should commit itself to achieving the goal, before the decade is out, of landing a man on the moon and returning him safely to earth.

He said on September 12, 1962, at Rice University in Houston, Texas: We choose to go to the moon in this decade and do other things, not because they are easy, but because they are hard.

About the Author

Dr. Diane Holloway Cheney is a psychologist, former Drug Czar (Coordinator) of Dallas, and member of the International Association of Chiefs of Police, International Society for Political Psychology, American Psychological Association, Arizona Authors Association, American Medical Writers Association, and Dallas Area Writers Group.

In the 1950s, after some college semesters, she moved to London and then Paris, where she ran a travel agency for Americans wanting to travel and earn college credit. Study Abroad, Inc. was owned by her Hungarian cousin. She set up tours for Americans for some two and a half years.

She then returned to the U.S. and took up her studies again as she completed studies to become a psychiatric nurse and then a psychologist. She has written several books and articles for various journals, such as the *International Social Science Review* and the *November 2020 Criminal Justice in America: The Encyclopedia of Crime, Law Enforcement, Courts, and Corrections,* produced by ABC-CLIO, Santa Barbara, California, and gave numerous presentations to medical and law enforcement groups.

Printed in Great Britain
by Amazon

46731154R10175